Translation Practices Explained

Translation Practices Explained is a series of coursebooks designed to help self-learners and teachers of translation. Each volume focuses on a specific aspect of professional translation practice, in many cases corresponding to actual courses available in translator-training institutions. Special volumes are devoted to well consolidated professional areas, such as legal translation or European Union texts; to areas where labour-market demands are currently undergoing considerable growth, such as screen translation in its different forms; and to specific aspects of professional practices on which little teaching and learning material is available, the case of editing and revising, or electronic tools. The authors are practising translators or translator trainers in the fields concerned. Although specialists, they explain their professional insights in a manner accessible to the wider learning public.

These books start from the recognition that professional translation practices require something more than elaborate abstraction or fixed methodologies. They are located close to work on authentic texts, and encourage learners to proceed inductively, solving problems as they arise from examples and case studies.

Each volume includes activities and exercises designed to help self-learners consolidate their knowledge; teachers may also find these useful for direct application in class, or alternatively as the basis for the design and preparation of their own material. Updated reading lists and website addresses will also help individual learners gain further insight into the realities of professional practice.

Dorothy Kelly
Sara Laviosa
Series Editors

LP

TRANSLATING PROMOTIONAL AND ADVERTISING TEXTS

Ira Torresi

Retiré de la
COLLECTION - UQO

St. Jerome Publishing
Manchester, UK & Kinderhook (NY), USA

Université du Québec
en Outaouais

1 5 SEP. 2010

Bibliothèque

P
306
.2
T67
2010

Published by

St. Jerome Publishing
2 Maple Road West, Brooklands
Manchester, M23 9HH, United Kingdom
Telephone +44 (0)161 973 9856
Fax +44 (0)161 905 3498
Email: ken@stjeromepublishing.com
http://www.stjerome.co.uk

InTrans Publications
P. O. Box 467
Kinderhook, NY 12106, USA
Telephone (518) 758-1755
Fax (518) 758-6702

ISBN 978-1-905763-20-7 (pbk)
ISSN 1470-966X (*Translation Practices Explained*)

© Ira Torresi 2010

All rights reserved, including those of translation into foreign languages. No part of this publication may be reproduced, stored in a retrieval system or transmitted in any form or by any means, electronic, mechanical, photocopying, recording or otherwise without either the prior written permission of the Publisher or a licence permitting restricted copying issued by the Copyright Licensing Agency (CLA), 90 Tottenham Court Road, London, W1P 9HE. In North America, registered users may contact the Copyright Clearance Center (CCC): 222 Rosewood Drive, Danvers MA 01923, USA.

Printed and bound in Great Britain by
T. J. International Ltd, Padstow, Cornwall, UK

Typeset by
Delta Typesetters, Cairo, Egypt
Email: hilali1945@yahoo.co.uk

British Library Cataloguing in Publication Data
A catalogue record of this book is available from the British Library

Library of Congress Cataloging-in-Publication Data
Torresi, Ira.
  Translating promotional and advertising texts / Ira Torresi.
     p. cm. -- (Translation practices explained, ISSN 1470-966X)
  Includes bibliographical references and index.
  ISBN 978-1-905763-20-7 (pbk. : alk. paper)
  1. Advertising--Translating--Textbooks. 2. Translating and interpreting--Textbooks. I. Title.
  P306.2.T67 2010
  418'.02--dc22
                                        2009043112

Translating Promotional and Advertising Texts

Ira Torresi

Promotional and advertising texts come in different forms and account for a considerable share of the translation market. Advertisements, company brochures, websites, tourist guides, institutional information campaigns, and even personal CVs all share a common primary purpose: that of persuading the reader to buy something, be it a product or a lifestyle, or to act in a particular way, from taking preventive measures against health risks to employing one candidate in preference to another. Consequently, their translation requires the application of techniques which, although they vary depending on the specific text type, are all aimed at preserving that persuasive purpose. This often requires in-depth cultural adaptation and, on occasion, thorough rewriting.

Translating Promotional and Advertising Texts covers different areas of personal promotion, business to business promotion, institutional and business to consumer promotion, including advertising. Numerous examples from a wide variety of languages and media, taken from the author's own professional experience and from real-life observation, are provided throughout. The volume is designed for use as a coursebook for classroom practice or as a handbook for self-learning. It will be of interest to undergraduate and postgraduate students, but also freelance and in-house translators, as well as other professionals working in sales, public relations or similar departments whose responsibilities include involvement in the management of multilingual advertising and promotion activities.

Ira Torresi has taught Translation from English into Italian for several years at the University of Macerata and at the Advanced School of Modern Languages for Interpreters and Translators (SSLMIT) of the University of Bologna, Forlì, Italy. She currently teaches Interpreting from English into Italian at the SSLMIT. Her research publications include studies on intercultural issues in the translation of advertising material. She also works as a freelance interpreter and translator, and has considerable experience in the promotional and advertising sector.

Contents

List of Tables and Illustrations

Tables

Illustrations

Acknowledgements

I have so many people to thank for this book that the only way to try and remember them all is to start from the beginning of the story. My first 'thank you' goes to Dorothy Kelly, who after a short accidental talk at the first IATIS conference in Seoul invited me to send in a proposal for a book on advertising translation when I was next to a perfect nobody, not only to her, but to the academic community in general. It would have been so much easier for any editor to invite an established academic to do the same. Her invitation, and then her acceptance of my draft proposal, gave me that little confidence boost that made me set my mind on continuing academic work and exploring ways to combine it with my professional practice. By the way, I would have never met Dorothy without the material support of Derek Boothman's research group on translation and identity of the University of Bologna at Forlì, a collective mentor that has meant, and still means, a lot for my research.

Moving on in time, a big thank you to Dorothy once again, and to Mona and Ken Baker, for their patience during the slow progress of the project – it took me a couple of years to classroom-test the format and materials you will find in the book. In this respect, I should like to thank my English translation students of the University of Macerata at Civitanova and the University of Bologna at Forlì for unwittingly providing the feedback that led me to expand and sometimes change my initial idea. And of course, no idea is really original – much of what I came to understand about promotion and advertising was shaped by my work with Rosa Maria Bollettieri Bosinelli, Raffaella Baccolini and Delia Chiaro.

During the writing stage, key input came from my revisers, Patrick Leech, Sam Whitsitt, Derek Boothman and Anthony Mitzel – thank you guys! And for their kind assistance in providing permission to reproduce copyright-protected material, my thanks go to Salvatore Casabona, Director-General of INCA; Titius Caius (he knows who he is); Barbara Amadori; Michael Grass, Marketing Communication Manager of WAMGROUP, and his assistant Silvio Bandi; Eleonora Zoratti of Zoratti Studio Editoriale; Ruggero Brunazzi of SIME Srl; the President of Fantini-Andreoli / Andreoli Engineering, Francesco Andreoli; Lester Trilla from Trilla Steel Drum Corp. and his efficient assistant, Nadine Lebensorger; Stefan Schulze-Sturm from ZDH; Tiziana Rambelli, the Communication Dept. Manager of the Forlì Health Unit (AUSL); Simone and Marcello Ruspi from Poliambulatorio Sanpietro and their press agent, Maria Cristina Lani; the President of Unione di Prodotto Città d'Arte, Cultura e Affari, Mario Lugli, and Celestina Paglia from APT Servizi Emilia Romagna; Andrea Pinchera, Communication and Fundraising Director at Greenpeace Italy, and Alexandra Dawe, Energy [R]evolution Communications Project

Manager at Greenpeace International; Nick Sharples, Sony Europe's Director of Corporate Communications; Candy Group Marketing Director Guglielmo Pasquali and his collaborators Franco Lualdi and Ramona Rotta; Giovanni Flamenghi of Moreno Motor Company Srl; and Eleanor Bowden, Press Office Executive at Unilever PLC.

Then came the editing stage, for which I have to thank first and foremost Sara Laviosa, a most valuable addition to the series editing team and a great editor and problem-solver. Dorothy and Mona, too, were very much present at this stage, helping me all along.

And last but not least, thank you Matteo and mum, for looking after me and bearing with me while I was writing this. Strange enough, all in all, it was a really nice summer.

Every effort has been made to obtain permission to reproduce copyright material appearing in this volume. Any omissions brought to the publisher's attention will be remedied in future editions.

1. Introduction

Why a Book on the Translation of Promotional Texts?

In introducing this volume, it is perhaps necessary to justify why one would write a book about the translation of a wide array of promotional genres, from advertising to institutional brochures, from company websites to personal promotion (CVs, job application letters, personal websites). One might argue that such text types have different topics and addressees, circulate across different media, and therefore have different linguistic and contextual characteristics that call for different translation strategies. What unites them, however, is that they all share a persuasive purpose. Or in more cynical terms, they all aim at selling something, be it a service, product, life-style, company (of any size), or public institution. For translators, this has one major implication: if a source text is intended to promote something or someone, then the one who commissions the translation of that text usually wants the same purpose to be re-created in the target (i.e. translated) text. This means that the translations of promotional texts are assessed in functional terms – i.e. for what they do rather than what they are, or for how well they affect the reader rather than how close they are to the original (§ 3.2). In other words, promotional translations, just like their source texts, are assessed in terms of their effectiveness or success, which means in terms of an increase in sales or, in the case of institutions, an increase in the number of contacts received as a token of visibility.

Thus, even if they belong to different genres, all promotional texts can be tackled within the same translational approach, which, in turn, needs to be adjusted to the specific nature of the text in question (for instance depending on its **information-to-persuasion ratio**, § 3.3), and the situational context of the translation job (for instance, a given commissioner might want a literal translation of a promotional text for non-promotional purposes, or for later re-creation).

For readers who may be interested in definitions, this shared translation approach can be broadly identified with **functionalism** or *Skopostheorie* (Reiss and Vermeer 1984/1991; Nord 1997; Schäffner 1998, 2009), and may be considered a kind of **consumer-oriented translation**, which applies to a larger number of text genres, including recipes, technical handbooks and instructions in general (Hervey and Higgins 1992/2002:196-204; Hervey et al 1995/2006: 145-154). It is also an instance of **covert translation**, which implies the naturalness of the target text, i.e. the translated text appears to have been written directly in the target language (House 1977/1981: 189). This implies that the source text is usually **domesticated**, i.e. made to conform as much as possible to the linguistic and cultural norms the target community attaches to that text genre (Venuti 1998b).

1.1   How to use this book

This book can be used in University classes as a coursebook, or as a self-learning handbook. In either case, note that chapters do not correspond to study units and require different periods of time and degrees of effort. In particular, the first three chapters are more general, and while they contain some examples, they do not have any exercises. They should not take more than one-tenth of the time you devote to the entire course or self-learning process. It is however important that practice-related and general issues (chapters 2 and 3) are studied before going on to practical examples.

As for timing, an adaptation of the book was piloted on an Italian undergraduate 30-hour (10-week) course focusing on translation practice. For shorter courses, I advise trainers to make a selection of topics from chapter 4 to chapter 7 rather than rushing through the whole coursebook. Professionals may also find it useful to skip sections about text types which they do not usually encounter in their work. To this purpose, I have designed chapters 4, 5, 6 and 7 in such a way to make it easier, I hope, for readers to select the topics and materials that best suit their own teaching or learning needs.

Teachers and trainers may also want to integrate this book with translation coursebooks and translation theory handbooks, such as the ones listed in the last paragraph of the Introduction above (especially Nord 1997), as well as a selection of relevant works from the further reading section in the References. Additionally, the materials provided in this book should be taken as examples, and should always be integrated with fresh real-life material that best suits learners' needs, including languages that are not accounted for here.

As far as activities are concerned, apart from individual translation exercises that can be corrected and discussed in class or among peers, roleplay can be useful to optimize classroom or individual study time, accommodate distance learning needs, and encompass revision as well as translation roles. This is especially useful with texts that lend themselves more easily to multiple versions (§ 2.2). Pairs or groups of more than two people can work together exchanging roles after each exercise: one component acts as the translator, the other as the commissioner's reviser/editor, and in larger groups additional members can be second-level revisers, or one of them can play the role of the end client. The reviser, or the end client where present, fills in the brief following the general model in table 1 or any other brief agreed by the group for the specific text to be translated. The translator translates the text following the brief, getting back to the end client or the commissioner's reviser to clarify the brief or negotiate choices when possible or relevant, and after self-revision hands in the final version(s) of the target text. The reviser revises the target text(s) taking the brief, the visual level and the target culture into account (see Mossop 2001/2007 for revision and editing strategies), and ranks alternative versions, when present, in order of preference and compliance with the brief. This first-level revision is then sent to the second-level reviser or the end-client, if the group includes such figures. At this point, individual choices and suggestions are critically discussed among all group members. In a face-to-face setting such as the classroom, oral communication has the advantage to be less time-consuming, but e-mail, Skype or Messenger communication are more realistic choices and help participants choose specific rhetorical strategies to motivate their translation and revision choices. Of course, given that power relations are non-symmetrical in the group, translators will need to be flexible and ready to accept equally or more fitting alternatives suggested by the reviser(s) or client, but equally ready to tactfully advocate for the validity of their translation options if they are sure about it. It might be a good idea to accompany the translation with a detailed comment that pre-emptively argues for translation choices; revisions should similarly be motivated with a comment. Revisers and end-clients should be well aware of their priorities from the start of each project when they fill in the brief, and investigate into any translation choice that they might interpret as challenges to such priorities. This should drill participants into the practice of negotiation (following § 2.2) and prepare them to face the complaints and claims that might arise during their professional practice.

1.2 Intended readership

This book is intended for both students/trainees and professionals.

Translation students, both undergraduate (BA level) or graduate (in master's or other postgraduate translation courses) may use it as a coursebook in class, or as a tool for individual training if promotional translation is not a topic of their translation courses.

Promotional translation may also be of interest for those professionals with different priorities. For instance, newly graduated translators who have not received specific training for advertising/promotional material, and who do not want to risk ruining their reputation by venturing into an unknown domain, may want to know more about this field, just in case one of their first clients asks them to translate texts such as a website or a company advertising campaign. As we all know, it is very difficult at the start of one's career, for both economic and psychological reasons, to say 'no' to any translation job. And clients do tend to turn elsewhere after the first refusals.

Similarly, well-established freelance translators or translation agencies specializing in other fields may wish to diversify their translation service offer, for at least two reasons: first, advertising translation is usually paid better than other fields; second, client fidelization is important, especially once one has won one's own pool of regular clients. For instance, if my clients are mainly small industrial companies, the bulk of my commissions will probably be made up of technical handbooks, but if I turn down, or translate badly, promotional texts, then my precious regulars might look for other providers, not just of promotional translation services, but of translation services in general.

This book, however, does not only address translators, but also in-house marketing people or sales personnel in charge of foreign markets, who work at small to medium sized companies that cannot afford to outsource their international advertising and marketing campaigns. Such professionals might be asked to develop and/or translate in-house the company's promotional texts (e.g. posters, leaflets and brochures to be distributed and displayed at international exhibitions, chapter 5).

Finally, other professionals working in the fields of marketing and advertising may be interested in gaining some insight into advertising and promotional translation. For instance, figures such as in-house copywriters, sales managers at advertising agencies, or the marketing staff of companies that outsource their promotional translations, may be asked to review or edit the target text produced by a translator, or may wish to have some degree of understanding of and control over the translation/adaptation process. After all, if translators need to learn to know their commissioners in order to work at their best, the reverse applies, too!

1.3   A short note on terminology

The trans-linguistic, trans-cultural, trans-market transfer of advertising and promotional material goes under a number of names. Just to name a few, 'translation', 'adaptation', 'localization', and 'trans-creation', each of them referring to different aspects of the same process.

Whereas **translation** might be considered as mainly connected to the written word and to the transfer of concepts from one language to another, **adaptation** and **localization** (a more specific term, which is mainly used for advertisements, websites and software) may be seen to stress the cross-cultural aspect of the process and the need to adjust the promotional text to the target market in order to preserve its persuasive function. This, in turn, might entail **trans-creation**, i.e. re-building the entire promotional text so that it sounds and reads both natural and creative in the target language and culture.

Given the practical approach of this book, however, I will use the term 'translation' for all such aspects, as long as they fall or can fall within a translator's field of action. In this sense, I give 'translation' its etymological meaning of 'transfer', i.e. the transfer of a text, concept, or promotional purpose across languages, cultures and markets. This by no means implies that translation is limited to the verbal dimension, nor to texts as seen out of their real-life contexts.

1.4   Structure

After this introductory chapter, we will first see a few notes and caveats concerning professional practice (chapter 2). Section 2.1 briefly outlines some of the non-linguistic abilities involved in promotional translation, while section 2.2 describes a few tools available to promotional translators and section 2.3 discusses the relative weight of advertising and promotional translation in professional practice. Chapter 3 focuses on a number of key issues such as the translatability of brand-names (§ 3.1), loyalty to the source text (§ 3.2), and the different strategies required by different types of promotional texts (§ 3.3). Chapters 4, 5, 6, and 7 are entirely practical and each chapter is devoted to a different text type. Texts are categorized according to their source, target, context of distribution, and information content, progressing from more informative text types such as self-promotion (chapter 4) to **business-to-business** (or **B2B**) promotion (chapter 5), institutional promotion and awareness-raising (chapter 6), and **business-to-consumer** (or **B2C**) promotion (chapter 7). The cultural side of advertising and promotional translation is then discussed in chapter 8.

The Appendix includes additional language versions of examples 10, 18, 19 and 20, for which several versions were available. Recurrent technical terms are listed in the Glossary; terms that are included in the Glossary are marked in bold the first time they occur in the book. Moreover, curious readers will find a further reading section in the References, with several suggestions on how to expand one's theoretical and practical knowledge about promotional translation.

1.5   What this book does and does not do

First and foremost, reading this book and doing all the translation exercises it contains is not, by itself, key to professional success. Secondly, although the book is meant to be as comprehensive as possible, there are entire areas that are not covered here. For instance, only printed promotional materials are accounted for, leaving out radio and TV commercials or promotional videos. The translation of these texts can be approached by combining this book with that of Díaz Cintas and Remael 2007.

What this book tries to do is to provide you with plenty of real-life examples, and information and hints that come from my own professional practice, which might help you recognize some of the main problems and opportunities of promotional translation. This, however, is far from being enough to make anyone a good translator of promotional and advertising material. As in other translation fields, it is vital that you seek as much practice, and expose yourself to as many promotional texts as you can. For instance, look closely at ads and promotional material that circulate in your own market, culture and language to spot recurrent linguistic forms and consumer values or fears that are used for leverage.

Additionally, my examples are mainly in English and will be old in a few years' time. Do not take them as universals, but always compare them with fresh material from your own country. And it would not be surprising to find that the more you are attentive to new trends and local peculiarities, the more you will have to adjust the general principles and approaches presented here which will serve, nonetheless, as solid guidelines to follow.

2. Promotional Translation and Professional Practice

Given the practical approach of this book, it seems appropriate to situate promotional translation within the working context of a professional translator before going on to translation exercises. This chapter, in spite of being short, influenced by my own professional experience, and given from the point of view of one who privileges freelance work, will hopefully put the translation of advertising and promotional texts in perspective – and perhaps provide students with a clearer idea about what it means to work with promotional and advertising texts.

2.1 Why advertising and promotional translators aren't just translators

If we understand translation in the broad sense mentioned at the end of § 1.3, no translator can really make it in the professional world by relying on verbal transfer skills alone. In each specialized field, a number of abilities that are not necessarily linguistic in nature are required, or at the very least, very useful: from the ability to detect and reproduce textual genres and their conventions, to familiarity with the subject-matter (e.g. in scientific or technical texts), and from ownership and proficient use of CAT tools and corpora to social and self-marketing skills (when working in a team and dealing with clients, respectively). No professional translator, therefore, is just a translator and the skills that one acquires in translation courses are seldom sufficient for survival when working in a highly diversified, constantly evolving market.

Promotional translation is a broad category, and it is impossible to list here all the non-linguistic abilities it requires. Some of these skills are very general and apply to all translation types, such as, for instance, a familiarity with the specific terminology and concepts concerning the field to which the object of promotion belongs, be it hair care, mortgages, or environmental activism. It is also necessary that one knows how to correctly assess both the constraints and the opportunities of the medium and channel being used for promotion, whether it be the press, posters, leaflets, the radio, television, internet, etc. To this purpose, other volumes in the series 'Translation Practices Explained' could be of help, and if one is interested in more theoretical issues, these can be found in literature on visual semiotics, film studies, multimodal analysis, conversation analysis (for the spoken parts of TV commercials), geosemiotics (for posters and other street-distributed material), and social semiotics. In the further readings section of the References, more information will be given on these resources.

To return, however, to those non-linguistic skills which are, if not required, at least extremely useful for promotional translators, we can begin with what may commonly be called **agility**: the ability to recognize different functions and purposes embedded in the source text, and approach them appropriately, without losing sight of the overall function of the text, its coherence and cohesion. We will see how this can be done in § 3.3 and in chapters 4, 5, 6, and 7.

Another quality which is often required of a promotional translator, in spite of it being rather vague, is **persuasiveness**, or the mastery of an emotional or evocative style that helps lure the addressee into the desired course of action. A component of persuasiveness is the ability to recognize and, where necessary or advisable, to adapt to culture-specific values in order to accommodate both the target audience's expectations and taboos (see chapter 8).

A third, much-abused word that recurs in the translation of promotional texts, and especially advertising, is **creativity**. It is often maintained, even by translation agencies specializing in the localization of advertising campaigns, that advertising should not be translated by professional translators, but by copywriters and/or creative people who are proficient in foreign languages (or who in any case, get to revise/recreate the translations, whether at the agency or client company). It is the same argument which claims that the best literary translations are not produced by professional translators but by authors who have already published their own books in the target language (sometimes regardless of their proficiency in the source language and familiarity with the source culture and literature). Needless to say, this has yet to be proved. It is true, however, that in promotional translation, the ability to devise and produce, within an extremely limited time frame, clever texts that play with language and visual cues makes things easier in professional practice, particularly in those cultures where witty promotion and advertising is more appreciated (see chapter 8). It should be also pointed out that this ability is not necessarily innate, or something that translators either have or have not: this is something that can be learned through constant exposure to and careful analysis of creative texts.

A fourth quality which is perhaps less vital for freelance translators, but crucial for agencies and company staff, is the knowledge of relevant **laws and restrictions** about advertising and publicly distributed material in the countries where the translated text will be circulated.

Finally, perhaps even more important for promotional texts than in other fields of translation is the ability to be **flexible** in the relationships one has with agencies, editors, and the end client. Promotion is a sensitive topic. After all, it is about the client's image, identity, and ultimately, money (in terms of prospective profits). This is why your translations, in spite of how good they may be judged by client and intermediaries, could still be laid aside, or used as raw material for in-house creative staff to re-write entirely. Promotional translators may be left free to express their creativity at its highest, but this does not mean that they are granted visibility or authorship status (incidentally, the same usually applies to copywriters and creative staff in general, no matter how glamorous the position may seem from the outside). So do not feel offended or frustrated if in addition to not seeing your name in the final text, you cannot even recognize any trace of your work there, even if you feel that you had followed the brief faithfully and the feedback was positive.

2.2 Valuable tools: the brief, visuals, multiple versions, and negotiation

After having examined some of the skills which are useful for promotional translators, we can move on to looking at some of the practical tools that can be particularly handy for them.

The first and perhaps most important of these tools is the **brief** – which includes the following detailed information about:

- the purpose
- the intended readership/audience
- the channel of distribution for which the target text is intended
- the values and brand/corporate image that should come out in the target text
- the product/service/institution/behaviour that is being promoted
- the producer/provider/promoting organization
- where possible, the authors of the source text, whether they are the end clients, and if not, the position of the end clients relative to the text.

The brief is of vital importance for our target text to keep its promotional function. At the verbal level, it gives us information which allows us to make decisions about lexis, register, and personal and social deixis (e.g. feminine/ masculine, singular/plural, degrees of social distance and respect). For instance, if we know that the intended addressees are young girls, we should normally employ feminine grammatical forms, an informal register, common words, and avoid distancing devices and indicators of formality such as impersonal forms; we could even opt for an informal second person singular or a first person if we wish to encourage identification.

While all translators should always receive a brief from their clients, when dealing with clients and/or agencies that are more familiar with non-promotional translation, a brief is seldom provided. To make things worse, insistent inquiries by the translator might even irritate the client or agency (who thus implicitly take upon themselves the responsibility for the effects of their reticence on the target text). In advertising translation, on the other hand, if the client and/or agency are accustomed to working with advertising agencies or staff, briefs are normally provided, and if critical information is missing, the translator is entitled to ask for it.

Things may be different when the translator works with smaller companies or agencies that have not had any lengthy experience with advertising translation, as well as non-advertising promotional text types (e.g. brochures or company presentations to be included in websites). In such cases, especially when one is working in direct contact with the end client, it might be useful to e-mail or fax your contact person a short list of the information you need. A model list is provided in English in table 1, but it is strongly advisable that you adjust it to your specific working conditions: in addition to translating the list into the language you use with the client, read the source text carefully, with the list at hand, and see what you can infer from the text. Sometimes information such as the intended audience and the product image emerge clearly, and it may be enough to ask the client whether s/he wishes to maintain the same in the target text. Keep the list as short as possible, avoid unnecessary or ambiguous questions, and give clear reasons for your requests, pointing to the client's interests (e.g. 'Information about the media involved would help me make the translated text as effective as possible for those media in particular'). If you are working through an agency, you can send the list to them and hope they will convey it to the end client. In any case, keep a record of all communication with your employer in order to clearly establish responsibilities for any interruption of the information flow. As already pointed out, promotional translation is a particularly sensitive field, and if problems arise, agencies or clients are quite likely to blame the translator for not guessing the information they withheld.

Table 1. *Model Translator-prompted Brief*

To be used when a brief has not been provided, and to be adjusted according to real working conditions

1. The translated text will be circulated (please tick all relevant options):
    ☐ as a brochure   ☐ as (part of) a website   ☐ via e-mail or snail mail
    ☐ as a leaflet/flier ☐ on the product's package ☐ at trade fairs
    ☐ in the press (title of publication/s _____)
    ☐ it is the script for a TV commercial to be broadcast on channel/s
    _____

    ☐ it is the script for a radio commercial to be broadcast on station/s
    _____

    ☐ other (please specify)   _____
    _____

2. What group(s) of people do you wish to reach and persuade? Please provide age range; nationality; gender; level of education; employment; degree of specialization with respect to the product/service; whether they are end-consumers/end-users, companies/organizations working in your field of activity, or companies/organizations working in other fields; any other relevant details.

3. Please list the brand values, corporate identity, and product/service image you wish to be conveyed in the translated text.

4. Please put an X where you would like to see your company/organization located on the following scales:

a. Degree of authoritativeness

Min   Max

b. Degree of proximity to the customer/user/public

Min   Max

c. Degree of deference towards the customer/user/public

Min   Max

5. What kind of effect(s) do you wish the translated text to have on the target group? Please provide full details and be as precise as possible.

6. Please enclose all visuals and other material that will accompany the translated text, or at least samples or descriptions of the final form it will have (e.g., for printed texts: layout, fonts, and colours to be used; for TV/radio commercials: music, sound effects, description of action, camera movements, etc.).

Other fundamental tools, which sometimes contain much of the information conveyed by the brief, are the **visuals** and any other **non-verbal elements** that accompany the verbal text. Apart from pictures and photographs, which may be quite descriptive and thus give translators significant input about the target group, the nature of a product, and the image attached to it, there are other elements, such as typography and layout (including the kind of font used for the characters and the colours used for the background), or the navigation structure of a website, which offer opportunities and pose restraints in the trans-creation process. Example 1 (at the end of this chapter) is a case in point; it shows that the visuals and the brief are complementary and should always be given to and/or actively sought by the translator.

Another tool that can, and sometimes must be used in promotional translation, but never with other translation types, is the possibility of providing **multiple versions**. It is a tool, and not just a waste of time and effort, for two very practical reasons: first, it is the client, not the translator, who takes responsibility for the final choice; and second, a translation with multiple versions is quite obviously paid better than a single version (assuming that the offer of multiple versions has been cleared with your client).

Multiple versions are likely to be explicitly requested for text types that are less informative, shorter and more emotional (§ 3.3), and by clients and agencies who fully appreciate the opportunities and risks connected with promotional translation, and wish to have more choices when revising and re-working the translation. In this book, the practice of providing multiple versions will be systematically introduced in § 7.1.2 (see table 3) for the following reason: it is for advertising that clients most often request multiple versions, whereas for longer promotional text types, it is far less practical to provide full alternative versions. In my own professional practice, however, I have sometimes been asked to provide alternative versions for key parts of non-advertising promotional text types, especially for less informative bits with a higher evocative, emotional value, and with a higher impact potential in terms of image. Quite predictably, these parts also require a translation approach that is more trans-creative and less close to the source text. These text types often include section or paragraph titles in websites and brochures, names of tourist packages, general profile descriptions in CVs or 'About us' web pages, extended metaphors in company/organization presentations, and the like. Quite obviously, the client does not expect to pay extra for multiple versions of very small portions of text (and even if the client does not pay, you might still want to provide them to foster client loyalty), but if requests of this kind are systematic, you might have good reasons to negotiate an increase in the translation price (see below).

It is important that all versions are valid in their own right, i.e. they comply with the brief and are free-standing, complete, and accurate. They should not be drafts or weaker versions of one final version; the client is not interested in seeing the phases of the translation process, but only in having a range of viable options, each of them with a different style that may be more suitable for a given reception context, or generate given nuances with respect to brand/product/company image. To facilitate selection, the differences between the versions and the specific properties of each one should be clearly outlined in a short comment. Example 2 (at the end of this chapter) is a real-life illustration of this process.

In any case, one should not provide alternative versions, even complimentary ones, unless asked to do so or before negotiating this possibility with the client or agency. For clients, choosing among a range of options can be a time-consuming activity; moreover, their staff might not be qualified to make the best decision with regard to translation solutions.

Example 2 also demonstrates the importance of the role of continuing **negotiations** between the translator and client in order to achieve mutual satisfaction, which does not necessarily apply only to promotional translation, but is particularly important in this sensitive field. In the example, it is the client who starts negotiations for the provision of alternative versions and gives input about translation choices that should be avoided. By asking for a range of possible solutions, the client also implicitly agrees to assume responsibility for the final translation choice. The translator, on her part, negotiates the amount of time to be granted for the new alternative versions. In similar situations, if alternative versions are required for longer parts of text, the translator should be in a position to negotiate higher prices (unless the first translation was badly done) and further extensions of the deadline.

Negotiations usually take place before a translation commission is accepted. In that phase, the translator ought to be able to point out to the client that that the process of trans-creating an entirely new text to accommodate the expectations of the target group requires more flexible deadlines and higher prices than the client is usually prepared to pay. But if the translator is just starting out, it is perhaps better to use such an approach with caution, and perhaps some time must be spent to educate those clients who may lack a genuine interest in obtaining functional target texts and may prefer any kind of translation at the lowest price. Promotional translation, on the other hand, does entail trans-creation and can therefore be much more time- and effort-consuming than other kinds of translation, and one should bear this in mind when drafting a quotation or accepting a commission, because your negotiation margin will be substantially reduced once you have agreed to certain conditions (§ 2.3).

2.3 A short note for freelance translators: can one live off promotional and advertising translation?

As with other specialized fields, especially at the start of your career, it is unlikely that you will be flooded with the kind of translation jobs you enjoy doing, or are more proficient in, although you can improve your situation by actively seeking such jobs and marketing yourself as a highly specialized translator. But even then, while we are surrounded by ads and publicity, these texts are often translated or recreated in-house. This happens not only in small and medium enterprises which do not have the resources to resort to professional agencies, but also in large multinational companies which have branches in the target countries. It is therefore advisable that you do not rely on promotional and advertising translation as your sole source of income, but diversify your offer in order to meet local market demand (§ 1.1).

It is also a fact, at least in the markets I know, that certain promotional text types (e.g. tourist promotion and company websites) are not regarded as belonging to a specialized field, which then has an inevitable impact on the price one can charge. When one gets to translate advertising texts, however, or succeeds in making clients realize that part of their income depends on the translation of promotional material, the pay is generally much better than in other specialized fields of translation. This implies that when you are asked for a quotation, it is not advisable to apply your standard prices. When in doubt, you can gather information about the prices for advertising translation which are being applied by others who operate on the same national or local market, and in the same language combination. You can do this by checking the mailing lists of translators' associations you are a member of, or other non-institutional mailing lists of professional translators, such as the Italian Langit (http://list.cineca.it/cgi-bin/wa?P1&L=langit).

Example 1
How the visual and the brief influence translation choices

Consider the following Italian source text:

Let us imagine that your client provides you with this text, but not a brief. Before sending them a brief to fill in, drafted following the list in table 1, let us try to draw up a list of cues that can be retrieved from the text, starting with the verbal components and then going on to the visual.

The large verbal print, which we can call the **headline**, literally means 'We help you extend your residence permit. And also defend it'. In the bottom left corner there is a telephone number, followed by words in small print which say: *Servizio telefonico multilingue. Costo 1 scatto a chiamata urbana. Giorni feriali h. 14.00-18.00* [multilingual telephone service. Cost: one local call. Weekdays 2 – 6 pm]. To the right of the logo, there is the name of the service sponsor: *Patronato INCA GGIL* [INCA CGIL aid society], followed by a website address.

This already contains a number of significant cues. First of all, the service being promoted is that of helping people extend their residence permits, which means that those targeted are immigrants working in Italy. Secondly, the service provider and promoting organization is an aid society (INCA) which is sponsored by a left-wing trade union (CGIL). As can be seen on INCA's website, it offers free assistance on issues connected with labour law.

This kind of promotion can be identified as **institution-to-user** (or **I2U**) (§ 6.1.2). The politicized nature of the provider is reflected by the choice of the verb *difendere* [defend], which implies that the residence permit is an immigrant's right that is worth fighting for and must be protected. INCA thus becomes an ally in the struggle as it helps the target group extend and defend its permits. And personal and social deixis confirm INCA's role as an institution that is strong enough to back migrants' rights because it is a collective and has more weight than a single person, while it also treats the persons it assists as peers by addressing them directly in the first person plural 'we' and not, for instance, by choosing a third person singular ('INCA helps you') or avoiding any personal self-reference ('you will find the help you need at INCA'). Referring to point 4 of table 1, this stance would score very low on the authoritativeness and deference scales, but very high on the proximity scale.

The war metaphor associated with migrant workers' rights is reiterated and made more explicit by the typography and layout. All letters are capitals, with the conventional exceptions of *h.*, from the Latin *hora(e)*, [hour(s)], and the website address. The headline is in boldface, and there is no concession to fancy formats; the colours are limited to black and red over a white background, which adds graphic emphasis to the verbal text by making it stand out on the page. Moreover, the use of the colour red, which is a high-visibility colour as well as the identity colour of CGIL, once affiliated to the now dismembered Italian Communist Party, further highlights the institution's logo and the main focus of the text, *il permesso di soggiorno* [the residence permit]. Such typographic choices, together with the particular font and the worn-out paint effect used for the headline, establish a clear intertextual link between this text and the writings on military vehicles and military property in general. Extending a residence permit, the verbal-visual metaphor implies, is no easy task: you will have to fight for it, and even if you succeed, you must then be prepared to struggle against those who want to take it away from you.

Any translation choice aimed at softening the image of the organization should therefore be avoided. It would not be appropriate to have a more friendly or affable text, such as: 'Need to extend your residence permit? We're here to help!'; nor should there be translations which would try to diminish the anxiety connected with extending residence permits (e.g. 'Residence permit extension? No need to worry!'). Such choices might work with other kinds of services, especially those which are not free, but they are out of place in this particular case. We must acknowledge however that in certain target cultures, INCA's aggressive stance might not be appreciated, and a milder tone therefore would be preferred, both in terms of verbal choices and visual encoding. In this case, nonetheless the service being discussed is in an Italian context, and INCA is quite proud of its militant mission.

At this point, there is actually very little we could get from a filled out brief. The only point in the brief in table 1 that cannot be inferred from the text itself is the media plan, or point 1. For the sake of the discussion here, we can say that If we were to ask our clients for clarification on this point, we would be told that the ad was one of three similar texts circulated in 2007 in the Italian free press (the kind of newspapers that are distributed free of charge in train stations and other public places). This further narrows the target group to financially disadvantaged migrant workers, who do not spend money on buying regular newspapers, and whom INCA is more interested in assisting. It also explains the discontinuous line around the ad which suggests that the square is to be cut, or ripped out for future reference when the rest of the newspaper is thrown away.

In order to reach a larger number of migrant workers, particularly those who did not read Italian, the ads were translated into English, French, Spanish and Arabic. The English translation of the Italian source text above is reproduced below.

The grammar of the English version, as you might have noticed, shifts between 'help' + infinitive without 'to' and 'help' + infinitive with 'to' mingling two usages that are usually associated with American and British English respectively. This approach should normally be avoided since it points to an inconsistent, sloppy style. When you translate into languages that have regional variation, the brief (or points 1 and 2 of table 1) should give you a clear indication of the local variety you should conform to. In this particular case, however, English is clearly used as a lingua franca to reach migrants who are likely to speak a number of different non-standard varieties of English as a second or third language. For INCA's purposes, then, a degree of variation from the standard cannot be considered a flaw, as long as it does not hinder comprehension nor the interlinguistic transfer of the organization values mentioned above.

There are two other interesting case-specific translation choices that are fully compatible with what has emerged from our analysis of the Italian text. The first is the elucidation of *giorni feriali* [weekdays] as 'Mondays to Fridays'. The tradition of considering Saturdays and Sundays as non-working days is clearly of the West, based on Christian norms, while migrant workers might originally come from other traditions and feel ill at ease with the Italian division of the week. The second is the choice to leave the word *patronato* in Italian. INCA probably wanted to introduce the word and the concept behind it into their users' vocabulary and reference systems, and the English term, 'aid society', might be mistaken for a religious organization, an association that INCA would not be too keen on encouraging.

In more general terms, and in other working contexts, choices such as these we have just discussed (especially grammatical variation and the no translation option) may expose the translator to the risk of being labelled inaccurate or to being accused of leaving words out. Such a risk can be avoided, however, by providing a short comment regarding the choices made, negotiating with the client and or employer, and providing, in the right cases, alternative versions.

Example 2
Alternative versions and negotiation

In a 2005 tourist guide of Emilia-Romagna, which was to be distributed free of charge at international trade fairs and local tourist offices, one of the sight-seeing tours of the town of Forlì was entitled, *Architettura fra le due guerre* [architecture between the two wars]. The reference is to functionalist architecture, which had become popular under the Fascist regime. I provided the client, a local tourist promotion organization, with the translation 'Mussolini Deco', a phrase that was quite shamelessly borrowed from a famous non-promotional English-language tourist guide of the region, as I noted in my accompanying remarks. In my mind, the authoritativeness and competence of the source from which I borrowed the phrase should have vouched for its validity. Moreover, the name, 'Mussolini', with all its negative connotations, not only denoted a particular historical period, but was also particularly appropriate in that context since it was either on Mussolini's orders or in order to please him that Forlì (a few miles from Predappio, the dictator's birthplace) was partly re-built and expanded in the official architectural style of Fascism, that of Functionalism.

I should have thought better, however. The text I was translating was promotional, whereas the guide with 'Mussolini Deco', was not, since it was aimed at giving its readership as objective an account as possible of Forlì's historical and artistic features.

Furthermore, my knowledge of current local policies should have helped me to foresee the client's reticence to use the name 'Mussolini'. I knew that the client worked in close contact with local authorities, some of which had announced in the local media that nostalgia tourism to Mussolini's places was to be staunched; and although the tour *Architettura fra le due guerre* was focused on architecture only, the very fact of mentioning Mussolini's name might have implied political exposure. All these considerations should have led me to keep away from 'Mussolini Deco', or at least to provide alternative versions.

During the in-house revision phase, in fact, my contact person called me to negotiate a new version of the title that did not contain the name 'Mussolini'. I asked for a few hours' time to produce a range of new translations from which she and her colleagues would then be free to choose, and proceeded to assess alternative options.

Given the premises, I immediately excluded any reference to Fascism or Fascist architecture. My first version was a literal

1. 'Inter-war architecture'.

As I pointed out in the comments that accompanied the new versions, however, I felt that while an Italian readership would immediately understand what type of architecture was typical of inter-war Italy, foreign readers might need more precise cues to figure out what kind of sights were being proposed as worthy of interest. I therefore brainstormed for a few alternative versions that integrated more precise references to the type of architecture involved, and came up with what follows:

2. 'Italian Functionalism in the 1920s and '30s';
3. 'Functionalist architecture, 1922-43';
4. 'Functionalism in Forlì before WWII'.

As you may have noticed, version 4 incorporates an explicit reference to Forlì, which may have been added to the other versions as well. The reason for its exclusion lies in the total length of the name of the itinerary which, just like an advertising slogan, should be kept as short as possible in order to capture the reader's attention, and also, in this particular case, to accommodate space restraints since the texts were to be printed in columns, and each title, where possible, was to be printed on the same line. I did not incorporate this remark in the accompanying comments, as the client was perfectly aware of the page-space issue.

Version 3, being precise about the dates marking the rise and fall of Fascism in Italy, may have led a foreign reader to associate Functionalism with the Fascist era. As indicated in the accompanying comments, I favoured this solution, as the reference was emotionally indirect and historically correct. I also pointed out that I had applied the opposite strategy in version 2, blurring the historical period into a generic reference to two decades, without any explicit mention of the sad milestones of Fascism and the two wars.

I stopped at four versions. I felt that although the client's staff had initiated negotiations, they were quite busy revising the rest of the book (some 150 pages), and I knew that they were under enormous pressure as the guide was supposed to be ready for an international trade fair that was only a couple of weeks away. Moreover, given the brevity of the title involved, I did not apply any additional charge to the price we had agreed on.

My agency and responsibility as a translator ended there. Just to tell the end of the story, however, the final version, which I saw in the proofs and which was not negotiated further, was the first, more neutral 'Inter-war architecture', perhaps the least problematic from the Italian organization's point of view.

This example also tells us something about the kind of hidden agenda an institutional client may have. Although the brief for a promotional text may be as generic as 'choose as persuasive and emotional a language as possible', other unspoken priorities (in our example, avoiding political exposure) may override it. Opening and maintaining a channel of negotiation with the client is always a precious tool that helps solve such communication problems.

3. Key Issues in Promotional Translation

This chapter addresses a number of key issues concerning the process of translating promotional texts. First, it focuses on the extent to which brand names are translatable; it then discusses the notions of accuracy and loyalty as they apply to the specific case of promotional material. The last part deals with the main features of different types of promotion and the translation strategies they require.

3.1   The brand name

Brand names are texts in themselves. They convey the brand's carefully constructed image and identity. Sometimes this is connected with the nationality traditionally associated with a kind of product: real pasta must be Italian, so non-Italian pasta makers choose Italian-sounding names for their brands (such as the French Panzani); in Italy, given the Americanness attached to products introduced by US troops during WWII, Brooklyn and Big Babol [*sic*] chewing gum (produced by Perfetti, until 2001 an all-Italian company) has been popular at least since the 1980s.

Given their importance for brand image, brand names are usually treated as proper nouns and left untranslated when a product is marketed abroad. There are, however, exceptions to this, and these can be divided into three groups:

- phonetic/graphic adaptation
- changes introduced to avoid taboos or undesired associations
- translation to make the meaning or implications of the brand name transparent in the language of the target market.

Phonetic and graphic adaptation

Graphic adaptation usually occurs between different alphabets or writing conventions. Normally, for instance, a Russian brand-name (or company name) has both a Cyrillic version and a version written in Latin characters for the benefit of foreign markets. The process of graphic adaptation may also carry some phonetic adaptation if the phonetics and alphabet of the target language do not include all the sounds that make up the original name.

Phonetic adaptation, however, can also occur among languages that share the same alphabet. This is common, for instance, in Italy, where foreign brand names are sometimes adjusted to the Italian phonetic reading to recreate a sound string that is similar to that of the source language, especially in down-market segments. Thus, before introducing the original name Pantene, a haircare line was marketed in Italy as Panten; Glade home deodorants were renamed Gled until a few years ago; and more recently, the registered mark Easy Peel (a pull-tab for tin covers) has become Isy-Pil, which had to be registered as a separate trademark. We may notice that none of these names were Italianized in any other respect than phonetically – rather, they were transformed into other foreign-looking and foreign-sounding words. In this way, the positive connotation associated with non-Italian non-food products was retained, whereas the right pronunciation was ensured even when the buyers had no idea of foreign languages. This kind of approach may be perceived as offensive by perspective buyers who feel that it presupposes their ignorance or unwillingness to take on new words.

Taboos and unwanted associations

When a graphic or aural element of the brand name or logo generates undesired associations or violates a taboo in the target language and culture, changes are normally made, since the negative connotation would directly affect sales. These changes are usually as unintrusive as possible, as in the case of the Italian marketing of Sega consoles and videogames. The word Sega, pronounced as /'sega/ in the rest of the world, in Italian commercials used to be pronounced /'si:ga/ with a heavy American accent. This was done to avoid the obscene associations that go with the written word, which in Italian would be pronounced /'sega/ and allude to male masturbation and to a low-quality product. The exotic pronunciation, on the contrary, made it apparent that the word was not to be associated with its Italian homograph. The original pronunciation was restored once the brand had conquered and stabilized its market share, and at the same time built a positive brand image. Failing to adapt a negatively connoted brand name may have high costs for a company launching a product on a new market. An example (which may actually be an urban legend) is the Chevrolet Nova, which is reported to have sold poorly in Latin America, where no va means 'it won't start'; while in the 1970s, the sales of a Chinese battery brand, which had already started to perform well on the British market under its original name, written in ideograms, plunged after the brand name was translated literally as 'White Elephant', a sacred animal in South-East Asia, and a useless but expensive thing in British English (Chuangshen 1997:182; other examples in Chuansheng and Yunnan 2003).

Translation

The last type of brand-name trans-creation that will be tackled here is the re-encoding of the name's meaning, either to convey the original meaning or to introduce a new one. Examples of transparent translation of the original meaning are the White Elephant case above or the successful localization of Procter and Gamble's brand Mr. Clean as Mr. Propre (France), M. Net

(French Canada), Mastro Lindo (Italy), Meister Proper (Germany), Don Limpio (Spain), Mastro Limpio (Mexico), and so on. Additionally, there are cases in which the brand is loaded with new meanings in the target language. This can be achieved more easily when the brand name is intersemiotically trans-created, i.e. totally replaced with a new one that has a different physical, as well as verbal encoding.

This can happen when Western brands are launched onto the Chinese market and vice-versa, when the name is trans-coded into or out of ideograms, and the gap between very different cultures and semiotic systems (the first logocentric, the second more visually-oriented), encourages the trans-creation of meanings that best accommodate the conventions of the target language and culture. When a Western brand is translated into Chinese, there are several alternative encodings of its phonetic component, and for each phonetic alternative there are several possible graphic encodings. Of course, translations that carry a positive meaning and therefore comply with the Chinese conventions of brand-name making are favoured. Successful examples of such trans-creation are the Chinese translation of Coca-Cola, which adopts a slightly different pronunciation (ke-kou-ke-le) with a set of ideograms which read 'tasty and happy'. The reverse also applies: of all the possible English words whose pronunciation would sound more or less like their brand-name, the managers of the Xiling company, a manufacturer of air conditioners, chose Serene by virtue of its connotation of quietness and comfort. The last two examples were taken from Chuansheng and Yunnan 2003, where many other interesting examples can also be found.

3.2 Accuracy and loyalty to the original text

In chapter 1, we saw that promotional translation is usually assessed in functional terms; in other words, the main concern in this field should be whether the target text works, i.e. fulfils the purpose for which it is intended in the target language, culture, community, and context. Similarly, it has already been pointed out that this may require a thorough trans-creation of the source text (§ 1.3), and that creativity is one of the abilities that are often required of promotional translators (§ 2.1).

Such arguments go against traditional concepts such as accuracy and loyalty to the source text. In fact, in promotional texts, the concept of loyalty applies neither to the letter of the text, nor to its original content or message, but only to its intended function. If this function is not preserved, the target text is disloyal to the source text, even if its content and literal meaning are accurately conveyed. If, on the contrary, the function is maintained, then the translation can be deemed loyal to the original text, even if this implies creating an entirely new text, with a new form and a new content. Of course, the notion of 'function' does not only pertain to the generic purpose of persuading the target group to buy a product or service, or modify the target group's behaviour or attitudes in some way or other, but also includes the specific indications contained in the brief.

It is easy to demonstrate this hyper-functionalist view through examples, especially in the case of advertising, where clients tend to give functionality of the target text priority over the close rendition of the source text. Sometimes this involves non-verbal as well as verbal aspects, which are totally or partially changed to accommodate the features of the target markets, or the sales strategies of national branches.

In example 3 (at the end of this chapter), for instance, the different definitions of the product's main ingredient, i.e. a protective 'UV FILTER' in the British version, and a 'NUTRI-FILTRO' [nourishing filter], in the Italian one, are reflected by the different encodings of the computer-generated images (the small boxes over the picture). In the British ad, the protective agent is visualized as a rigid, semi-transparent and shiny ribbon, apparently in line with its function of shielding the hair from UV rays. In the Italian version, on the other hand, the nourishing substance – probably to convey its supposedly organic nature – is a floppy double filament that hangs onto the surface of the hair, which is superimposed onto a part of the model's real hair, not a computer-generated background of stylized hair as in the British example.

The two ads in the example were independently developed in-house by the respective national marketing departments from a range of visuals, a loose brief and a draft copy (in English) provided by the company's central marketing department. The values attached to the product were adapted according to the expectations of the British and Italian markets (protection and nourishment, respectively), or the marketers' perceptions about them. In such cases we can still talk of translation if we intend it in the broad sense used in this book, but a more specific term would be **glocalization** (Adab 2000:224).

The phenomenon of glocalization suggests that a holistic view of advertising translation, which embraces all its semiotic dimensions and the functionalist view of loyalty explained above, is possible and viable. Even when the end client is not a multinational company, but perhaps a small company interested in translating a few business-to-business posters to be shown at international trade fairs, this holistic approach may be extremely productive in marketing terms, because it caters for cross-cultural as well as cross-linguistic adaptation. Translators or in-house marketing staff may therefore propose or be asked to re-create a new campaign that best suits the expectations of the target group. Of course this does not mean that translators or in-house copywriters should acquire the skills of art directors, typographers, and the like. They can, however, suggest how non-verbal elements may be adapted in order to match new values or new figures of speech that were not present in the source text. In order to do this, however, it is vital that they are ready to forfeit the traditional concept of loyalty to the source text, and re-locate it within the text function and the client's brief.

The same can apply to non-advertising promotional genres, even if clients may be less prepared to spend a significant amount of time and money on a complete re-thinking of their promotional material. In such cases, if a translator spots an opportunity to trans-create the text, negotiation becomes vital to defend that opportunity (§ 2.2). Also, in such cases it is important to identify or investigate any hidden agendas the client may have: for instance, spending as little as possible on translation at the expense of the prospect of higher profits – perhaps because the efficiency of the members of staff entrusted with finding a translator will be assessed in terms of costs and timing, rather than according to possible higher company profits. In such cases, after careful negotiation, translators may have to find a compromise between their own loyalty to the function of the promotional text and the client's hidden agenda.

Even in non-advertising promotional genres, however, holistic trans-creation becomes necessary when given elements of the source text, if translated literally or (in the case of non-verbal elements) left unchanged, may offend or be negatively received by the target group. Examples of this might be a hypothetical brochure developed in the United States for a German language course, written in a gothic typographic style like the *Fette Fraktur* font shown in Schopp 2002, which in Germany (and Europe at large) would evoke neo-Nazism; or a website or brochure decorated with pictures of chrysanthemums, a symbol of nobility and power in many Asian cultures, but usually associated with death in Italy. (Other examples of cultural taboos can be found in chapter 8; see also § 3.1). At the verbal level, any incompatibility of the source text with the genre conventions that apply in the target language should be pointed out to the client and amended. Normally, however, the degree of freedom in trans-creation is directly dependent on the information/persuasion ratio (§ 3.3): the higher the persuasion and the lower the information, the higher the possibility, and potentially the need, to trans-create. For example, normally a business-to-consumer website offers much more leeway for trans-creation than a CV.

This does not only apply to the text as a whole, but also to its parts. Any part of the promotional text that contains specific and/or technical information, and serves the overall promotional purpose of the text through its local informative function rather than through an emotional or evocative language, should be approached with an accuracy-oriented approach. In other words, the local function of the informative parts of a promotional text should be preserved by conveying their content as accurately as possible. On the other hand, any part of the source text that appeals to the addressees' impressions, feelings and emotions rather than their rational judgement can be trans-created more freely. This point will be analysed further in § 3.3.

3.3   Different text types

As pointed out in chapter 1, we are dealing with a vast array of texts which share the same purpose: selling something (a product, a service, a person, a company, an attitude, or a behaviour). Of course, different categories of addressers and addressees determine different genres, each of them being characterized by specific stylistic conventions both in the source and target language. This is why, in the following chapters, a distinction will be made between different kinds of promotion, i.e. business-to-business (or B2B), **institution-to-institution** (or **I2I**), business-to-consumer (or B2C), and institution-to-user (or I2U) (see example 1 in chapter 2). Another contextual characteristic that contributes to genre definition is the kind of medium employed, the limits it poses and the opportunities it offers, all of which account for the general division of brochures and websites from advertising, and for the division of advertising texts according to the medium of distribution (the press, TV, posters, etc.).

The main characteristics of each (sub-)genre that are relevant for translation will be analysed in chapters 4-7. Before moving on to more particular issues, however, a general concept must be introduced here, as it will be mentioned throughout the following chapters and it is critical for the selection of appropriate translation strategies. It is the information-to-persuasion ratio of a text, that is the extent to which the text can be defined as informative or technical, compared with the extent to which it appears to aim at persuading the addressee by means that do not include the provision of objective data or facts.

'Information' and 'persuasion' are intended here as stylistic traits rather than textual purposes. Of course all promotional texts are ultimately persuasive, but in some promotional genres this persuasive purpose is best not made explicit and is thus left to impersonal, non-emotional information that is presented in such a way that it speaks for itself. In such genres, adding evocative language, or trying to get emotionally closer to the addressee (e.g. by speaking or writing in the first person to an interlocutor identified as a 'you') would be interpreted as a less than serious attempt at biasing the addressee's assessment of the qualities described in the text. In Great Britain and other Western European cultures high information, low persuasion texts include: CVs, business-to-business technical brochures and catalogues, and institution-to-institution literature. Whenever the texts within such genres are seen, both in the source and target language and culture, as objective and based on facts rather than argumentation and emotions, they are usually translated as closely as possible, i.e. reproducing the information as accurately as possible, while adjusting the form to the canons of the same genre in the target language.

High persuasion and low information genres, on the other hand, include most business-to-consumer texts, especially ads. Such texts tend to rely more on emotional, evocative language which is often used creatively, e.g. in word-play. When they do convey technical information, they may not be aimed at informing as much as impressing the addressee, as is evident when pseudo-technical jargon is used or scientific-sounding neologisms are specially coined to promote a given product. Such texts normally require thorough re-writing or trans-creation to preserve their persuasive effect.

As can be seen from the tentative collocation of some promotional genres in table 2, however, there are several genres that are located half-way across the information-to-persuasion ratio continuum. Additionally, it should be pointed out that there may be persuasive elements in the most informative of texts, and conversely, even the most persuasive texts may include facts and data. What kind of strategy should one adopt in such cases? Here agility (§ 2.1) comes to the translator's aid: as will be seen in the following chapter, informative texts can suddenly shift to a persuasive style and vice-versa, and such shifts can occur several times in a single text, paragraph, or even sentence, requiring a prompt adjustment of strategies from literal to creative translation, and back.

Example 3
The following two-page spreads were respectively circulated on the British and Italian press (mainly women's magazines) in 1999. Notice the different visual encoding of the product's main ingredient in the two CGIs (computer-generated images) in the small boxes

Table 2. *Visual indication of the collocation of different promotional genres on the information-to-persuasion ratio continuum*

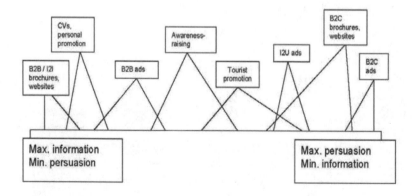

4. Translating Promotional Material
Self-promotion

This chapter first introduces four interrelated features of promotional texts, which the translator needs to consider when dealing with this text typology, i.e. the source, the target, the context of distribution, and the information-to-persuasion ratio. It then analyses, through real-life translation assignments, the characteristics of three types of text (CV, job application letter and promotional personal website) that share the same type of source: individuals who want to promote themselves as professionals.

4.1 Source, target, context of distribution, and information-to-persuasion ratio

Why is it particularly important to assess the source, the target, the context of distribution, and the information-to-persuasion ratio when translating promotional material? Knowing the source – where a promotional text comes from, or for whom it speaks – is vital not only to correctly assess the client's potentially hidden agenda (see chapter 2), but also because certain categories of persons or organizations have typical ways of using language, or addressing their clients. In Italy, for instance, public institutions and those who want to be associated with the public sector by their target audience/readership tend to use a rather impersonal, unemotional style when promoting their services, especially in sensitive fields such as healthcare. In their promotional texts, then, it is likely that the information-to-persuasion ratio will be oriented towards information, so that the overall impression is that the receiver of the text is being informed rather than persuaded to use a service. This is precisely what triggers persuasion in Italian users, because they expect an unemotional style from that type of source, and because they tend to associate it with objectivity and reliability, which is important in the scientific or medical sphere. In this chapter, sources will be categorized as: single individuals, as in personal promotion, private companies, as in business-to-business (B2B) or business-to-consumer (B2C) promotion, and institutions, as in institution-to-institution (I2I) or institution-to-user (I2U) promotion. Institutions include public entities, NGOs, or even private companies that aim at being identified with public organizations, usually to partake of their authoritativeness.

Knowing the target, i.e. whom the text aims at persuading, is important because it helps us make specific practical choices about the kind of language we should use. For instance, as pointed out in § 2.2., the definition of the target may be essential for decisions about the gender, number, register and lexical complexity to be used in the target text. Target identification is also essential to define the values and/or fears that are employed in texts with high promotion and low information content (see table 2 in chapter 3); this is especially important for copywriters and market researchers, but translators, too, should be aware that target characteristics may vary across markets and cultures, and sometimes it may be useful to warn commissioners that the product/service benefits present in the source text may not work in the target culture (see chapter 8). In this book, targets are categorized as collective entities, such as businesses or public organizations (as in B2B or I2I promotion), or individuals (as in B2C or I2U promotion).

The relationship between the source and the target is equally important. In some cases, it helps us assess the client's agenda, which often has to do with power relations. For instance, I2I promotional communication usually proceeds from the dependent or funded organization to the principal or funding one. The main purpose of such communication, therefore, will be that of showing the target that the source of the text is worth the support it receives (or more), even if the client labels the purpose of the text as 'informative' in the brief. In more general terms, however, the relationship between the source and the target is essential for establishing a correct information-to-persuasion ratio (§ 3.3.), that is to say, the amount of information regarding what is being promoted that is shared by both the source and the target. If the target readers already know the promoted product/service, and have very well-defined needs that cannot be easily changed (as usually happens in B2B genres, for instance), then they will expect very specific information. Not complying with such expectations – for example choosing a boastful or argumentative style rather than a factual and technical one – might irritate the target and undermine the source's reliability. In B2C promotion, on the other hand, the target is not likely to know what is being promoted yet, and his/her needs and desires are assumed to be induced or manipulated by the promotion itself. This justifies the use of a more openly promotional, less informative style.

Another factor that influences the encoder's and the translator's choices is the context of distribution, meaning the space (either physical or virtual) in which the text is circulated. The amount of other semiotic stimuli, especially other promotional texts, that occur at the same time or in the same space as our text tells us how hard the text will have to fight to get the target's attention. This information, too, helps us assess how far we should go towards the promotion end of the information-to-promotion ratio, using both verbal and non-verbal means, to give our text a chance to be seen among its potential competitors.

The last (but by no means least) factor that we will take into account is the information-to-persuasion ratio. As is clear from the previous discussion, it is a consequence of all the elements listed above: it is influenced by the type of source and target, their mutual relationship, and the context of distribution.

Moreover, for certain promotional genres or sub-genres, it varies substantially across cultures, depending on specific textual conventions. For instance, the promotion of private healthcare or educational services is deeply influenced by the country's economic history: in countries where government-funded systems are more widespread and/or are recognized to provide higher quality than private entities, private schools or healthcare providers will usually adopt a factual I2U, rather than a boastful B2C, style which, on the other hand, may be favoured by the same kind of sources in those countries where public services are non-existent or seen as less efficient. In such cases, special attention should be devoted to relevant target culture conventions, and, if necessary, raise or reduce the amount of promotional **boost** contained in the text. Generally speaking, however, if the source and target cultures share similar conventions (as usually happens in international B2B promotion, for instance), the translator is required to treat factual, neutral information as an **anchor** that should be manipulated as little as possible (i.e. translated as accurately as possible), so as to avoid the risk of the text going adrift and missing the target. On the other hand, less informative, more promotional texts or parts of texts can be trans-created, provided that the overall amount of boost is preserved, otherwise the text may either outrun or fall short of the target.

4.2   Self-promotion

The texts analysed in this chapter share the same type of source: individuals who want to promote themselves as professionals, whether they are applying for a job or trying to reach new customers for their activity. Translating this kind of text is not as unusual as one may think. In the global market, people may seek a job abroad, and require a professional translator's services if they recognize the importance of a well-written CV and cover letter. Moreover, professionals who use the Internet to make connections with their prospective clients or customers may need a multilingual website because they operate in a multilingual area, or they may be seeking to expand their market internationally by having their websites translated into foreign languages.

Individuals are usually aware of the competition they are exposed to. Their drive towards visibility, however, is usually mitigated by the need to build a reliable image, one that does not give away the professional's naturally limited resources (after all, they are individuals, not a company or institution) or, even worse, their limited knowledge of the conventions the target readership is used to.

The following sub-sections will examine the characteristics of self-promotion texts, dividing them according to whether their main targets are potential employers (as in the case of CVs and job application letters, which will be treated separately because they follow different textual conventions), or potential clients/customers (as in personal websites).

4.2.1 CVs

Curricula vitae are highly formal and standardized texts. Different conventions for CV writing exist in different countries; within the European Union, to reach formal equivalence and thus grant better understanding of the skills and abilities of applicants coming from different member states, the Europass CV model (http://europass.cedefop.europa.eu/europass/home/vernav/Europasss+Documents/Europass+CV/navigate.action) is currently used. It is a template, written in all the languages of the Union, which caters for the needs of those who apply for a job in both the public and private sector across the EU, both in their own country and abroad. If the person one is translating for falls within this category, then suggesting the Europass template for the relevant target language may be a good idea (with the proviso that in some sectors, such as academia, it may not be appropriate).

There are cases, however, in which the client may not wish to resort to a fixed model or template, either because it does not cater for his/her specific needs (e.g. a freelancer who wishes to list all his/her working experiences) or because s/he knows the potential employer as someone who may appreciate people who do not necessarily conform with the standard. In such cases, it is always better to make it clear that the responsibility for such deviation from the canon lies with the client, not the translator. Moreover, it is advisable that the degree of deviation from the standard is assessed and negotiated with the client depending on the kind of target, the kind of job that the client is applying for, the extent to which the client is sure of his/her knowledge of the potential employer or the person who will be receiving and selecting the CVs, and other important details that at first sight may seem minor. For instance, the client may want to mark out key elements (the ones that would be in bold and/or capital letters in the Europass and other traditional CVs) in dark red or blue rather than through other graphic conventions, but can s/he be sure that the person who receives the CV will not print it out, or photocopy it, in black and white, thus missing all emphasis?

At any rate, there are certain conventions that are best retained if the client wants to convey an image of professionalism and reliability, which are generally appreciated virtues in job applicants or freelancers seeking to expand their client pool. For instance, graphic consistency should be sought throughout the CV, with as few changes as possible in formatting (e.g. type and size of fonts, spacing, alignment, etc); bright or varied colouring and fancy graphic styles should be avoided, even if the context of distribution of CVs is usually characterized by fierce competition; and information units should be clearly separated, so that each relevant item can be easily spotted on the page and identified in terms of information type. Generally speaking, when writing or translating a CV, typography and layout play an essential role (Schopp

2002). Even if CVs are usually seen as a kind of text where the information conveyed is more important than the style of the language that conveys it, the very existence of rather strict semiotic and linguistic conventions for CVs bears witness to the contrary.

Titius Caius's CV (see example 4a) is an illustration of CV translation which entailed substantial negotiation with the client. I was commissioned the translation of the CV into Italian by the end client's wife, who owned a translation agency. Translation choices were negotiated with the end client either directly or through his wife. The text is reproduced faithfully except for proper names, which have obviously been changed.

Example 4a
English CV of a German professional working in the banking system

Curriculum Vitae	**Dr. Titius Caius**
	Steubenstraße 16, D-47100 Fantatown, Germany Phone: +49 777 66 55 444, Mobile +49 111 222 333 55 Fax +49 666 88 99 000, e-mail: drtitiuscaius@aol.com
Statement	A professional with a sustained record of achievement within the financial sector. Quick to grasp new ideas and concepts and to develop innovative and creative solutions to problems. A team player with highly developed communication and people skills. Proficient in English, German, Italian and Spanish and good knowledge of French and Luxemburgish
Career History	
10/03 – present	**PARIBAS FUNDSHUB, Luxembourg** **10/03–present: Manager, Dealing and Client Services Team** (8 people) • Supervise and manage all operational processes of a Fundsupermarket dealing and client service desk (UK, German and Swiss Market) on a daily basis • Co-operated in the start-up and production set up of a Fundsupermarket in Germany with special emphasis on taxation aspects • Involved in business analysis and development of new functions and applications • Validate and ensure the application of internal procedures and guidelines • Recruited and integrated a number of new Team members

Major achievements: Efficiently re-engineered operations to enhance performance and improve customer satisfaction

06/01 - 09/03   **AGENT INVESTMENT OPERATIONS S.A., Luxembourg**
05/02 – 09/03: Team Leader, International Team

- Overseeing all daily operational processes in the transfer agency area (incl. Dealing, Registration, Euroclear/Clearstream operations, trailer fee management, distribution processing etc.)
- Managing relationships with key TA clients and assisting in winning and integrating new TA clients
- Managing a team of 6 TA Administrators – recruitment, motivation, appraisals, delegation of duties

Major achievements: Restructured work flow in the transfer agencies in Luxembourg and Dublin and ensured full promotion and utilisation of electronic commerce applications

ASSET INVESTMENT OPERATIONS S.A., Luxembourg
06/01 - 04/02: Administrator

- Delivered and improved reliable shareholder record keeping
- Implemented an internal communication program
- Instructed and monitored new staff members

Major achievements: Reorganised reconciliation of accounts.
Designed and implemented new procedures in the transfer agency area

10/97 - 05/01   **UNIVERSITY OF BERLIN, Berlin**
05/98-05/01: Academic Assistant

- Researched and published on Spanish and Italian Culture and Literature
- Managed human and financial resources
- Co-ordinated national and international symposiums
- Wrote course design documents

Major achievements: Published several articles and held conferences.
Ph.D. degree with highest honours

10/97 - 05/01: Lecturer for Spanish & Italian Literature

- Taught Italian and Spanish literature
- Prepared and scored student exams, tutored and advised students
- Lectured on interpersonal communication topics

Major achievements: Organised and led internet and HTML workshops.
Developed training schemes for lecturers.

08/96 - 02/97   **TRAINER AT PHOENIX INSTITUTE** (Institute for Job Information and Training, Berlin)

- Developed and implemented training programs
- Advised clients and conducted negotiations with institutional clients

04/88 - 08/00   **GUIDE AT BERLIN TOURIST INFORMATION**

- Guided tourist groups and translated publications into Spanish and Italian
- Organised training for guides

Education

06/96 - 03/02   **Ph.D. in Spanish Literature** (University of Berlin)
Grade: summa cum laude

02/00 - 03/00   Research activities at the Universidad Nacional Autónoma de Argentina, Argentina

03/96   **M.A. in Political Science, Romance Philology and History** (University of Berlin)

10/92 - 10/93   Studies in Political Science and Italian Philology at the University of Bologna (Italy)

10/90 - 05/96   Studies in History, Romance Philology and Political Science at the University of Berlin

08/86 - 05/90   Berliner Gymnasium Berlin, school-leaving certificate: Abitur

08/87 - 07/88   Exchange student in Argentina

08/80 - 06/86   Staatliche Realschule Fantasberg, school-leaving certificate: Mittlere Reife

Language Skills   German (mother tongue); Proficient in English, Italian, Spanish; good language skills in French and Luxemburgish

Communication Skills
- Group leading and event management practice
- Published several articles and a Ph.D. thesis

	• Extensive experience in public speaking and lecturing • Strong multinational culture formed through extensive travel and living in Argentina and Italy for more than two years
PC Skills	Very good working skills in **Office programs** (Word, Excel and MS Project), in the **DTP Area** (e.g. Power-point, Photoshop), as well as in the **Internet Publishing Area** (HTML, Homepage, Frontpage)
Personal Details	**Nationality:** German **Date of birth:** 12th February 1970 **Place of birth:** Fantasberg, Germany **Civil status:** married, two children

Example 4b *Translation of 4a*	
CURRICULUM VITAE	DOTT. TITIUS CAIUS
Dati personali	Titius Caius Steubenstraße 16, D-47100 Fantatown, Germania Tel: 0049 777 66 55 444, Cell : 0049 111 222 333 55 Fax : 0049 666 88 99 000, E-mail: drtitiuscaius@aol.com Nato a Fantasberg (Germania) il 12 febbraio 1970 Coniugato, due bambini
Profilo	Comprovata esperienza nel settore finanziario, prontezza nell'apprendere nuovi concetti e nell'elaborare soluzioni innovative e creative. Propensione per il lavoro di squadra, elevate competenze sociali e organizzative. Ottima conoscenza di inglese, tedesco, italiano, spagnolo; buona conoscenza di francese e lussemburghese
Formazione	
06/96 - 03/02	**Dottorato di ricerca in Letteratura Spagnola** (Università di Berlino), con eccellenza
02/00 - 03/00	Visiting Scholar presso la Universidad Nacional Autónoma de Argentina, Buenos Aires
03/96	**Laurea magistrale in Scienze Politiche, Filologia Romanza e Storia** (Università di Berlino)
10/92 - 10/93	Studi di Scienze Politiche e Filologia Italiana presso l'Università di Bologna

08/86 - 05/90	Maturità classica (Abitur) presso il Berliner Gymnasium di Berlino
08/87 - 07/88	Scambio studentesco con l'Argentina
08/80 - 06/86	Licenza media (Mittlere Reife) presso la Staatliche Realschule di Fantasberg

Esperienze professionali

10/03 – oggi   **PARIBAS FUNDSHUB, Lussemburgo**
Responsabile unità di negoziazione e servizi alla clientela (8 persone)

* Supervisione e amministrazione costante di tutti i processi gestionali relativi a un'unità di negoziazione e servizi alla clientela (mercati britannico, tedesco e svizzero) di un supermercato di fondi
* Assistenza all'avviamento e al set up produttivo di un supermercato di fondi in Germania, con particolare riferimento agli aspetti fiscali
* Contributo alla business analysis e alla creazione di nuove funzioni e applicazioni
* Approvazione e controllo dell'applicazione di procedure e linee-guida interne
* Assunzione e integrazione di diversi componenti dell'unità

Principali successi: Efficace riorganizzazione delle operazioni nel senso di una migliore performance e per soddisfare al meglio le esigenze della clientela

06/01 - 09/03   **AGENT INVESTMENT OPERATIONS S.A., Lussemburgo**
05/02 – 09/03: Team Leader unità operatività estera

* Supervisione costante di tutti i processi gestionali dell'area Transfer Agency (ufficio registro e trasferimento), incluse le operazioni di negoziazione, iscrizione, Euroclear/Clearstream, gestione commissioni di intermediazione, distribuzione ecc.)
* Gestione dei rapporti con i principali clienti della Transfer Agency e contributo all'acquisizione e integrazione di nuovi clienti nella stessa area
* Gestione di un team di 6 amministratori dell'area Transfer Agency: assunzioni, motivazione, valutazione, assegnazione delle mansioni

	Principali successi: Ristrutturazione del work flow nelle Transfer Agencies di Lussemburgo e Dublino; promozione e garanzia dell'utilizzo a pieno regime delle applicazioni di e-commerce
	06/01 - 04/02: Amministratore • Tenuta e ottimizzazione dell'archivio azionisti, mansione svolta con la massima affidabilità • Implementazione di un programma di comunicazione interna • Tutoring e supervisione di nuovi colleghi **Principali successi:** Riorganizzazione dei controlli della concordanza dei conti. Elaborazione e implementazione di nuove procedure nell'area Transfer Agency
10/97 - 05/01	**UNIVERSITÀ DI BERLINO, Berlino** **05/98-05/01: Dottorando titolare di borsa** • Ricerche e pubblicazioni accademiche su Letteratura e Cultura Spagnola e Italiana • Gestione risorse umane e finanziarie • Organizzazione conferenze nazionali e internazionali • Compilazione di programmi di corsi universitari **Principali successi:** Pubblicazione di vari articoli accademici e partecipazione a convegni. Dottorato di ricerca conseguito con eccellenza **10/97- 05/01: Docente di letteratura spagnola e italiana** • Corsi di letteratura spagnola e italiana • Preparazione degli studenti agli esami e loro valutazione, attività di tutoring e orientamento • Lezioni sulla comunicazione interpersonale **Principali successi:** Organizzazione e direzione di workshop sull'uso di Internet e del linguaggio HTML. Ideazione di piani di formazione per docenti
08/96 - 02/97	**ISTITUTO PHOENIX (Istituto per l'Informazione e la Formazione Professionale, Berlino): Istruttore** • Ideazione e implementazione di programmi di formazione • Consulenza ai clienti e negoziazioni con i clienti istituzionali
04/88 - 08/00	**UFFICIO INFORMAZIONI TURISTICHE DI BERLINO: guida turistica**

	• Guida turistica per gruppi e traduzione di pubblicazioni in spagnolo e italiano • Organizzazione della formazione delle guide turistiche
Lingue straniere	Tedesco (madrelingua); ottima conoscenza di inglese, spagnolo e italiano; buona conoscenza di francese e lussemburghese
Competenze sociali e organizzative	• Esperienza di ruoli direzionali e organizzazione eventi • Pubblicazione di vari articoli accademici e della tesi di dottorato • Esperienza pluriennale di public speaking e docenza universitaria • Cultura di forte impronta internazionale, formata grazie a frequenti viaggi e lunghi soggiorni in Argentina e Italia, questi ultimi della durata di oltre due anni
Competenze informatiche	In ambito lavorativo, uso assiduo del **pacchetto Office** (Word, Excel e MS Project), di software **DTP** (come Powerpoint e Photoshop) e **Web editing** (HTML, Homepage, Frontpage)

Although the client was German, he had developed his CV in English, as he had worked for multinational financial corporations and was seeking a job outside Germany. In particular, he hoped to be employed by an Italian bank, with which he had already arranged an interview, and move to Italy. He believed that his knowledge of Italy and the Italian culture, which emerged from the CV itself, could be an advantage in obtaining the job, but did not feel up to writing an Italian CV that could persuade the potential employer that he could function smoothly in an all-Italian workplace, in other words that he 'thought like an Italian'. Accordingly, the first and main input I received was to make the CV 'as Italian as possible'.

After reading the source text, I asked the client whether he wished to comply with Europass standards, as the CV clearly broadly followed them in some respects (for instance, in the general graphic layout composed of a left-hand column bearing the labels of the CV sections, and a larger right-hand column describing the contents) but also differed from them in other details (for instance, in the Europass CV, labels in the left-hand column are much more detailed and sometimes redundant, as they identify items such as 'surname', 'name', 'address' and the like). The client answered that he had not chosen a Europass CV because he wanted to be recognized as somebody who was capable of taking independent decisions, and he knew that his potential employers would appreciate this approach in connection with the kind of position he was applying for.

After this second input, I then proceeded to re-organize the information structure of the CV in such a way that it would seem logical to an Italian reader. When I had a clear idea of how to arrange the target text, I contacted the client with a series of proposals, some of which were accepted, some other rejected. These proposals are listed below; the result of the negotiation can be seen in the target text (see example 4b).

The first step was to group contact information and personal details together and place them directly under the applicant's name (originally the contact information was placed under the applicant's name, whereas personal information was provided at the end of the CV). It is true that, from an applicant's point of view, contact information may be the most important item in a CV, because the purpose of the CV is in fact to have the potential employer call or write back to the applicant. It is also the kind of information one would find on a business card, which is a promotional text in its own right. From the employer's point of view, however, it is also useful to know the applicant's age, nationality, and whether s/he has a family. Having to look through the CV in order to find such information may be frustrating when its standard position would be together with the contact data (see the Europass model). The client agreed with this rearrangement.

The second consideration was linked to the 'Statement' originally placed directly under the contact data. It summarizes the entire CV in a few short sentences, highlighting the applicant's best qualities with a positively con-noted language that is quite unusual in Italian CVs, which are normally more oriented towards a neutral, informative style rather than rhetorical or lexical boost, as can be seen from the tentative collocation of this genre along the information-to-persuasion ratio continuum in table 2 in chapter 3. This kind of language is usual in English cover letters; in this case, however, the client did not wish to enclose a job application letter, which he knew would prob-ably be discarded, but stated his intention of also preserving the same kind of summary in the Italian version of the CV.

I therefore proceeded to adjust the style of the statement according to what would be found in an Italian job application letter (§ 4.2.2.), making it as impersonal as possible. This was done mainly at the grammatical and lexical level. At the grammatical level, the logical subject and theme of all sentences was changed from the applicant: *A professional... quick... a team player... proficient* to his skills and abilities, transformed from adjectives into nouns: 'Comprovata esperienza... prontezza nell'apprendere... propensione al lavoro di squadra... ottima conoscenza' [Proven experience... readiness to learn... inclination towards team-work... proficiency]. In this way, the focus was shifted from the person to his qualities, which were presented as facts. The same strategy was employed throughout the text, for instance changing verbs into nouns in the career history sections. e.g. *Efficiently re-engineered operations*, with the applicant as logical subject, became an impersonal 'Efficace riorganizzazione delle operazioni' [effective re-engineering of operations].

At the lexical level, the promotional boost inherent in words such as *new, creative, innovative*, and *highly developed* was preserved: 'nuovi', 'innovative', 'creative', 'elevate'. On the other hand, the *Statement*, which implies a subject that states, namely the applicant, became a more objective 'Profilo' [profile]: something that is stated about the applicant by an external, although indeterminate, logical subject. Moreover, the *sustained record of achievement*, once again something that implies the applicant's active role in achieving success in his work, was turned into 'comprovata esperienza', where the applicant's experience is backed by some indeterminate material proof or authoritative testimony. The omission of the *achievement* element is a clear loss of boost, but makes the target text seem much more objective and less boastful, following the Italian stylistic conventions for CVs and cover letters. In fact, CVs and cover letters are two examples of promotional genres where conventions concerning the information-to-persuasion ratio vary across cultures. In such cases, then, decreasing emotional boost to bring it within the target culture's conventional limits (or increasing it, as might be the case when translating from Italian into other languages) may become necessary to preserve the text's overall promotional purpose.

Following the same logic, the *Major achievements* items in the Career History sections should have been reworked into the rest of the text, or at least their graphic emphasis should have been eliminated or attenuated. The client, however, chose to keep them lexically and graphically conspicuous because he knew the target reader as someone who would appreciate a summary of what the applicant had achieved in different workplaces in addition to, and possibly more than, an account of what responsibilities he had covered, so my suggestion on this third point was dismissed on valid grounds.

The fourth major difference concerning the adjustment of the information structure of the text was the anticipation of the education section, which was relocated before the career history. This was not done in order to comply with conventional Italian standards, but to highlight the applicant's high educational level (he held a PhD) and inclination towards international relations, as shown by his in-depth knowledge of Romance languages and cultures. The client agreed with this strategy.

In translating the section, however, I realized that most of the items in the education list were redundant, as in Italian CVs it is customary to include only the degrees and diplomas obtained after each cycle of studies (e.g. BA, MA, and PhD) and not the period of study that leads to them. Additionally, lower education level such as primary and junior high school (*Mittlere Reife* in German, 'Licenza Media' in Italian) are generally not accounted for, as they do not qualify the applicant's specialization in any way. At this point, however, the client had already received two e-mail inquiries, one about the Europass model, and one consisting in a list of proposals for the rearrangement of the information structure. Not wishing to overtax the client's patience, I took the initiative of omitting the period of university studies (10/90 - 05/96), explaining in the e-mail that accompanied the target text that the information could be easily retrieved from the items about his MA and high school diploma. For the rest, for the sake of completeness I did translate the *Mittlere Reife* item, but advised the client to take it out, and left the start and finish dates of each period of study even if the corresponding items stated the kind of diploma obtained (e.g. 'Maturità classica'), suggesting that only the finish dates be used except for exchange programs with foreign institutions.

Clumsy choices like these could have been avoided by further negotiation, or much better, by including relevant proposals in the second e-mail inquiry. By including suggestions about the final editing of the text in the accompanying e-mail, I placed the responsibility for the corresponding choices upon the client, as I would have done by negotiating them beforehand; in the latter case, however, the target text would at least been a truly turnkey version. As usually happens in professional practice, such considerations had to be balanced against other ones, such as time constraints (the deadline, and the lack of time to draft a first version that would have helped spot the need to rearrange the text at the micro level) and the wish not to irritate the client with too many questions about what s/he may perceive as mere details of translation.

Example 4 is a good illustration of negotiation strategies and introduces an aspect that will·be brought to the fore in the following section: the need to adjust the amount of boost used in personal promotion to the conventions that apply in the target culture.

4.2.2 Job application letters

Job application letters have the same source, target, and context of distribution as CVs. Usually, they actually accompany curricula vitae, in which case they may be termed cover letters. In the e-mail era, cover letters may be included in the text of the message, whereas the CV would normally be attached as a separate file. This can have an impact on the length of the cover letter, as e-mailed letters are usually shorter than hard copies sent via surface mail.

Like CVs, job application letters are formal texts that follow culture- and language-specific conventions. It is therefore advisable that in translating such texts attention not be paid only to rendering the factual information which makes up most of the letter (and makes it a high information, low persuasion kind of text in comparison with other promotional genres, see table 2), but also to the functional equivalence of the target text as a persuasive piece of writing. For instance, it is not unusual to find enthusiastic and self-assertive statements in American English cover letters, which are not necessarily bound to the neutral objectivity that is normally found in CVs, and also follow a less schematic style. American guides to cover letter writing (see for instance http://owl.english.purdue.edu/owl/resource/527/03/) suggest that the body paragraphs contain 'strong claims' that the applicant is the right candidate for the employer, and is better than others. In Italian cover letters, on the other hand, even in the face of less schematic, more argumentative language, one would more often find an objectivity and neutrality that reflect those contained in the CV itself, and seem much less assertive than American letters in the description of the applicant's qualities. This difference equals a shift of job application letters along the information-to-persuasion ratio continuum across languages and cultures, which should be taken into account in translating this kind of text.

The tendency towards less assertive CVs and cover letters is by no means limited to Italian linguistic and cultural conventions. This is how the Dutch authors Hofstede and Hofstede (2005:116) describe the matter from their own point of view:

> American applicants, to Dutch eyes, oversell themselves. [...] Dutch ap-
> plicants, in American eyes, undersell themselves. [...] To an uninitiated
> American interviewer, an uninitiated Dutch applicant comes across as
> a sucker. To an uninitiated Dutch interviewer, an uninitiated American
> applicant comes across as a braggart.

Hofstede and Hofstede explain the difference between assertiveness and modesty on the workplace with a specific cultural dimension that they call "masculinity vs. femininity", and provide a list of 74 countries and regions with their respective Masculinity Index Scores (ibid.:120-121). Their conclusions, however, should be taken with a pinch of salt: Italy seems to rank higher than the US on the masculinity scale, but Italian CVs and cover letters seem to be more on the Dutch than on the American side.

Examples 5, 6, 7a and 8a below are the result of a rewriting process based on sample letters found in various online and offline sources. Even if they are not real texts, they reflect the conventions by which cover letters are written in American English and in Italian, since the texts that were used to draft them are in fact produced and circulated as models to be followed by applicants in the respective languages and cultures. They can therefore be used as parallel texts to compare respective textual features. More examples for the same and other languages can be easily found in professional writing manuals and online career guides.

Taken two by two, same-language examples display obvious differences (for instance, example 6 is clearly shorter and more informal than example 8a, and can be used for e-mail transmission as well as surface mail). Overall, however, they share several features. In the two American examples (5 and 7a), self-assertiveness emerges clearly from sentences and phrases such as *My levels of enthusiasm, experience and team-building skills provide an excellent match for the requirements of this position*; *I performed an active and significant role*; *formidable challenge*; *daily contact with dozens of customers, effectively prioritize tasks, optimize my time and maximize the results of my efforts* (example 7a). Some of the words underlined here (*excellent, formidable, optimize*, and *maximize*) are instances of what Teh (1986) and Bhatia (1993: 51-52) call **lexical boost**, that is to say, words with an inherently superlative meaning that are used to boost the applicant's qualities without resorting to grammatical devices such as the grammatical superlative form.

Lexical boost proper is not found at all in the two Italian examples. We only find some degree of boost, but with no inherently superlative words, in '*buon* livello' [good level], referred to the applicant's knowledge of English (example 6) and, in example 8a, one instance of '*particolare* interesse' [special interest] (example 8a), which, however, does not count as a quality or past experience, and one '*importanti* istituti bancari' [important banks]. (Note that in the rest of the book, the term *boost* will be used in this broad sense rather than in Teh and Bhatia's specific one, for which the term *lexical boost* is used instead.)

Verbs are perhaps the most telling elements with regard to self-assertiveness: in example 5, we find *I believe that my enclosed resume will demonstrate that my characteristics match such requirements*, whose closest match in example 8a is '*spero* che la mia formazione e le mie esperienze lavorative possano interessarLa' [I *hope* that my education and professional career *can be of interest for you*']. The style of the Italian example would certainly seem too weak to an American employer, whereas the American style would appear over-confident to an Italian reader. A functional translation of letters such as those contained in the examples, then, would imply shifting the position of the text along the information-to-persuasion ratio continuum. American source texts intended for an Italian audience would need to be pruned of some of their boost, which would tip them closer to the maximum-information, minimum-persuasion end of the line. Conversely, a job application letter written by an Italian for an American potential employer would probably need to be trans-created in such a way as to sound more persuasive; the operation would in turn require close cooperation and much negotiation of choices between the translator and the client. Two possible results of such processes, in both directions, can be seen in example 7b and example 8b.

Example 5
American English job application letter

789 Rhododendron St.,
Madison, WI 53703
February 19, 2008

Ms. Jennifer White
Human Resources Manager
Health & Safety Corporation
P.O. Box 411
Houston, TX 77002

Dear Ms. White:

Prof. John Doe, a consultant to your firm and my Marketing professor, has informed me that Health & Safety Corp. is looking for someone with excellent communication skills and leadership background to train for a management position. I believe that my enclosed resume will demonstrate that my characteristics match such requirements. In addition, I should like to mention how my recent work experience makes me a particularly strong candidate for the position.

As a promoter for Fireproof Textiles at the 2007 Birmingham (UK) Safety & Health Expo, I discussed Fireproof Textiles' products with marketing and sales personnel from all over the world. I also researched and wrote reports on the development of new products and compiled information on safety apparel trends. The knowledge of the health and safety industry I gained from this position would help me analyze how H&S products can meet the needs of regular and prospective customers, and the valuable experience I gained in promotion, sales, and marketing would help me use that information effectively.

I would welcome the opportunity to discuss my qualifications with you. If you are interested, please contact me at (111) 222-3333 or by e-mail at margegreen@server.com. I look forward to meeting with you to discuss the ways my skills may best serve Health & Safety Corp.

Sincerely yours,

Marjorie Green

Enclosure: resume

Example 6
Italian job application letter

Spett.le Macchine Srl,

mi chiamo Eugenio Bianchi, sono un ingegnere elettrico con indirizzo automazione industriale, ho 26 anni ed attualmente sto svolgendo servizio civile che terminerà il 30/07/08.

Sono interessato ad approfondire sia argomenti tecnici sia argomenti di marketing.

Durante gli studi universitari ho studiato per sei mesi in Gran Bretagna come vincitore di borsa Socrates. Questa esperienza mi ha consentito di imparare l'inglese ad un buon livello.

Sono una persona curiosa cui piace viaggiare, incontrare nuove persone ed imparare.

Vi autorizzo all'utilizzo dei miei dati personali ai sensi del D. lgs. 196/03.

Cordiali saluti

Eugenio Bianchi

Example 7a
American English application letter

RODERICK BROWN
789 Rhododendron St.,   Office: (000) 555-6666
Madison, WI 53703   Mobile: (000) 777-8888

February 19, 2008
Letter of Application

To Whom It May Concern:

With reference to the employment opportunity advertised on your website, I have noted that the Senior Account Manager position you are offering strongly appeals both to my experience and personal goals. My levels of enthusiasm, experience and team-building skills provide an excellent match for the requirements of this position.

As an Account Manager at Smith & Smith, I performed an active and significant role in the development of new business relationships. I met the formidable challenge of coordinating daily contact with dozens of customers and suppliers by learning to effectively prioritize tasks, optimize my time and maximize the results of my efforts. Regardless of workload, I took care that each contact received an appropriate level of attention as to portray them as the only organization that mattered to S&S.

Now, I am looking for a new opportunity where I may continue to provide innovative direction as a member of your team. I will welcome a personal interview at your convenience to discuss this opportunity with you. I can be reached at the contacts above and look forward to hearing from you soon.

Thank you for your time and consideration.

Sincerely,

Roderick Brown

Example 7b
Translation of example 7a into Italian

RODERICK BROWN
789 Rhododendron St.,
Madison, WI 53703

Ufficio: (000) 555-6666
Cellulare: (000) 777-8888

19/2/2008
Lettera di presentazione

Spett.le <company's name>,

Scrivo in risposta all'annuncio di lavoro relativo alla posizione di Senior Account Manager pubblicato sul vostro sito web.

Nelle mie mansioni di Account Manager presso la Smith & Smith, mi sono occupato della presa di contatti con nuovi clienti e fornitori, gestendo considerevoli moli di lavoro su base quotidiana. Questa esperienza mi ha insegnato a ottimizzare tempo e risultati, e a mantenere un'immagine aziendale positiva attraverso una cura costante e personalizzata delle relazioni esterne.

Sono una persona che si dedica con entusiasmo al lavoro e possiede spiccate doti di team-building.

Spero che le mie esperienze possano essere di vostro interesse. Rimango a disposizione ai recapiti contenuti nell'intestazione della presente per un eventuale colloquio in merito alla mia candidatura.

Vi autorizzo all'utilizzo dei miei dati personali ai sensi del D. lgs. 196/03.

Nell'attesa di un vostro cortese riscontro, vi ringrazio e porgo i miei più

Cordiali saluti,

Roderick Brown

Example 8a
Italian job application letter

Marcella Rossi
Via Garibaldi, 9
95124 Catania
tel. 095 -333333
Cell. 320-001122334
e-mail marcella.rossi@server.com

Gent. Responsabile del personale,

con la presente desidero sottoporre alla Sua attenzione il mio curriculum vitae.

Sono laureata in Economia e Commercio e già durante la formazione accademica e post laurea ho mostrato particolare interesse per l'analisi economico-quantitativa con riguardo agli aspetti matematico-finanziari. Ho successivamente sviluppato esperienze professionali presso importanti istituti bancari italiani, nell'ambito del Risk Management e dell'area titoli e derivati.

Spero che la mia formazione e le mie esperienze lavorative possano interessarLa e resto a Sua disposizione per ogni chiarimento in merito alla mia candidatura.

Nell'attesa di un Suo cortese cenno di riscontro, porgo i miei migliori saluti.

Vi autorizzo, limitatamente allo scopo per cui Vi scrivo, all'utilizzo dei miei dati personali ai sensi del D. lgs. 196/03.

Marcella Rossi

Example 8b
Translation of example 8a into English

Marcella Rossi
Via Garibaldi, 9
95124 Catania
tel. +39 (0)95 -333333
mobile +39 320-001122334
e-mail marcella.rossi@server.com

Dear Human Resources Manager,

Please find enclosed [*or 'attached' if the CV is sent via e-mail*] a copy of my CV for your consideration. I believe that my experience and qualifications make me an ideal candidate for a managerial position in the financial areas of <company's name>'s business. Other positions in any other areas of your company will also be considered.

Ever since my time at University, both before and after my MA in Economics, I have been developing and cultivating a special interest in quantitative economic analysis, particularly concerning the application of mathematics to finance. I have also had the opportunity to effectively put such knowledge into practice during my professional experience at several major Italian banks, where I performed an active and significant role in Risk Management as well as Securities and Derivatives.

I would welcome the opportunity of a personal interview to discuss how my qualifications and skills may best serve <company's name>. To this end, I can be reached at any time at the contacts above.

Thank you for your time and consideration,

Sincerely,

Marcella Rossi

In example 7b, the first major transformation is the substitution of the generic salutation *To whom it may concern* with the company's name. This operation could be carried out on the source text as well, as the letter is clearly written for a specific company and, therefore, it does not count as a translation-driven modification.

When we come to the first paragraph, however, we find that, whereas the source text states that the position appeals to the applicant, and why he would be the best person to fill the vacancy, the Italian text only states the subject of the letter. This is motivated by the fact that in Italian job application letters, writing that the position for which you are applying is interesting for you is equal to stating the obvious. Also, it is usually left to the reader to assess whether the applicant's experiences and characteristics match the requirements for the position in question. For this reason, the information content (but not the general attitude, or the boost) of the last part of the first paragraph of example 7a have been postponed to the third and fourth paragraph of 7b.

The reduction of self-assertiveness and boost to a more impersonal, neutral style is evident in the second paragraph, where the applicant's work experience is outlined. Here several elements have been omitted, some of them (*active and significant role, formidable challenge, effectively*) carry a type of boost that in an Italian setting would be more appropriate in a past employer's letter of recommendation. Some others, that shorten the distance between the applicant and the prospective employer through colloquialisms (e.g., *dozens of customers and suppliers*) are generalized in a more formal, although equally boosting, 'considerevoli moli di lavoro' [considerable workloads], which at the same time partially makes up for the omission of *regardless of workloads* below.

Similarly, the boosting triad, *prioritize tasks – optimize time – maximize efforts* is subsumed in one action verb only, 'ottimizzare tempo e risultati' [optimize time and results]. The semantic component of the first element that indicates organizational skills, *prioritize tasks*, is partly recovered in 'gestendo [managing] considerevoli moli di lavoro' above. In the last sentence of the second paragraph, the reason why the company should care about its contacts feeling as *the only organization that mattered* is made explicit in 'mantenere un'immagine aziendale positiva' [maintain a positive corporate image]. This operation helps shift the focus from the emotional impact of the applicant's work to the importance of such work for the company's interests.

The third paragraph of example 7b is an integration that recovers the semantic content of part of the last paragraph in example 7a, *My levels of enthusiasm ... and team-building skills.* The relocation was necessary because in Italian formal professional communication, personal characteristics are usually regarded as less important than work experience, and occupy the last part of CVs and job application letters.

The rest of the last sentence of the first paragraph in the source text, ... *provide an excellent match for the requirements of this position,* has been relocated as the first sentence of the fourth paragraph of the target text, where it introduces the closure. Notably, the self-assertive original wording has been changed into a much more hypothetical '*Spero* che le mie esperienze *possano* essere di vostro interesse' [I *hope* that my experience *may* be of interest to you]. In Italian applications, such non-committal strategies do not denote a weak personality, but are widely used to make professional relations more impersonal, less loaded with emotions. This is not only meant to make things easier on both parts in case the application is turned down, but is also motivated by the traditional clear-cut separation between the kind of language one uses for professional purposes and the one that is used in personal life. Emotional language, even when applied to professional relations, such as in *the only organization that mattered to S&S*, is usually avoided in Italian professional writing, as are colloquialisms and the constant use of boost.

Going back to the first sentence of the fourth paragraph of example 7b, it actually replaces the sentence that had the same metatextual function of introducing the closure in the source text, *Now, I am looking for a new opportunity where I may continue to provide innovative direction as a member of your team*, which was omitted. Indeed, it is quite obvious that the applicant is looking for a job at the company he is addressing, and the only other element in the sentence, *innovative direction*, does not have a formulaic value or a specific information content that would motivate its translation. It is only another instance of boost, which would be particularly inappropriate in this section of the letter, where formality is even higher than in the paragraphs introducing the applicant (the second and third paragraphs of the target text). Here, boost and self-assertiveness are actually countered by additional non-committal strategies, such as in 'per un *eventuale* colloquio in merito alla mia candidatura' [if the opportunity arises for a *possible* interview regarding my application].

The following paragraph of the target text is a formula that must be added to Italian cover letters and/or CVs following an act on personal data protection issued in 1996 and modified in 2003. This takes us back to the importance of knowing relevant laws and restrictions that apply to the promotional texts we translate (§ 2.1). Finally, the closure of the letter is highly formal and formulaic, and does not pose particular translation problems.

The resulting target text is shorter that the source one, although it has more paragraphs, but, most notably, it contains much less boost, is more formal, and is worded in such a way that the applicant does not appear over-confident or even arrogant, as he would probably appear if he sent in a more literal translation of the original text. When working in the opposite direction, of course, reverse strategies should be employed, or the Italian applicant would fail to impress the American prospective employer as a self-confident individual with strong qualities. Example 8b illustrates how this can be done.

Whereas in 7b the first paragraph had to be pruned of boost and the information content of its last part postponed to the third and fourth chapters, the reverse happens in example 8b. Boost is added ('ideal'), and self-confidence is shown clearly rather than downplayed ('I believe', 'Other positions ... will also be considered'). Additionally, the first part of the second sentence of the target text is a boost-enriched version of the first sentence of the third paragraph of the source text. Finally, the kind of position the applicant is applying for is specified in order to add relevance to the letter. The information content of this specification, '...a managerial position in the financial areas of <company's name>'s business. Other positions in any other areas of your company will also be considered', should be negotiated with the client. Here, the assumption is that the applicant is looking for a managerial position, but is ready to settle for less and does not want to lose the opportunity to be hired by this particular company by seeming too demanding.

In the first sentence of the second paragraph, the deliberate addition of the verb 'cultivated' qualifies the applicant as a person who is capable of constant and active dedication. This is equal to adding boost, because the added notion has a positive connotation, even if this is done by manipulating concepts rather than just words. On the other hand, 'quantitative economic analysis, particularly concerning the application of mathematics to finance' is factual information. It consists in the enunciation of a discipline that has a domain-specific name and extension in both languages, plus a specific technical qualification; it is therefore translated as accurately (or literally) as possible, without much adding or pruning. If we were to place the phrase on the information-to-persuasion content ratio continuum (table 2), it would be right at the maximum-information, minimum-persuasion end.

In the last sentence of the second paragraph, significant additions include the notion of 'put[ting] such knowledge into practice', which makes it explicit for the prospective employer that the applicant's studies have a practical use (and thus counts as another instance of conceptual boost), and, additionally, several instances of boost, including 'effectively', 'several' (quantitative boost), 'major' (an over-translation of *importanti*, which shifts from a generic boost to lexical boost proper), 'active and significant role', and arguably even 'as well as', which, being a more marked conjunction than the simple 'and', makes the two linked elements stand out as more relevant. Adding this kind of boost in this kind of texts is reasonably safe in this particular translation direction (Italian into American English), provided that the information content of what one adds is sufficiently generic and cannot be easily refuted. For instance, unless the applicant did a particularly bad job or was particularly lazy during one of her past experiences, it is unlikely that any of her past employers would refute her claim that she put her knowledge 'effectively' into practice, or that she played an 'active and significant role'.

The third paragraph of example 8b recovers the last sentence of the third paragraph of 8a, while the information content of the first sentence of the same paragraph of 8a has been anticipated to the first paragraph of the target text. The addition of 'how my qualification and skills may best serve...' conveys an image of self-confidence, regarded as a virtue rather than a weakness in an applicant for a job with an American company. The closure is once again adapted to the formal conventions of the target language, and the Italian legal formula in the fifth paragraph of the source text has of course been deleted, assuming that the addressee of the letter is located outside Italy. If the prospective employer were an American company with an Italian branch, however, and if selections were carried out at that branch, the formula should either be translated literally, or left in Italian. In the latter case, it can be relocated at the very end of the letter, and put in inverted commas to mark out that it is a legal formula that only applies to the Italian legal situation.

4.2.3 Personal websites with a promotional purpose

Self-employed professionals and sole proprietor businesses increasingly use the web to seek new clients, expand their markets internationally, and build an image of reliability and professionalism. In this section, only texts promoting individuals who provide a given service or product as professionals, rather than promoting the service or product itself, will be taken into consideration. Texts that promote the services or products offered by sole proprietor businesses can be considered B2B or B2C communication, depending on their targets (chapters 5 and 7). Personal websites that do not have a professional use are of course excluded from the scope of this book.

The potential targets of personal promotion websites may be either businesses or individuals. This largely depends on the kind of services or products offered by the professional in question, and sometimes the website is intended for both categories of targets. This may happen, for instance, with a plumber working for construction companies as well as private houses, who may live in a multilingual country or require the contents of her/his website to be translated from a working draft because s/he is not a native speaker of the language of the host country. It is therefore important for the translator to define the target together with the client, as it may be difficult to infer this information from the kind of text one is dealing with. Knowing the target and the kind of relationship our client wishes to establish with them is important not only because it helps us make choices about the degree of formality and detachment vs. friendly, emotional language that we can use. It is also important to assess the extent to which the target knows the kind of services or products offered by our client, that is to say, whether the target does, or does not, work in the same field as our commissioner. Going back to the previous example of the plumber, a webpage addressing construction companies would normally require a much more technical and specific information content, conveyed, and translated, in a much more concise style, than a webpage addressing private individuals who are perhaps more interested in prices and availability and can be addressed in a persuasive and less informative style. If our client has mixed targets and does not have the resources to create separate sections in the website, then a compromise has to be struck between the two strategies, and discussed with the client.

In either case, since the main object of promotion is the producer or provider, not the product or the service, it is likely that at least the 'About me' page of the website will share some of the information content of CVs or application letters, that is to say, the professional's education and work career. The style in which it is conveyed, however, changes substantially depending on whether the main target is expected to appreciate a truly CV-style detailed list (which is thought to provide an impression of professionalism) or a more narrative account, perhaps in the first person singular, which builds an emotional bridge between the addresser and the addressee.

In the following example, two 'About me' pages, one in Italian (the source text) and the other in English (the target text) are analysed. They are extracted from the website of a professional astrologist operating in Italy, who, after gaining a certain international renown thanks to conferences and private contacts in the UK, contacted me through the website of the TradInFo association to commission me to translate her site into English.

Of course, a personal promotion website can consist of many more sections, but their nature may change depending on the kind of service/product offered, and they may have less relevance for personal promotion than for the promotion of what the professional provides. Additionally, the 'About

me' page is usually the first page of the site, either coinciding with, or coming immediately after, the homepage, and it is always present, even when the
website only consists of one or very few sections.

Example 9
*Barbara Amadori's homepage (© Barbara Amadori) – Italian version at http://
www.barbaramadori.com*

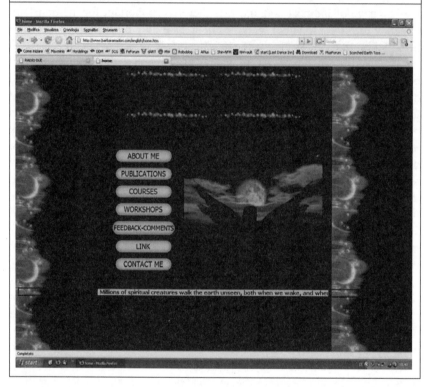

Unlike what we saw in § 4.2.1 and § 4.2.2 with CVs and job application
letters, the text in Example 9 did not require substantial re-writing on the
translator's part. This is due to the fact that, unlike the previous two genres,
personal websites are not usually subject to rigid conventions. Additionally,
when translating a website into English, the target cannot be clearly defined
in geographical or cultural terms, since English is commonly used as a lingua
franca for international web communication. Therefore, even if there were
specific conventions (e.g., concerning politeness, formality/informality, boost,
etc.) in one of the cultures that may be reached by the English version of the
website, or in the corresponding variety of English, they would not apply to all
of the potential addressees of the website, unless the commissioner specified
one or more priority geographical targets.

The target readership of the two texts is clearly composed of individuals

Example 9a
Italian 'Chi sono' page, with graphic adjustments (http://www.barbaramadori.
com/chi%20sono/chisono.htm)

Barbara Amadori

Sensitiva, Master Reiki, Astrologa e giornalista, Barbara Amadori ha una formazione culturale che spazia dalla musica classica (ha studiato presso il Conservatorio di Musica "B. Maderna" di Cesena), a quella letteraria (Diploma Magistrale), linguistica (First Certificate conseguito c/o British School) al giornalismo.

Appassionata ed attenta studiosa delle discipline esoteriche quali Qabalah, Numerologia, Astrologia Karmika, Evolutiva, al fine di completare adeguatamente la proprio cultura personale in merito alla Qabalah ebraica, consegue il diploma di II livello in ebraico antico.

Da oltre 25 anni si dedica al mondo delle Dimensioni Sottili che permeano l'esistenza di ciascuno di noi.

I seminari da lei condotti vertono su alcuni importanti aspetti della Medianità e soprattutto si svolgono con l'intento di insegnare a tutti i partecipanti, la possibilità di contattare, attraverso i propri doni intuitivi, la propria Guida spirituale. Diversi pertanto i "passaggi" che vengono esaminati in merito: prima di affrontare l'anelato momento in cui si effettua il contatto con le Guide, Barbara Amadori conduce le persone attraverso l'apprendimento della lettura energetica e medianica delle fotografie, degli oggetti, dei nastri, nonché esercizi pratici sulle possibilità di comunicazione fra i partecipanti del seminario attraverso l'utilizzo di tecniche meditative e di unione con l'aura.

Inoltre sia corsi che seminari prevedono parti pratiche e teoriche e dipanano le proprie forme partendo dalla teosofia fino a giungere, seppur in modalità breve e superficiale, a qualche elemento di fisica quantistica.

Il curriculum di Barbara Amadori inerente l'affascinante mondo dell'ignoto, vanta, nel 1997, unica donna in Italia, la pubblicazione del rinomato Saggio "L'Albero della Vita" trattato sulla Qabalah ebraica, riconosciuto dal Centro di Cultura Ebraica di Bruxelles e da alcune comunità rabbiniche americane.

Relatrice presso Associazioni ed Accademie italiane, nonché presso Convegni internazionali, ultimo dei quali in Svizzera, docente di tecniche evolutive, Barbara Amadori partecipa alla trasmissione televisiva "Maurizio Costanzo Show" in qualità di esperta in reincarnazione. Partecipa quale sensitiva ai Convegni Internazionali di Parapsicologia a Bellaria, Modena, Assisi, Palermo, Milano, Locarno, Lugano, Zurigo.

Frequenta il prestigioso Arthur Findley College di Londra per confrontarsi con i più qualificati medium inglesi.

Tiene abitualmente conferenze e seminari in Svizzera ed in Italia.

E' in fase conclusiva "La nostra storia scritta nell'Infinito" trattato incentrato sulla Medianità odierna.

who probably do not know the details of astrology and mediumship, i.e. prospective clients rather than colleagues of Barbara Amadori's. This accounts for the inclusion, in the source as well as the target text, of clarifications on the courses and seminars held by the professional, and for the use of a language that is usually not over-technical or cryptic, so that it can be understood by laypersons. It should be noted that, had the original author wished to impress (rather than inform) the reader, she could have used a much more specialized approach, building the text in such a way that her prospective clients would not understand what she does, but only get the impression of a highly qualified, reliable and trustworthy professional. In so doing, she would have adopted a style and language that is more in line with B2B communication (see chapter 5), and in translating, I should have adjusted my techniques accordingly. This kind of approach is seldom employed in personal promotion. It might work for professionals offering highly technical products and services, from whom the prospective client/customer may expect data rather than explanations (and be prepared not to understand them in full). However, such a strategy is a risk when the target readership cannot be easily identified in terms of age, level of education, and other indicators that may influence their inclination towards trusting (and paying!) someone they do not understand.

In our source text, the author is clearly concerned with helping the readers understand, without giving the impression of patronizing them. This creates a mix of high information content anchors that require an accurate rendition and in-depth research for lexical equivalents of specialized, often **monoreferential**, terms (e.g., numerology, karmic astrology, evolutionary astrology, subtle dimensions, mediumship, clairvoyant reading, quantum physics, etc.) and bits of text with lower information density that allows a freer approach, although their limited extension does not yield easily to thorough rewriting. Moreover, following the reader-friendly, non-cryptic approach to the client adopted by the original author, I thought it appropriate to insert additional clarifications for references to the Italian media (as in 'the popular Italian talk-show, "Maurizio Costanzo Show"', 7th paragraph) and suggest literal English translations for the titles of the author's publications, even if these works do not circulate outside Italy.

Since this example is the first text that we have encountered in this book to show such a rapid succession of high- and low-information content points, it is perhaps worthwhile analysing a few paragraphs in deeper detail. Let us take the second paragraph, which consists of one sentence only:

9a: Appassionata ed attenta studiosa delle discipline esoteriche quali Qabalah, Numerologia, Astrologia Karmika, Evolutiva, al fine di completare adeguatamente la proprio cultura personale in merito alla Qabalah ebraica, consegue il diploma di II livello in ebraico antico.

Example 9b
*English 'About Me' page, with graphic and other minor adjustments (http://www.
barbaramadori.com/english/about%20me/aboutme.htm)*

Barbara Amadori

A Sensitive, a Reiki Master, an Astrologist and a journalist, Barbara Amadori
has a liberal education that ranges from classical music (having studied at the
"B. Maderna" Conservatoire in Cesena) to the humanities (she has a high school
degree in pedagogy), from foreign languages (she holds a Cambridge ESOL
First Certificate) to journalism.

In order to get the best possible insight into the Hebrew Kabbalah – one of
her chief interests, together with other esoteric subjects such as Numerology,
Karmic Astrology, and Evolutionary Astrology – she has obtained a 2nd-level
diploma in Ancient Hebrew.

Barbara has been studying the world of the Subtle Dimensions that permeate
our life for over 25 years.

Her workshops are focused on several important aspects of Mediumship; their
specific aim is to teach participants how to use their intuitive abilities to contact
their Guiding Spirits. This is achieved through a number of "steps", the final one
being the long-awaited contact with one's Guide. Before that, Barbara Amadori
takes participants through intermediate steps such as the energy and clairvoyant
reading of photographs, objects and tapes, and practicing communication with
other participants through meditation and aura connection techniques.

Both courses and workshops feature theoretical as well as practical sessions
and cover a variety of disciplines, from theosophy to a quick glance at some
concepts of quantum physics.

Barbara Amadori's curriculum in the field of the fascinating world of the Unknown
also includes a yet unchallenged record – in 1997, she was the first and only Italian
woman to write a treatise on the Hebrew Kabbalah, the renowned "L'Albero della
Vita" (The Tree of Life), acknowledged by the Brussels Jewish Culture Centre and
by several American rabbinic communities.

Barbara presented papers at several Italian Associations and Academies as well
as at International conferences – most recently, in Switzerland; she teaches
Evolutionary Techniques and is the reincarnation expert of the popular Italian
talk-show, "Maurizio Costanzo Show". As a sensitive, she also takes part in the
International Parapsychology Conferences held in Bellaria, Modena, Assisi,
Palermo, Milan, Chieti, Locarno, Lugano, Zurich.

Being a student of London's prestigious Arthur Findlay College, she is familiar
with the most outstanding British mediums and their work.

She holds frequent conferences and workshops, both in Switzerland and
Italy.

Barbara is currently completing a new treatise on Mediumship, "La nostra storia
scritta nell'Infinito" (Our Story Written in Infinity).

Literal translation: A keen and scrupulous scholar of esoteric subjects such as the Kabbalah, Numerology, Karmic and Evolutionary Astrology, in order to adequately complete her personal culture about the Hebrew Kabbalah, she obtains a 2nd-level diploma in Ancient Hebrew.

9b: In order to get the best possible insight into the Hebrew Kabbalah – one of her chief interests, together with other esoteric subjects such as Numerology, Karmic Astrology, and Evolutionary Astrology – she has obtained a 2nd-level diploma in Ancient Hebrew.

Of course the sentence might have been translated in several different ways, for instance splitting it in two for better readability. What we have in our version of 9b, however, is one long sentence that particularly emphasizes the Kabbalah above the other disciplines, which are reduced to 'other ... subjects' in an interpolated clause. The choice is motivated by the further recurrence of the Kabbalah in the 6th paragraph, where the client claims her primacy in the field as she was 'the <u>first and only Italian woman</u> to write a treatise on [it]'. In the second paragraph of 9a, too, the other disciplines are only mentioned once and do not recur again in the text, whereas Barbara specifically mentions her education in Ancient Hebrew in connection with the Kabbalah. This further justifies the transformation of the theme/rheme structure in 9b, even in the face of the Italian syntax of 9a, which apparently puts the Kabbalah on the same level as the other subjects in the first part of the sentence (see the literal translation).

This, in its turn, allows for the shift of boost from the client's research activities concerning the whole group of disciplines (*appassionata ed attenta studiosa*, literally, 'a keen and scrupulous scholar') to her specific commitment to the Kabbalah ('the best possible insight into the Hebrew Kabbalah', which more precisely translates *completare adeguatamente*). In the process, boost has been increased through the deletion of *personale* (literally, 'personal'), which in English might have suggested that the scope of the client's culture is limited to her own personal knowledge rather than being valuable in absolute terms, while in Italian it has a positive connotation, as it implies that Barbara has actively and independently sought to broaden her knowledge instead of receiving it from educational institutions. Further boost is then provided by the superlative, 'the best possible insight'. Such operations make up for the loss of boost in the under-translation of *appassionata e attenta studiosa* with 'her chief interests', where, despite the inherently superlative adjective 'chief', the idea of active commitment to research is only partially conveyed by the more neutral 'interests'.

The group of modifications that alter the boost structure of the text also includes the change of the tense from a historical present to a past perfect, which causes a shift from narration about past and concluded events to the positive assertion of Barbara's current titles. On the other hand, the high information content parts of the paragraph, which here consist in field-specific terms, are translated using the tools that are typical of technical or scientific translation. The equivalents for *Qabalah, Numerologia, Astrologia Karmika, [Astrologia] Evolutiva*, for instance, were obtained by using the web as corpus. (At the time when the translation was made, no lexicological databases or ready-made corpora were available for esoteric domains). Self-evident as several of the equivalents may seem, such approach was vital to assess the most reliable and consistent spelling of Kabbalah (rather than Qabbalah, Cabbalah, Kabala, and the like).

Paragraph 5, too, is interesting for its intertwining of high and low information content parts:

9a: Inoltre sia corsi che seminari prevedono parti pratiche e teoriche e dipanano le proprie forme partendo dalla teosofia fino a giungere, seppur in modalità breve e superficiale, a qualche elemento di fisica quantistica.

Literal translation: Moreover, both courses and workshops feature theoretical and practical parts, and unravel their forms [structure] starting from theosophy and coming, however briefly and superficially, to a few elements of quantum physics.

9b: Both courses and workshops feature theoretical as well as practical sessions and cover a variety of disciplines, from theosophy to a quick glance at some concepts of quantum physics.

Two main boost-related interventions can be observed here. The first is the replacement of the visual metaphor, *dipanano le proprie forme partendo da...*, with a less figurative but more assertive 'cover a variety of disciplines', where 'cover' suggests thoroughness and 'a variety of' adds quantitative boost, which in the original was only hinted at through the construction *partendo da... fino a giungere a* (literally, 'starting from... and coming to'). The second operation of partial rewriting is the alteration of the extremely cautious clause, *seppur in modalità breve e superficiale* (literally, 'however briefly and superficially') into a much less self-diminishing 'quick glance'. Technically speaking, the notion of treating quantum physics only in passing remains, so there is no real addition of boost here. Rather, by avoiding negatively connoted words such as 'superficially', and turning the concept into a positive one (a quick glance is better than a superficial one, or no glance at all), boost is simply not removed.

Of course one could push the re-boosting operation further by completely deleting the reference to 'a quick glance' and 'some concepts'. This, however, would be inadequate in this working situation, as it would dismiss the author's clear concern about conveying an impression of reliability and professionalism rather than inflating the readers' expectations at the risk of losing credibility. That concern is particularly important for Barbara, given that some readers might disbelieve not only her, but the entire field she works in. Face issues, however, are usually relevant in all kinds of personal promotion: after all, the object of promotion here is a person who puts her or his own personal, as well as professional, face and credibility on the Web.

Example 9 is also a good illustration of another issue that, although not strictly verbal, should be taken into account when translating for the Web. It should be noted that in the online version of example 9a, the last paragraph becomes visible only when the text is selected (for instance, to copy it). The text that can normally be seen from the screen ends with *Svizzera e Italia*. This is a perfect example of a layout issue that is recurrent in website translation (or, as happens here, website copywriting): target text length. When frames are used in the website, the target text cannot exceed a certain length, or its end will just be cut off. This is exactly what happened in the source text in 9a; the target text in 9b, being shorter, did not require trimming.

It is worth mentioning here that – probably due to the traditional ancillary role attributed to layout and composition – commissioners may leave details such as space constraints out when briefing the translator. For this reason, it is important to know whether a text is intended for the web or other media that tend to pose the same space-related issues, such as brochures or tourist guides. If this is the case, it is better to get back to the commissioner and ask whether specific space constraints apply to each page of the site (or brochure, or guide), or even to single paragraphs or sections. It is also advisable to keep all communications regarding such instructions for future reference. For instance, should the limitations to the number of characters change after you have started translating, an adjustment to the final price and deadline can be negotiated, as the operation of culling what has already been translated is time- and effort-consuming, and the responsibility for the change lies with the commissioner or the end client.

5. Translating Promotional Material
Business-to-Business

This chapter outlines first of all the main features of business-to-business (B2B) promotional communication in terms of information-to-persuasion ratio and distribution context. Next, it illustrates a variety of B2B promotional texts, which are characterized by different information-to-persuasion ratios, which are in turn influenced by their contexts of distribution.

5.1 B2B promotional texts

Business-to-Business (or B2B) promotional texts are produced by a commercial enterprise to promote its products or services to one or more other commercial enterprises that are regular or prospective customers of the source company.

The bulk of B2B communication occurs between companies in the same market segment. Since these segments may be quite specialized, target enterprises are typically well informed about the kinds of products/services they need. Their requirements will be mainly related to increasing production, enhancing quality and/or cutting costs. For this reason, B2B promotion tends to be technical and information-oriented rather than based on persuasive devices; in other words, its information-to-persuasion ratio is rather high. The persuasiveness of this kind of promotion is often based on the amount and quality of information provided, and on the neutral, impartial style in which it is presented. Additionally, target companies usually have qualified technical staff able to assess whether or not the object of promotion meets their needs, and whether the source company's promotional communication is accurate and complete.

From a translator's point of view, therefore, omitting or over-generalizing what the inexperienced reader may perceive as small technical details or trifles, or failing to identify a translation that the source company deems fitting for monoreferential terms (i.e. terms which have only one referent in the real world) or other technical words, may lead to the translation being rejected by the client (the source company), seen as inappropriate by one of the target companies, or at the very least less functional with respect to its promotional purpose. Any of these outcomes would cause the source company to lose money, mainly in terms of prospective profits, even if its regular customers/ clients would probably overcome the language barrier. Obviously, this could potentially negatively impact the translator's work and career.

The highly technical nature of B2B texts usually calls for a translation approach that is similar to that of technical translation, making it convenient to use CAT tools, especially when the client employs specific terminology and provides past translations or ready-made translation memories. When working with technical B2B promotional texts, it is therefore a good idea to ask clients whether they can provide any terminological support such as translation memories, glossaries, or at least the telephone number or e-mail address of a member of staff who can assist you with company-specific terminology. If your client is a direct one, you can actually include a specific item in your translator-prompted brief (see table 1). Terminology alone, however, is not always the key to a good B2B promotional translation: it is always important to assess whether the technical anchors that force us to stay close to the source text are complemented by devices that serve to boost the quality of the product/service, and might require adaptation and rewriting rather than close rendering.

Moreover, not all B2B promotional texts are extremely technical in nature. Some products or services offered by the source company are of a more general nature, i.e. they can be used by various types of client/customer companies, for instance toiletries, or Internet connections. Also, the advertised product/service may pertain to a field in which the use of creative language and persuasive devices alongside more technical information is generally appreciated, and the translator will find more leeway for rewriting (see § 5.1.1).

Additionally, the distribution context has an impact on the information-to-persuasion ratio. If a text is circulated in response to a prospective customer's specific request, or it is published on a company website that is intended to be purposefully navigated by well-informed users, it will not need attract the reader's attention, and will most likely include only technical information in verbal form, possibly with pictures or technical drawings describing the product. An advertisement published in the trade press, on the other hand, will have to compete for the reader's attention, as it is published alongside articles and other promotional material. It is thus more likely to rely on visual suggestion and perhaps some emotional or creative language.

One other important point that must be mentioned about B2B communication in general is that, given their modes of circulation, such texts may be subject to space constraints. As already seen at the end of § 4.2.3, website (and brochure) layout may be done using frames. In the case of websites, frames can sometimes be altered to accommodate the text, but this may come at a cost for the end client, either financially, if the alteration has to be outsourced to an external webmaster, or in the form of staff working time if it is done in-house. It is therefore important that any space constraints, or the possibility of restyling the website layout, are negotiated at an early stage with the end clients, if the translator has direct contact with them.

Brochures often have a fixed layout that is more rigid than a website layout, since brochure space is physically limited by the edges of the sheet of paper it is printed on. Moreover, multilingual brochures may be laid out using grids that allow a fixed amount of space for each paragraph of the source text and its translation(s). Of course, this hinders major rewriting attempts that entail major omissions or integrations, paragraph order reversal or paragraphing revision, even when such efforts would make the target text stylistically more functional. In any case, the layout structure may have an influence on target text length and/or on translation choices. If you have direct contact with the client or know the agency you are working through would appreciate initiatives of this kind, it is advisable to inquire about how long the target text and/or its individual paragraphs should be in order to accommodate the layout.

Length is an equally important issue in advertising. B2B advertisements have limited space, which will most likely be taken up by the product/service's essential technical features or simple information about its existence, perhaps referring the reader to a website address for further details. Furthermore, shorter advertising copy, especially headlines and payoffs, tend to attract and retain the reader's attention more than lengthier, more boring ones. This also goes back to the need for these texts to compete for attention with articles and other advertisements in the same trade magazine. In B2B advertising, however, such concerns may not be as overriding as in business-to-consumer (B2C) or traditional advertising, and compromises tend to be struck between the goal of capturing readers' curiosity and the need to inform them about the technical reliability of the product/service advertised.

B2B promotional literature containing exclusively factual information, such as price-lists, e-commerce web pages, catalogues and fact-sheets listing only product names and a fixed number of characteristics (price, item code, colour, size, etc), will not be taken into consideration here, even though this also has a basic promotional purpose, served namely by its technical nature and factual style. Similarly, unsolicited sales letters circulated via snail or electronic mail will not be treated in this volume, as they are usually taken care of in trade correspondence handbooks. In the following sections, text types will be divided according to their distribution context, which, as we have just seen, has a direct influence on their space constraints and information-to-persuasion ratio and, as a consequence, on the translation approach they require.

The first section groups together websites and promotional brochures, based on the fact that both text types are circulated in distribution contexts that do not usually require them to compete for the reader's attention. This implies that they can be comparatively long and detailed. Differences in information-to-persuasion ratios, however, can be observed across B2B websites and brochures, depending on the specific market of the company, product or service advertised. For this reason, the examples in § 5.1.1.1 and § 5.1.1.2 illustrate a range of information-to-persuasion ratios from very high (characterized by high frequency of technical terms and numerical figures, lists of noun phrases, and raw facts in general) to medium-low (with a more complex interplay of specific information and evocative style, see in particular example 14). This will hopefully serve as a reminder of the fact that one cannot always rely on text type categorization to pre-determine a text's information-to-persuasion ratio.

The second and final section devoted to B2B promotion (§ 5.1.2.) is about advertisements in the specialized press. Here a few elements about advertising proper (B2C advertising in § 7.1.2) will be introduced, and we will see how these elements can interface with the technical and information-specific nature of B2B communication.

5.1.1 Brochures and websites

As mentioned before, for the purposes of this book, B2B brochures and websites can be approached in the same way; the very same texts sometimes appear both in brochure format and on the source company's website. They vary in length and can be designed to promote a specific product or a company as a whole. Their information-to-promotion ratio varies depending on the object of promotion and how much the target company/ies are expected to know about it. The more the target company knows about what is being advertised, about its purpose and how it may serve the prospective buyer, the more factual and informative the text is likely to be.

Another common feature of B2B brochures and websites is that their respective distribution contexts are both non-competitive, although different. Brochure distribution presupposes direct contact between the source company and the target one, as printed literature is usually sent via snail mail or handed out to persons visiting the company or otherwise coming in contact with people from the source company (agents, salespeople, marketing personnel, trade fair staff, etc.). For websites, on the other hand, distribution is usually target-initiated: the website is there for virtually anybody to visit. At the same time, however, the explicit B2B nature of the site – i.e. allusions to products or company types that are only interesting for other companies rather than for the man or woman in the street – immediately selects the appropriate type of target readership by discouraging occasional web surfers. Such a difference, then, does not have an impact on the information-to-persuasion ratio of B2B brochures and websites, since an informed and purposeful target readership is presupposed by both, and usually neither needs to compete with similar texts in order to be noticed and collected. Additionally, brochures are increasingly made available on company websites, in .pdf or other downloadable formats.

Here B2B brochures and websites are presented in two separate sub-sections, respectively dealing with product presentation and company presentation texts, only to arrange examples more clearly with a progression from higher to lower specificity and information-to-persuasion ratio. Brochure and website examples will also be presented in a similar way in chapter 6 and chapter 7.

5.1.1.1 *Product presentation websites/brochures*

We have just seen that the distribution contexts of product presentation websites and brochures are not highly competitive. Obviously in the long run, only truly interesting promotions will be kept or remembered, but more often than not, the assumption is that interest will stem from the product's quality and price rather than how well the brochure or website is written and designed. For this reason, across the commercial world, B2B product presentation brochures and websites are usually drafted and translated so that the product's technical or otherwise specific qualities emerge as objectively and neutrally as possible. Translating the kind of text contained in example 10, then, is to a certain degree comparable to technical translation; at the same time, the overall purpose of the text is promotional, and parts of the brochure or website may contain boosting elements (as happens in the part of example 10 analysed in example 11).

The excerpts in example 10 were taken from the online catalogue of an Italian company, Oli, specializing in vibration technology. The company has branches in Germany, France, the USA, Spain, India, Romania and Malta, each one with its own website, and is a member of Wamgroup, an Italian-based corporation operating in the field of bulk solids handling and processing. 10a is the source text; 10b is the English version that can be accessed from the Italian homepage, it serves an international readership, and is reproduced as such in the websites of the Indian and Maltese branches of Oli; while 10c was found on the website of the US branch of Oli. The Romanian, French, Spanish and German versions of 10a, extracted from the websites of the respective branches of Oli, can be found in the Appendix (chapter 10).

In all versions of example 10, emotional language is purposefully avoided at both the verbal and visual level. Finite verbal forms are avoided in the last two sections, entirely formed by nominal clauses; and even in the first two sections, no first- or second-person verb or pronoun is used. Similarly, the pictures lack any kind of background; the products are displayed in such a way as to provide a clear and detailed view of them while getting rid of all non-essential information, including the context of use that should already be familiar to the target reader. The sense of objectivity and neutrality is further enhanced by the form taken by the description of specifications in the last two sections (a list) and the numerical data strewn across the text.

As we will see in chapter 7, § 7.1.2, technical terms, numerical data, diagrams, lists and objective drawings or pictures can be employed even in business-to-consumer communication, where target readers are not supposed to have in-depth knowledge of the subject discussed. In such cases, they are mainly supposed to convey a sense of objectivity and present information as factual and non-negotiable. In B2B promotion, on the other hand, they are supposed to give the reader what s/he expects, i.e. technical information rather than generic boost, in an easy-reference, down-to-earth format. As such, in translation they should normally be treated as technical anchors that are best translated as accurately as possible, without creative rewriting.

This, however, does not mean that the text should not be adjusted to the target readership's expectations and experiential context. It is interesting to note that in 10b, which is aimed at a global readership, international measurements are translated into feet, inches, and pounds for the benefit of non-metric-system customers. At the same time 10c, which is meant for the American market, offers non-metric measures as the only option. The only other difference between 10b and 10c is the rendering of the Italian *ago* as 'needle' or 'tip' in 10b and as 'head' or 'tip' in 10c, clearly responding to different traditions of technical terminology.

Example 10a

From http://www.olivibra.it/ (the page below can be reached from the homepage by selecting the links 'Prodotti', 'Vibratori e agevolatori di discesa', and finally 'VN - VNP - Vibratori immersione ad alta frequenza')

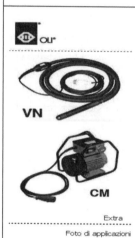

VN

CM

Extra

Foto di applicazioni

Descrizione

VN (OLI® Standard Line) e VNP (OLI® Professional Line) sono vibratori elettrici ad immersione ad alta frequenza. La VNP Professional Line sviluppa forze centrifughe più elevate e dispone di un albero dotato di 4 cuscinetti (più uno ad aghi) il che rende questa linea adatta per applicazioni particolarmente gravose. Entrambe le linee sono dotate di 5 mt. di tubo protettivo, 10 mt. di cavo elettrico con spina CE e di un interruttore manuale ABS.

Funzione d'uso

La capacità di compattazione sensibilmente più elevata della VNP Professional Line porta alla completa eliminazione di bollicine d'aria compatibilmente con la tecnologia del calcestruzzo più recente. Con 42V/200Hz o 230V/200Hz e con 6 diametri di aghi la gamma è adatta a qualsiasi tipo di servizio in cantiere nonché per l'utilizzo in impianti di compattazione del calcestruzzo (produzione di pavimenti).

Prestazioni e caratteristiche tecniche - Vantaggi

- Protezione del motore tramite termistori
- Diametro dell'ago: 36 mm, 50 mm, 57 mm, 60 mm, 65 mm, 70 mm
- Ampiezza: da 1,2 mm a 3 mm
- Diametro di efficienza: da 60 cm a 180 cm
- Ago fabbricato in acciaio o Vulkolan
- Rivestimento dell'ago rinforzato
- Basso consumo di elettricità
- Altamente performante

- 2 anni di garanzia

Opzioni e accessori

- VN line con protezione termica
- Standard 42 V, 200 Hz, optional 230 V, 200 Hz

Example 10b
*From http://www.olivibra.it/ (the page below can be reached from the homepage
by first selecting the English language from the 'Lingua' menu, then the links
'Product Range', 'Vibrators and Flow Aids', and finally 'VN - VNP - High-
Frequency Internal Vibrators'). It can also be viewed following the same path
from http://www.olivibra.in/ and http://www.olivibra.com/malta/*

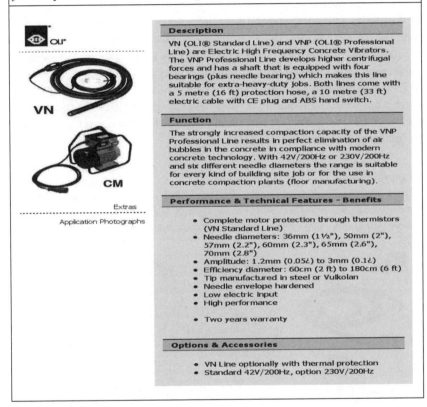

Generally speaking, in a B2B product presentation website or brochure,
terminological accuracy, compliance with the company's terminology, a non-
emotional style (short nominal sentences, lists without verbs and articles rather
than discursive descriptions) and compliance with layout constraints seem to
be more important than linguistic accuracy and stylistic flair.

In local or national companies that do not have foreign branches, but
nonetheless sell internationally, target texts may be produced or revised in-
house at the source company by non-native users of the target language. In
such cases, minor grammar or spelling deviations from the standard may be
tolerated if they do not hinder comprehension. On the other hand, since such
texts are likely to be revised by the client's in-house staff, who are used to a

certain kind of company-specific technical terminology, revisers might consider departures from that terminology to be mistakes. It can turn out to be difficult for a freelance translator to negotiate other terminological solutions found in external reliable sources and that fit the original terms equally as well, or even better than, the equivalents normally used within the client company. This is especially true when the translator is not in direct contact with the end client, but is working through an agency, or s/he is a newly employed member of staff of the source company and does not wish to start off on the wrong foot with her/his supervisors. In the worst cases, clients who have not provided the translator with any terminological source or support might not even acknowledge their responsibility in what they may judge a poor translation of technical terms, because they assume their own terminology to be the only correct one, and might claim that their level of terminological experience in their own field of activity is more authoritative than the translator's (which, incidentally, is often difficult to refute).

Example 10c
From http://www.olivibrator.com/ (the page below can be reached from the homepage by selecting the links 'Product Range', 'High-Cycle Concrete Vibrators', and finally 'VN - VNP - High-Frequency Internal Vibrators')

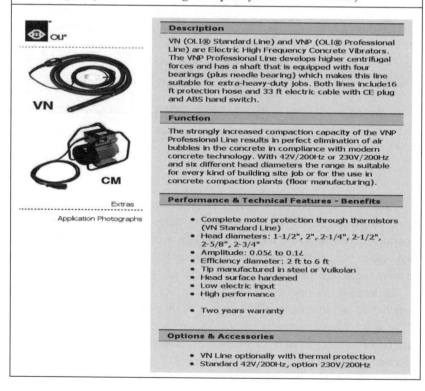

For all these reasons, before starting the translation it is important to ask for any specific terminology the client would like the translator to use, or at least for parallel texts, such as a multilingual company website. If no internal source is provided and you do not trust the client (or the agency) to be impartial in the case of terminological disputes, then it might be a good idea to keep track of your terminological sources, so that you can argue in favour of your diligence should claims about terminological accuracy arise.

Example 10 is quite easy to locate towards the maximum information, minimum persuasion end of the information-to-persuasion continuum (table 2). In fact, with this kind of text, as long as one knows it is intended for a B2B technical brochure or website focusing on a specific product or product line rather than generically introducing the company, one might do without a detailed brief following the model of table 1, since all information contained in the table is either clear from the text type or irrelevant. For instance, as an answer to question 2, we can easily infer that the target readership is made up of organizations working in the same field as the source company, and they are well-informed about the promoted product or service. Similarly, answers to questions 3 to 5 emerge clearly from the objective and neutral style adopted in the text: the company is not close, nor deferent, to the target reader, on the other hand it appears to be detached even if not particularly authoritative (since it is not supposed to know more about the product than the reader). Company values come down to technical know-how, quality, precision and reliability; and the text is aimed at persuading the prospective customer of the product's characteristics that objectively make it something to buy. In the end, the commissioner should only be consulted about visuals (if not originally provided), plus two items that were not originally included in the list: company terminology and, if relevant, space constraints.

If we look closer, however, even in example 10 there are instances of boost that may require, or allow, some rewriting, although not an extensive one. The following example is the transcription of the second section of example 10c; technical or informative anchors are underlined, while boost elements have been italicized. As you may remember from § 4.1, persuasive components should not be translated as much for accuracy as for functionality, and therefore their rendering might actually require some rephrasing. The reverse is true for underlined technical anchors. In this particular example, however, the close intertwining of the two categories does not allow for substantial re-writing, as the boost tends to refer to specific anchors that cannot be easily moved around in the text, and the lexical meaning of boost words such as 'suitable' is closely linked to the immediate co-text.

Additionally, some elements are both informative and persuasive, and appear in example 11 as both italicized and underlined. For instance, in 'six different head diameters', 'six' quite obviously counts as the prototypical kind of objective data (precise figures), and on top of that it refers to head diameters, i.e. a measurable technical characteristic. This phrase, then, has a high density of objective information; at the same time, it is not presented in a neutral way, since the one-digit figure is boosted by 'different', which turns it into a wide range of diameters that can cater to all requirements. In this context, then, the use of 'six different' adds implicit boost as well as numerical precision. In this case, it would be hard to creatively rewrite the phrase in such a way that the same objective data fit into a dramatically different boost structure.

The close intertwining of boost elements and anchors can thus be an obstacle to significantly rewording this type of B2B text; it is often much easier and less time-consuming to limit rewriting to the minimum required so that the target text works well in the target language and context. Such a conservative attitude might also be safer because for clients commissioning this kind of translation, technical accuracy is the priority, and they may not particularly appreciate creative initiatives.

Example 11
From the 'Function' section of example 10c

The strongly increased <u>compaction capacity of the VNP Professional Line</u> *results in perfect elimination* <u>of air bubbles in the concrete in compliance with</u> *modern* <u>concrete technology. With 42V / 200Hz or 230V / 200Hz and</u> <u>six different</u> <u>head diameters</u> *the range is suitable for every kind of* <u>building site job or for the use in concrete compaction plants (floor manufacturing)</u>.

5.1.1.2 Company presentation websites/brochures

The examples in this section are taken from company homepages, the only kind of page present in all, or most, company websites. Naturally each website has additional sections. Some of them may be recurrent across B2B sites (e.g. 'Products', 'About us', etc.), but overall they are so variable that it would be impossible to give a full or even partial account of them here. It is important to bear in mind, however, that different B2B website (and brochure) sections usually have different information-to-persuasion ratios. Whereas homepages and 'About us' pages, or introductory sections to brochures, usually display a mix of technical information and boost, product- or service-related pages of company websites intended for a well-informed target readership are likely to favour an information-oriented communication strategy that is more similar to that of examples 10 and 11.

Additionally, as in the previous section, here we will only be referring to the translation of the (verbal) texts to be inserted in websites, not the localization of websites as a whole. Localization is a more complex process that entails adapting the site structure (which requires programming skills) as well as translating its verbal contents. For an account of general localization issues, see Sandrini 2005-2007 in the References.

The first example (12a through 12d) consists of a series of homepages of the same company, Papertech, respectively in English (the version that appears by typing the URL www.papertech.com), and, in the same order as they appear at the bottom of the English homepage, in Chinese, Spanish, and Indonesian. The range of languages stems from the geographical location of the company's paper mills: one is in Spain, one in China, and two in Indonesia. Quite obviously, English was chosen as the site's main language in order to reach an international pool of prospective customers. The international English text is also likely to be the source text from which the others were translated. In fact, Papertech is part of the multinational group Texpack, which has locations in the US and UK, and whose website also has Chinese and Spanish versions.

Example 12 therefore reflects the trend towards glocal (global+local) strategies that tend to adjust texts developed in global English (i.e. a kind of English that is not conspicuously recognizable as American English, British English, or other geographical macro-varieties of English, and thus addresses a global readership) to other national or local languages and cultures. In this case, the very existence of the other versions (in which, however, visuals and layout were not changed) reflects the company's interest in appearing as an industrial concern with roots in real geographical places, each one with its language. This glocal strategy is especially common among large multinationals which feel they might lose their corporate identity by presenting only an English institutional face, disembodied from their real-world, physical presence. In similar cases, translating from the international English version into the other languages chosen by the company is the common translation direction.

In terms of information-to-persuasion ratio, the text contained in each homepage shows several characteristics in common with example 11. Try and separate the boost elements from the objective data in the same way as was shown in example 11 (a key is provided at the end of § 5.1.1.2, but do not look at it before trying yourself). Also, pay attention to the close interplay of objectivity and boost. Notice, for instance, how large numbers are used to support general boost, thus retaining their objective nature but losing in neutrality. You can check how the translation was approached by comparing 12a with one or more of the other versions.

One last teaser: why is it that, in all four homepages, Papertech mainly refers to itself in the first person plural, while Oli avoids personal pronouns altogether and when possible, even personal verbal forms? The issue of personal deictics in B2B promotion will be discussed further, with reference to example 14, but perhaps you can reach an independent conclusion. (Hint: where would you locate Papertech on the scale of items 4.a and 4.b of table 1? And where would Oli be on the same scale?).

Example 12a
Detail of the English homepage of Papertech, a cardboard supplier (www. papertech.com)

Example 12b
Detail of Papertech's Chinese homepage (www.papertech.com/papertech_ ch.asp)

Example 12c

Detail of Papertech's Spanish homepage (www.papertech.com/papertech_sp.asp?portalid=1)

Cartón para Tubos
Fabricamos uno de los cartones para tubos de mayor calidad en el mundo. Los tubos que se fabrican con él giran a 25.000 r.p.m. y resisten tensiones extremadamente altas en todas las aplicaciones.

Máximo Nivel de Ply-Bond
La estrategia de Papertech se basa en la I+D y la mejora continua. Recientemente hemos desarrollado Core HP10 y Core A51 con valores de plybond que sobrepasan los 1.000 j/m².

Amplia Gama de Calidades
Hasta 12 calidades distintas de cartones para tubos, adaptadas a las necesidades específicas de nuestros clientes dedicados a la manipulación del papel. No importa lo complejas que sean sus necesidades, nosotros proporcionamos la calidad que se ajusta a sus operaciones.

Experiencia

Basamos nuestra fiabilidad en nuestra capacidad total de producción que supera las 200.000 toneladas anuales. Durante mas de 50 años hemos respondido a las necesidades de nuestros clientes suministrándoles cartón de calidad y un servicio puntual.

Example 12d

Detail of Papertech's Indonesian homepage (www.papertech.com/papertech_in.asp)

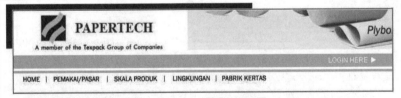

Spesialis Coreboard
Kami memproduksi beberapa dari coreboard kualitas terbaik di pasar dunia sekarang ini. Tubes yang dibuat dengannya berputar pada kecepatan 25,000 RPM dan tahan akan tekanan yang sangat tinggi dalam semua aplikasi.

Plybond tinggi
Pabrik Papertech berdedikasi untuk melakukan R&D dan peningkatan yang terus menerus. Baru baru ini kami telah mengembangkan Core HP10 dan Core A51 dengan nilai plybond yang melebihi 1,000 j/m2.

Skala yang luas
Sampai dengan 12 grade coreboard yang berbeda, dibuat sesuai dengan kebutuhan khusus dari pelanggan converting kami. Bagaimanapun kompleksnya kebutuhan anda, kami menyediakan grade yang tepat untuk operasional anda.

Keahlian yang mendalam

Kehandalan kami berakar pada kapasitas tahunan kami yang 200,000 ton, dan 50 tahun sejarah kami akan menjawab kebutuhan pelanggan dengan mengirimkan board berkualitas dengan servis yang memuaskan.

Example 13 is made up of the two homepages, one in Hindi and the other in English, devoted to a textile product of Kamadgiri Synthetics Ltd. (KSL), called True Value. In terms of information-to-persuasion ratio, the texts seem to display the same features as examples 11 and 12: several high-informa-tion-content or objective anchors linked by a boost structure. Try and divide the two categories of elements, as was done with the previous two examples; this time, no key will be provided. Also, compare the effect of third-person-singular deixis to indicate the manufacturer ('Kamadgiri Synthetics Ltd. is...') with that of the first-person-plural observed in example 12.

In example 13, however, there is more than information-to-persuasion ratio and personal deixis to be discussed. KSL is based in India, and therefore it seems obvious for its site to feature a Hindi version that is likely to be the source text, even if it can only be accessed from the English homepage. Since this B2B website is meant for a global market, it also has a version in Indian English that, while fully ensuring international readability, at the same time proudly states the Indian identity of the company and its products. This is made clear not only by the syntax and grammar, but more prominently by the use of an Indian numerical unit, the *lac* (also transliterated as *lakh*).

Example 13a
Hindi homepage of KSL True Value, http://www.ksltruevalue.com/index-1.html

Example 13b
English homepage of KSL True Value, http://www.ksltruevalue.com

In examples 11 and 12 we have already seen how figures can be loaded with boost even if they are presented as inherently objective data. In *60 lacs meters*, however, we do not only find the use of objective information for the purposes of boost (6,000,000 meters of fabric produced each year is, after all, a considerable quantity). Here we find a corporate image and identity that has its roots in a local culture that, in turn, points out its connection to the current global economic situation in which Indian-ness has turned into a value-added quality for industrial businesses. In example 10, quantities expressed in international metric measurements were accompanied by their translation into inches, feet and pounds, reflecting the company's desire to make non-metric-system customers feel at home. The reverse applies here: it would be a rash choice to translate *lacs*, a strong indicator of identity, into hundreds of thousands without negotiating this choice with the end client. So, translators beware: a number is not always just a number, and even in promotional translation, domestication is not always the obvious choice.

In example 13, then, we have a new combination of global interests and local identity. This time, the company is not a multinational one that localizes its corporate image in order to make sure that its local dimension is not overlooked, as occurred in example 12. Here the company is inherently and inescapably local, and lets this local identity show through the windows it opens onto the world. The direction the company is moving is no longer from global to local, but from local to global, which implies a translation direction from the local language into English, that is, the reverse of what applies to the glocalization observed in example 12.

Incidentally, this is the usual direction when translating promotional material for local businesses wishing to expand their market internationally, even for those that do not seem as proud of their local identity as KSL but only have an English website developed from ghost local-language originals. In such cases, local companies usually either use in-house staff or seek the assistance of freelance translators operating in their own countries and are more easily accessible to them, both in terms of proximity and price. This in turn implies that, in countries where English is not one of the national languages, this kind of B2B materials is often translated by non-native speakers of English. This contributes both to spreading global English(es) in international business environments and to breaking the taboo of L1 → L2 translation.

The last example of B2B websites was mainly chosen to remind readers that the general guidelines for the text types described in this book should always be taken with a pinch of salt. We have seen that B2B brochures and websites can have an information-to-persuasion ratio that oscillates between the maximum information, minimum persuasion end of the continuum and a point that is not far from there, as visualized in table 2. It is quite rare for a B2B text to be thoroughly rewritten, and those who commission the translation of such texts do not usually look for creative trans-creation as much as terminological accuracy. Every rule, however, has its exception, and a translator must be ready to assess the nature of a text and the approach it requires, independently or with the client's help, without uncritically applying what can be found in the textbook. (This might seem a foolish thing to write, but in my teaching experience, and a short one it is, I have heard quite a few 'But I read it in the book' replies.)

Example 14 consists of the German, English and Italian homepages – in the same order as they appear in the site itself – of Zoratti Studio Editoriale (formerly Durante&Zoratti), a Germany-based, Italian-owned publishing studio specializing in international publications. The target readership and the pool of prospective clients consist of publishing houses, i.e. companies that work in the same field as the source company and should have a clear idea of this type of studio's activities and the services they provide. This notwithstanding, Eleonora Zoratti, in agreement with Raffaella Durante, the co-owner at the time, chose to make the site a practical example of the studio's work, rather than focusing on factual information only.

Example 14a

Detail of the German homepage of Zoratti Studio Editoriale, http://www. studio-editoriale.com

Bücher sprechen viele Sprachen. Die assoziative Sprache kreativer Gedanken, die logische überzeugender Ideen, die unmittelbare berührender Bilder, die individuelle eines kultivierten Stils, die spielerische innerhalb etablierter Genres.

Wir bringen Ihre Bücher ...

Entdecken Sie Ihre internationalen Leser. Zoratti studio editoriale unterstützt Sie mit langjähriger Erfahrung und einem Team hochqualifizierter, buchbegeisterter Übersetzer und Lektoren, Gestalter und Setzer, Redakteure und Produzenten.

... zu Lesern in aller Welt.

The translation process for example 14 was rather complex. The first source text to be developed by professional copywriters was a German one, which was then translated into English by two professional translators. The English text in turn became the source text for the Italian translation, entrusted to two translators, including myself. The brief was to adapt the target text as much as possible to the target culture and the literary style of the target language. The two Italian translators were also asked to provide multiple versions of specific metaphors and other parts of the translation as they saw fit. The clients would then choose from the array of proposals, and it was clear from the start that they would do a final round of revision/rewriting. Partly due to the clients' direct involvement in the adaptation process, and perhaps more importantly, given that the visuals and layout had not yet been decided at the translation stage, no space constraints were specified. Close negotiation of individual translation choices was made possible by constant contact with the end clients and by their manifest interest in the outcome of the project.

After the clients had all translations/adaptations in their hands, they proceeded to a sort of reverse rewriting not only of the target texts but also of the originals, so that in the end it would be impossible to tell which was the source text and which were the translations. They treated all three versions (some of them including multiple solutions) as alternative proposals, and chose the individual solutions they felt best suited the studio's image. For each version, they kept the selected solutions and replaced the rest with translations of the winning solutions chosen from either one of the two other versions. Finally, the original German version and the Italian translation were re-adapted by the clients, whereas a British professional copywriter was asked to revise and adapt the English translation.

Example 14b
Detail of the English homepage of Zoratti Studio Editoriale, http://www.studio-editoriale.com/e01-home.htm

Books speak many languages: the associative language of creative thought, the logical flow of persuasion, the directness of touching images, the individuality of a cultivated style, the play with established genres.

Your books ...

Discover an international readership. Our highly specialist bibliophile team of translators, designers, producers, typesetters, copy editors and proofreaders can help you with any or every stage from initial idea to finished book on a distant shelf.

... for readers the world-over.

The final result is a multi-language site whose versions, while generally consistent, retain several points of stylistic departure, due to the need to functionally adjust texts not only to the target language and culture, but also to the space constraints posed by the newly developed site layout. In the English version of the homepage, for instance, shorter solutions towards the beginning of the final three-line copy leave room for a highly evocative coda, *from initial idea to finished product on a distant shelf,* which is not present in the other two versions. This vivid image would be perfect for the Italian target readership, and it would translate quite well into Italian, but in 14c, precious space is consumed by a long but stylistically functional translation of the term *bibliophile* and other lengthy solutions that also account for the intentional omission of the initial catchphrase and professional figures such as producers, typesetters or proofreaders (among the few technical anchors of this text). Zoratti's website is clearly an exception in the B2B scenario.

Example 14c
Detail of the Italian homepage of Zoratti Studio Editoriale, http://www.studio-editoriale.com/i01-home.htm

Un libro parla molte lingue. Vi è il linguaggio associativo della creatività, quello logico della persuasione, l'immediatezza di un'immagine, il codice individuale di uno stile colto, il gioco consapevole *con i generi.*

I vostri libri ...

Lo studio editoriale Durante & Zoratti è il partner ideale per le vostre produzioni internazionali grazie alla solida esperienza e allo staff di traduttori, redattori e grafici altamente qualificati, uniti dall'entusiasmo per i libri e per tutti i nuovi media.

... per i lettori del mondo.

The texts in example 14, and Zoratti's website as a whole, are similar to B2C texts in that they rely more on figurative language and emotional style rather than technical or objective data. Neutrality here is decidedly not an issue, as shown by the use of personal deixis. Let us briefly recall other examples of B2B promotional texts: in example 10 personal pronouns and verbal forms are carefully avoided, and the company never refers to itself in the first person; the same happens in CVs (see example 4), which usually totally lack personal deixis with reference to the person being promoted, and in personal promotion websites, where the standard deictic for the professional promoting his/her activities is the third person singular. Both the impersonal form and the third person create detachment between the text and its object of promotion (i.e. the source company or professional), suggesting an objective, neutral stance vis-à-vis the contents of the text and implicitly presenting the promotion as a series of facts to be taken for granted.

Here, on the other hand, Zoratti studio reveal themselves as a *we*, as Papertech does in example 13. Unlike example 13, however, here the client, too, is addressed directly, through a second person, the English *you*, that is disambiguated to be a plural in the other two versions. Thus, the *we*/plural *you* deixis in example 14 creates an emotional bond between the source and target companies that is much closer than what we find in examples 10 to 13, but at the same time does not infringe the B2B conventions of the respective languages and cultures or irritate prospective clients with an over-friendly tone. We find *voi* in Italian, without the capital *V*, which is typical of more official and highly codified text types, such as formal application letters (compare with *Sua* in example 8a), and the formal *Sie* in German.

Such plural reference to the target readership is standard across all types of B2B communication using personal deixis: it makes it clear that a company in the form of a plural entity, *we*, is addressing a peer, another collective entity. The degree of formality in such situations should be adjusted according to the specific conventions that apply to the B2B context in the target language and culture. This is an important point when translating from English into languages that distinguish between singular and plural forms as well as the formal and the informal *you*. As a rule of thumb, it is usually inappropriate to address a company using singular or colloquial second person forms, just like it is usually off-target to address individual consumers with a highly formal plural form in B2C promotional communication (we will see a purposeful exception to this in example 33c).

5.1.2 B2B advertisements

B2B advertisements share some of the characteristics of ads as we all know them (i.e. B2C ads) – in particular, space constraints and the predominant presence of visuals. The latter is mainly due to a distribution context that is different from that of brochures and websites. B2B ads are mainly developed to be circulated in the trade press, which does not only contain articles and informative materials, but also other B2B ads. This generates a certain degree of competition for the reader's typically short attention span. Like B2C ads, B2B advertisements also try to generate curiosity or interest and transmit their message in the shortest time possible, and with the least effort from the reader. This is why visuals are preferred to verbal text: they are thought to be easier and quicker to grasp and remember. The visual dimension of verbal elements, too, is often emphasized with the use of larger and/or coloured prints, or unusual fonts and layouts. Following the same logic of fast communication, short nominal sentences are preferred to an argumentative or descriptive style.

On the other hand, the kind of advertising we are dealing with here is B2B, which means that the target is usually supposed to know the object

Key to the separation of objective/technical/informative data vs. boost in example 12a. Boost elements are italicized, objective data are underlined. Boldface is only used for emphasis and was present in the original.

*[**Please** note that this is just one possible interpretation; figures, in particular, can be counted as both boost and objective/technical/informative data, as only large ones have been selected to portray the company's activity. However, from a translator's practical point of view, in this kind of text and with this kind of client, they cannot be normally treated with the same freedom as 'normal' boost elements. The same applies to lexical items that, although technical or highly informative in nature, have an inherently positive connotation (and, therefore, a boost value) in this context, such as 'R&D' and 'continuous improvement'. The reverse also applies: several boost elements appear to have informative value, or are so closely linked to technical/informative anchors that a translator might find it difficult to detach him/herself from the original structure of the text.]*

Coreboard Specialists

We <u>manufacture</u> some of the *highest quality* <u>coreboard</u> *in the world market today.* <u>Tubes made with it spin at 25,000 rpm</u> and <u>resist</u> *extremely high* <u>tensions</u> *in all applications.*

High Plybond

<u>Papertech mills are</u> *committed to* <u>R&D</u> and <u>continuous improvement</u>. *Most recently we have developed* <u>Core HP10</u> and <u>Core A51</u> with <u>plybond values that exceed 1,000 j/m2.</u>

Wide Range

Up to <u>12</u> *different* <u>grades</u> of <u>coreboard</u>, *tailored to the specific needs of our* <u>converting</u> <u>customers</u>. *No matter how complex your needs, we supply the right* <u>grade</u> *for your operations.*

Expertise and Depth

Our <u>dependability</u> *is rooted* in our <u>annual capacity of 200,000 tons</u>, and our <u>50-year history</u> of *responding to our customers' needs* by delivering *quality* <u>board</u> with *exceptional* <u>service.</u>

being advertised (or at least the category of products/services it belongs to) and expects technical details or specific advantages compared to competing items. In some cases, therefore, both the verbal and visual levels of B2B ads reflect the objective and neutral stance observed for instance in example 10, albeit with a different layout that gives prominence to the visual part of the text and accommodates the one-page format.

Example 15 is one instance of this approach. The priority here seems to be information rather than persuasion. The page is rather full, with several visuals illustrating the referents of the two nominal sentences, which simply state the categories of products depicted. Each category name is provided in Italian, English and French, the same three languages of the multi-brand catalogue where the ad was published. The inclusion of more than one language in the same ad allows the company to cover a broader international readership without resorting to multiple ads, and thus save on costs. At the same time, it imposes significant space constraints, which might force translators to save even on hyphens, as in 'self-propelled', which here becomes 'selfpropelled'.

Example 15

Fantini-Andreoli multilingual one-page ad, Directory of Farm Machinery, three-language edition, Bologna (Italy), Edagricole, 2000, p. 245

Example 16 follows the same multilingual strategy as example 15, adding German and Spanish to the language list. Overall, however, this ad appears much more oriented towards persuasion than the previous example. Why?

As mentioned above, the visual level is particularly important for advertisements, because images and graphic elements do not only convey information but also carry suggestions, metaphors, and symbolic links (several of which are culture-bound) in a denser and more direct way than verbal elements, which may take more time and effort to read and understand.

In example 15, visuals mainly provide concrete referents for the general categories enunciated verbally, and verbal elements are rendered in a formatting style that is more standard than that of example 16. The colour of the print is always black, no italics are used, and capitals are employed throughout the text, ensuring overall visibility but without emphasizing any element in particular. Fonts, moreover, especially the one used for the product categories, are rather square-angled; the overall impression is one of objective information rather than emotional involvement. This serves several purposes. First of all, the company is presented in a way that is familiar to, thus reassuring for people who are used to doing business in the B2B environment. Secondly, as we have already seen in B2B brochures, the impersonal, neutral style adopted at the verbal and visual/graphic levels conveys a no-nonsense company image and makes product characteristics emerge apparently naturally and objectively from what is presented as a series of facts. Thirdly, the amount of specific information conveyed by this single one-page ad, especially by its visuals, is quantitatively comparable to that of a brochure. The reader is informed about the existence and names – if not technical specifications, which would not have fit into the space – of as many as nine products, two of which are shown in three variants each.

In example 16, on the other hand, the background picture has an important two-fold purpose. It not only describes the scope of application of the advertised product (agricultural rainguns), but also has an evocative quality to it. The picture is undoubtedly a cultivated field, but it does not depict an area of freshly tilled or sown land, the kind of soil we see in the three smaller pictures. It is a golden field of blooming sunflowers accented by the contrast with the dark trees on the horizon, the blue sky above, and the red of the company logo. Colour saturation and contrast make the picture, and consequently the superimposed verbal text, more evident and likely to attract the reader's attention. Also, the page is less crowded with specific information, which is confined to the pre-headline announcing the company's production (*irrigatori*, in English 'rainguns') and the three smaller pictures depicting products of three different categories (respectively indicated in English as 'sprinklers of medium and small capacity', 'slow reverse rainguns', and 'gears' rainguns').

The rest of the verbal text, which again, is highlighted with the use of white print over the saturated colours of the background picture, does not contain any technical anchor, but consists entirely of boost: 'The widest range for the best choice', in the sub-headline, and '50 years of quality + performance + safety' in the payoff. It should be noted, however, that the specific layout of the ad in example 16, with five language versions bullet-listed one after the other, suggests that the overall layout should be kept symmetrical, since, as mentioned before, the visual level is more important than the verbal one. This, in turn, coupled with the extreme simplicity of the boosting nominal sentences, advocates literal translation rather than rewriting, which is exactly what happens in example 16.

In some cases of B2B advertising the persuasive element is much more dominant than in example 16; the text is catchier and the language is more emotional than neutral. Example 17, for instance, displays a layout that is

Example 16
SIME multilingual one-page ad, Directory of Farm Machinery, three-language edition, Bologna (Italy), Edagricole, 2000, p. 243

clearly designed to capture one's attention and ensure high visibility for the text, which is even shorter that in the previous two examples. This monolingual ad also has more space for the visual, and much larger print. Colours and slanted lines are repeated several times across the ad, reinforcing each other and making the overall message more powerful, easier to grasp and remember. Thus, example 17, although curiously included in the 'Brochures' section of the Trilla company website, appears to be more persuasion-oriented than example 16, and much more so than example 15. Actually, the only product-specific information – the main benefit of the product, its advantage vis-à-vis other competitors – is conveyed by the picture alone: the advertised steel drums are not only 'new', as stated by the capitalized word opening the slanted part of the copy, but also coloured. It is this characteristic that helps the addressees enhance their product image.

Example 17
English-only ad, Trilla Corp, downloadable from http://www.trilla.com/trilla/ ENHANCE_YOUR_PRODUCT_IMAGE_BROCHURE.pdf

Here, persuasive intent emerges on a verbal as well as visual level. In example 17, we find two imperatives, one of which is made relevant by its initial position, *Enhance*, the other by the larger print, the use of italics, and the high-visibility background, *buy*, in the left-hand red wedge. In advertising and low-information, high-persuasion promotional genres, imperatives and other devices, like rhetorical questions are used to elicit the addressee's direct involvement in the message. Additionally, by using second-person verb forms, they address the reader directly, creating an emotional bridge between addresser and addressee. In example 17, this is reinforced by the personal adjective, *your*, which further highlights that buying the product is important for the reader, not in general terms.

Second person forms, however, pose a practical translation problem when one translates from English into a language that distinguishes between plural and singular as well as formal and informal *you* forms. We have seen in § 5.1.1.2 that, as a rule of thumb, in B2B communication, *you* should normally be interpreted as a plural, given that the target is made up of collective entities. This general condition still applies here, but one should also take into account the extent to which the ad mimics B2C communication, where *you* is usually singular. In cases such as example 17, then, when it is difficult to disambiguate the nature of *you*, it is essential to ask clients how they wish to be portrayed in terms of authoritativeness and closeness/deference to the target readership (see item 4 of table 1). If the working context makes it impossible to retrieve such information from the client, and if multiple versions are not an option, then the only thing that can help a translator is to carefully assess the position of the text on the information-to-persuasion ratio continuum (table 2). In example 17, as we have just seen, there are several elements, both graphic and verbal, that suggest an intention to position the text slightly more towards the maximum persuasion end of the continuum. In particular, the establishment of an emotional bond between the addresser and the addressee seems to suggest a high degree of closeness between the two. In similar B2B contexts, if the target language favours singular and/or informal second person forms in B2C advertising, it would not be a mistake to opt for such forms.

In the light of the latter comments and of the whole discussion about B2B advertising, try and translate example 17 into your working language(s). Pay special attention to space constraints, typography and layout issues (use of capitals, etc). Remember that the use of space, geometrical shapes, and other visual devices also carry meaning, and can be adjusted to the conventions applying in the target language and culture. Also remember that each culture has a visual language that may differ from the American (or more generally, Western) one. Colour symbolism, in particular, may be an issue here or in similar cases (see chapter 8). (See also Schopp 2002 and works on visual semiotics, social semiotics and geosemiotics in the further reading list in the References).

6. Translating Promotional Material
Institutional Promotion

This chapter briefly outlines the main features of promotional material produced by institutions and addressed either to other institutions or to individuals. It then analyses two examples of institution-to-institution (or I2I) promotional texts and a variety of institution-to-user (or I2U) promotional materials.

6.1 Institutional promotional texts

By 'institutional promotion' I mean all forms of materials that are produced by institutions (both public and not-for-profit private ones) to acquire visibility. They may be self-referential, e.g. inform the public about what the institution does and how to access/use its services, in which case the information content will be higher, or present its achievements. Alternatively, they may give visibility to something other than the institution itself, if this purpose falls within the institution's mission. The latter case applies to materials produced by tourist promotion boards or charities, foundations or organizations that seek to change people's behaviour (e.g. 'Quit smoking' campaigns promoted by hospitals, health ministries, or cancer leagues).

Institutional promotion can be circulated in all media. It is not unusual, however, that the same materials are made available across different media that would normally require different verbal and visual encodings: for instance, the same text can be found as a brochure and on the institution's website. This is a way to save money, which might be frowned upon in the case of private companies, who risk appearing mean or even worse, poor, but is taken as a virtue in the case of institutions, especially public ones.

For this reason, in this chapter institutional promotion material will not be divided by medium, but by addressee. The first section will be about texts that are produced by institutions to gain positive visibility with other, usually superordinate, institutions. Drawing a parallel with B2B, I will call such promotion 'institution-to-institution' (or I2I). On the other hand, the target of the texts discussed in the second section is the individual user. This type of promotion will accordingly be called 'institution-to-user' (or I2U). In the I2U section, texts will further be divided by field (health service promotion, tourist promotion, and awareness-raising).

Differences that can be ascribed to specific media and circulation contexts will be accounted for in the discussion of individual examples. One media-related characteristic, however, that applies in particular to web-circulated materials and brochures (i.e. the totality of the examples that will be analysed here) is space constraints. As we have seen in the previous chapters, it is always important to clear this aspect with the client prior to starting the translation. If no space constraints are specified in the brief or after the translator's inquiry, then the translator may either disclaim any responsibility concerning the downsizing of the target text to accommodate the final layout, or accept that responsibility as an additional commission at an additional price.

6.1.1 *Institution-to-institution (I2I)*

The addressees of institutional promotion are usually the general public, or the users of the institution's services. Institutions, however, may need to produce material which motivates or justifies the funds they receive from higher-level institutions, for instance through a list of achievements that implicitly vouch for the good use of such funds. Using a neologism, this kind of promotional material can be called institution-to-institution or I2I. Even if it is produced by public-owned or public-funded organizations and it targets similar organizations, it is similar to B2B in at least three respects. First, it usually circulates in narrow circles, such as other institutions or the decision-makers from whom the existence and funding of the institution depends. Secondly (and as a consequence of the first aspect), the information it conveys tends to be more specific than in public campaigns. And thirdly, since it is not supposed to be promotional but informative, it contains data presented as objective and usually avoids emotional language.

In multilingual countries, I2I material often needs to be translated into all national languages, or the main working language(s) of the addressed institution(s). Even in monolingual countries, however, this kind of promotional material might need to be translated whenever the addressee is an international organization. In the EU, for instance, several national or local organizations receive funds from European institutions and, additionally to producing official reports, might wish to produce easy-reference literature about their virtuous use of such funds. Such literature is made available to the general public, but is really aimed at gaining visibility at the institutional level. Moreover, public documents produced in the framework of European projects are often translated into the respective languages of all participants, in addition to the usual English translation that is provided for general and public reference.

In a different scenario, European or international projects might aim at supporting national or local institutions that are different from the partners to the project, so that the documents produced by the participants need to be translated into the national language(s) of the targeted organizations. In the latter case, I2I takes on a different meaning; the targeted institutions do not give out funds or support, but are the recipients of the work of the institutions participating in the project.

The style of I2I promotion may at times overlap with that of institutional

Example 18

From the homepage http://smetypo3.stage-server.de/

About the project

The project's vision as part of the European Year of Workers Mobility is supposed to support qualified workers to take well informed decisions concerning taking up employment in a different country, either temporarily or permanently, either deliberately (as a career move) or out of necessity (for instance unemployment). The project will encourage young and older skilled workers to get work experience abroad to considerably increase their chances on the labour market. The project will also help European small and medium-sized enterprises to recruit suitable staff for their needs which, again, will contribute to achieve the Lisbon objectives – competitiveness and job creation.

This project therefore aims to provide

- targeted information on demand and supply of skilled labour
- comparable data to skilled workers to help them develop a decision based on solid information when they want to work abroad
- material for training support to help mobile employees to prepare adequately for working abroad
- a platform for European recruitment of skilled workers, based on an already existing and functioning database, managed by EFKA

The platform will offer an additional service: enterprises who register and declare availability to recruit workforce coming from different countries, will have the opportunity to acquire visibility towards European workers who are interested in getting work experience in their field.

Example 19

From the brochure downloadable from http://smetypo3.stage-server.de/ fileadmin/sme/download_assets/pdf/Eu-brochure-do-you-want-to-work-in-another-EU-Member-State.pdf

Introduction

Free movement of persons is one of the fundamental freedoms guaranteed by Community law. EU citizens can move to another Member State in order to work or to study there, to provide or receive services, to set up a company, to settle there for retirement or, in the case of economically inactive persons, simply to reside there.

This guide describes **only the legal position of persons who migrate within the European Union for reasons of employment.** Its aim is to provide you with information about your rights as a migrant worker in an easily understandable questions and answers form.

Do you want to take up a job in another Member State? Are you working in another Member State and wondering what your rights are in comparison with workers from that country? What happens if you work in one country but reside in another? This guide will provide you with answers to those and many other questions.

This guide has been published in the framework of the European Year of Workers' Mobility 2006, which has been organised to raise awareness and understanding of the benefits of working abroad.

public campaigns (institution-to-user, or I2U, § 6.1.2), but sometimes it is quite easy to tell the two apart. For instance, before reading further, compare the excerpts in examples 18 and 19. They refer to the same issue, workers' mobility across the EU, and both can be accessed from the same website. One of them, however, is clearly I2U, while the other seems to have a more institutional stance that makes the reader think that it is not primarily or exclusively targeted at individual service users. There are several linguistic features, which have already been mentioned in the previous chapter with reference to B2B, that tell them apart. There are also clues that can be retrieved from the contents of the texts. Draw a list of relevant differences between the examples before reading the continuation of this section. If you use this book for classroom practice, discuss these differences in class. Where do they locate the respective texts on the information-to-persuasion ratio continuum (table 2)? And with respect to question 4 of the model brief in table 1? Please note that one of the two texts was probably written by non-native speakers. Stylistic differences that can be ascribed to this characteristic should not be taken into account here.

(Please do not resume reading before you have completed your list of differences!)

First of all, a few contextual elements might make the difference clearer. Example 19 is the introduction to the brochure 'Do you want to work in another EU Member State? Find out about your rights!', issued by the European Commission Directorate-General for Employment, Social Affairs and Equal Opportunities, available in 20 EU languages from http://bookshop.europa.eu/uri?target=EUB:NOTICE:KE7506930:EN (the URL in the caption only refers to the English version). The fact that EC Directorate-Generals do not depend on external funding discourages the I2I interpretation, even if this conclusion needs to be supported by text analysis.

On the other hand, those who are familiar with the kind of texts produced by European-funded projects will have recognized, at the very least from the recurrent reference to 'the project', one such text in example 18, which, in fact, is the homepage of the Skilled Mobile European project. The site is multilingual, with versions in seven different languages, the national languages of the partners, plus English. European projects are proposed by organizations that apply for European Commission funds through special calls for proposals. The proposals are assessed by a group of specialists and the winners are then closely monitored during all stages of the project, both in terms of results and expenditures. For this reason, as already mentioned, several materials originating from European projects are intended for I2I communication, even if this is not always the case. This particular project, for instance, is intended to have relevance for individual workers migrating across the EU as well as for small and medium-sized enterprises hiring them.

The site also contains several downloadable materials that address the end users of the project, some of them with more direct and emotional style than others. In this case, therefore, context is not enough to let us decide clearly whether this text is I2I or I2U. To make this decision, and therefore as translators decide whether we can address the reader as an individual or it is better to leave the text impersonal, we have to look at the text in more detail.

The section of the homepage contained in example 18 does not seem to seek direct contact with the end users, at least from a linguistic point of view. For a start, the project is presented as a work-in-progress initiative, and its final results, which should benefit individual workers and small and medium-sized enterprises (SMEs), had not been achieved yet at the moment when this webpage was written. The vision *is supposed to support... workers*, the project *will encourage, will... help, aims to*, and so on. Moreover, Lisbon objectives, *competitiveness and job creation*, are in a position that grants them high relevance both linguistically and graphically, since they are the rheme of the last sentence of the first paragraph, followed by a blank line. Such objectives, however, are not presented in a way that has a clear practical relevance for individual workers or enterprises. This would have entailed a different emphasis structure, for instance,

> In line with Lisbon objectives, the project will also help European small and medium-sized enterprises to recruit staff that suit their needs, which will contribute to making them more competitive at the same time as they create new jobs for European workers.

Here, competitiveness is presented as a potential point of interest for SMEs and job creation as something relevant to workers. Well-informed readers might still link them back to the initial parenthetic clause about Lisbon objectives, but the end users of the project's services would recognize the final pieces of information as relevant for them as enterprises or workers, rather than in general or for European institutions. In the original, on the other hand, the focus is on the project's compliance with a specific institutional strategy, which seems to imply that the primary addressees of the text are European institutions, not European citizens or businesses.

Such considerations are confirmed by what is perhaps the most obvious difference between examples 18 and 19 in terms of I2I vs. I2U language. In example 19, after one and a half paragraphs which appear objective and informative, the text starts addressing the reader as a *you* that is immediately disambiguated as a singular (*as a migrant worker*). In other language versions the second person plural is used, which is either more formal (as in German) or betrays that the source institution looks at the addressee as a collective mass rather than a set of individuals (as is usual in Italian I2U communication issued by public bodies where personal deixis is used). Moreover, the third paragraph of example 19 seeks the readers' active participation through three questions that are supposed to make them identify with the situations described, and call on them to provide an answer, i.e. to actively complete the meaning of the message. No such devices are employed in example 18.

At the same time, examples 18 and 19 also share some common features. For instance, the first and last paragraphs of example 19 contain information about EU laws and the Union's official position vis-à-vis workers' mobility, presented as general statements rather than something that has special relevance for the reader. Such institutional parts of the text are, accordingly, rather impersonal; no personal deixis is used, no emotional bond is created, the reader's active participation is not an issue. The latter elements are only found in the middle part of the text. Moreover, in both example 18 and 19, the addressers never reveal themselves in the first person, or even as organizations. In example 18, the topic is always *the project*, never its participants (whose logos and contacts, however, are displayed on the site, to the right of the text shown in the example). In example 19, the addresser is identified as *the guide* itself, not its source institution. Both strategies convey the impression that the two texts are intended for information only, not for persuasion. In fact, this is exactly their purpose; we have already seen that, in institutional promotion, the term 'promotion' often refers only to 'visibility', especially when the object of promotion is not something that can be bought, or a change of lifestyle that is pushed on the addressees.

Now that we have outlined differences and similarities between our I2I and I2U texts, use examples 18 and 19 as source texts for translation practice. For a comparison with other language versions, example 18 is available at the URL contained in the caption, as well as in the Appendix of this book (chapter 10), in six other versions (German, Finnish, Hungarian, Italian, Danish and Slovak) provided by the national partners of the project. Example 19 can be found in 19 other European languages also in the Appendix, while the whole brochure 'Do you want to work in another EU Member State? Find out about your rights!' can be downloaded in 20 EU languages from http://bookshop.europa.eu/uri?target=EUB:NOTICE:KE7506930:EN.

6.1.2 Institution-to-user (I2U)

Institution-to-user communication originates from institutions and addresses the end users of the institution's services, or, in the case of awareness-raising, the general public. The addressee, therefore, is always an individual who is not supposed to have any special knowledge about the institution's field of activity. This accounts for a density of specific information that is generally lower than in B2B or I2I texts. Not all I2U texts, however, resort to high-persuasion devices such as personal deixis, emotional language, or the active involvement of the reader through imperatives or questions that elicit the reader's action or answer, or through tropes or puns that require a non-literal, creative interpretation. Thus, the information-to-persuasion ratio of I2U texts is highly variable, depending on a number of factors.

For instance, in cultures where hierarchies and public face are important, public institutions are usually more oriented towards an institutional image that is more dignified than humanized, which prevents them from using emotional language or fancy wordplay. Texts produced by such sources will tend to be more informative than persuasive, even if the information provided is not particularly specific. Conversely, in cultures where those who hold power are expected to wear a human face and be close to the people who depend on them, public agencies might find it more effective to put on a friendly image and address the reader as a peer, increasing their visibility with highly captivating or even amusing devices at the same time as they provide useful information. The same cultural differences apply to private organizations that choose to portray themselves as institutions rather than companies, perhaps because they provide services traditionally associated with the public sector, or are partly owned by public entities, or receive public funds. Such companies, too, will tend to keep a distance from the addressee in large-power-distance cultures, whereas in small-power-distance cultures they are more likely to choose a B2C-like approach.

This creates a major problem for translators, since the functional translation of an I2U text coming from a public source, or a source that imitates public promotional discourse, can require heavy trans-creation, similar to what we have discussed with regard to CVs and job application letters (§ 4.2.1 and § 4.2.2). How does one decide whether the target culture is based on small or large power distance, and if institutions are supposed to have a friendly human face or an impassively dignified image? Hofstede and Hofstede (2005) help us with their investigation of cultural dimensions in 74 countries. Besides "power distance" (ibid.: 39 and following), other relevant dimensions here are "individualism vs. collectivism" (ibid.: 73 and following) (in collectivist societies, institutions are supposed to serve the common good seen as an abstract entity rather than provide services to and seek contact with individual citizens) and "masculinity vs. femininity" (ibid.:115 and following) (in feminine societies, institutions are expected to be more caring and closer to citizens as service users). It is however important to complement Hofstede and Hofstede's data, which are not meant to suit a translator's specific needs and require some interpretation, with real-life observations. In other words, read as many parallel texts as possible in the target language, after making sure that they are comparable with the text to be translated in terms of source, target, and distribution context, including the source organization's field of activity and whether it operates in the public or private sector.

These considerations do not necessarily apply only to those cases when the target text is intended for users who live outside the borders of the source institution's country, and therefore clearly belong to a different culture. Even within the borders of a multilingual state, different language communities may score differently on one or more cultural dimensions. For instance, Hofstede and Hofstede show that, compared with the total Canadian population, Québec is characterized by higher power distance and lower individualism and masculinity rates. The same applies to the Flemish part of Belgium when compared with the Walloon population. Secondly, even when the translation is intended for migrants residing in the same country as the source institution, translators may choose to exploit the conventions that apply in one or more of the countries where the target language is spoken, in order to accommodate the cultural expectations of the target readership.

It is obviously impossible to cover all fields of I2U communication. The following sections concern the fields of healthcare, tourism, and awareness-raising. Trade union communication was already discussed in example 1 (chapter 2), which also championed the distribution context of I2U print ads, and will not be discussed again here.

6.1.2.1 I2U promotion in the healthcare field

In addition to what has been discussed about power distance, individualist vs. collectivist, and masculine vs. feminine cultures, there is an important contextual element that one should take into account when translating healthcare promotion across languages and cultures. Some countries have highly developed public-funded healthcare systems that provide citizens with services free of charge or at low prices. In such countries, citizens tend to resort to private healthcare institutes outside the public circuit only when local public structures cannot grant a timely or highly specific service. Moreover, since profit is supposed to be less of an issue for public healthcare units than for private entities, the general assumption is that their main priority should be citizens' health rather than economic performance. Under such circumstances, the public tend to trust the public healthcare sector namely for its institutional nature, and are likely to be negatively influenced by linguistic (or visual and graphic) strategies that may be perceived to belittle the source's authority, public face, or neutral stance.

This is particularly true for cultures that have relatively large power distance combined with relatively high scores in another cultural dimension, that of "uncertainty avoidance", which for the purposes of this discussion can be taken to mean a preference for everything reassuring and familiar (Hofstede and Hofstede 2005: 163 and following). Italy is one such culture; the United States, English-speaking Canada, Great Britain, Ireland, New Zealand and Australia, conversely, all have low power distance and uncertainty avoidance scores. In the following two examples we will see how this influences brochure and website copywriting and translation.

The first example comes from the public sector. It is taken from a guide to the services of the Forlì hospital, written by the Public Relations office of the Forlì Local Health Unit (AUSL) and circulated both in printed form and as a .pdf file available from the institution's webpage. A reduced version of the original brochure, translated into English by a Dutch translator, is available only as a downloadable file with a simplified layout. (French, Chinese, Albanian and Arabic versions of the reduced guide can also be downloaded from the webpage indicated in the two captions; see Appendix for the respective translations of example 20.) Once again, the purpose of the brochure might seem to be only informative, but at a deeper level the issue here is institutional visibility and putting on a public face that is well accepted by the citizens.

Example 20a
From page 14 of the Italian brochure "Guida al Polo Ospedaliero 'G.B. Morgagni – L. Pierantoni' Forlì", Forlì AUSL (Local Health Unit), downloadable from http://www.ausl.fo.it/tabid/444/Default.aspx. With graphic adjustments

A chi chiedere informazioni

[...]
Nell'atrio del padiglione "Morgagni" ci si può rivolgere allo sportello informativo. Gli operatori risponderanno a tutte le domande relative ai servizi offerti. Possono fornire informazioni sulla modalità di accesso a ricoveri ed esami, visite ambulatoriali e in libera professione, tempi di attesa, funzionamento di tutte le strutture operative dell'Azienda e altre informazioni per garantire la soluzione di problematiche relative ai servizi socio sanitari come esenzioni, rimborsi, altre strutture sanitarie a cui rivolgersi.

Il personale favorisce l'accoglienza, è disponibile nei confronti dei cittadini per ascoltare e comprendere le richieste ed offre l'aiuto necessario a limitare i disagi che possono verificarsi durante la fruizione dei servizi e risolvere eventuali problemi pratici collegati alle prestazioni erogate dall'Azienda.

Example 20b
From page 1 of the English translation of a reduced version of 20a, downloadable from http://www.ausl.fo.it/tabid/444/Default.aspx. With graphic adjustments

Where to get information

[...]
In the entrance-hall of the Section "Morgagni" you can turn to the information desk. The operators will respond to all your questions about the services offered. They can give you information about the modality of access to hospitalization and examinations, surgery visits and private visits, waits, the functioning of all the operative structures of the Centre and other information to guarantee the solution of problems related to social health care, such as exemptions, refunding and other health services where to turn to.

> Our staff gives priority to hospitality, and is at the disposal of the citizens to
> listen and comprehend their requests, offers the necessary help to limit the
> inconveniencies during the use of the different services and resolves practical
> problems related to the services lent by the Centre.

The target text in example 20b is a literal translation of 20a, at times so
close to the original that the reading becomes awkward, e.g. in 'at the dis-
posal of the citizens to listen and comprehend their requests'. The principle
of accuracy appears to override that of functionality, except for one important
element: personal deixis.

In both languages, this excerpt of the guide is supposed to explain where
people can find information once they get to the hospital and what kind of
information they can find there. This content is very practical and is supposed
to be especially relevant for the person who has taken the initiative of picking
the brochure from an information point or downloading it from the Health
Unit's website. This is why the English text routinely turns impersonal sentences into personal addresses ('you can turn to'), and adds personal pronouns
or possessives ('They can give you', 'Our staff') to make communication
personal, between a plural *we* and a singular *you*, as is in the nature of things
as well as in English conventional I2U writing.

The Italian text, on the other hand, never uses personal deixis. It does
not define the hospital as a *we*, which is probably due to the need to make it
clear that the source institution, AUSL, is not the same as the object of promotion, i.e. the hospital, a subordinate institution. This need is clearly only felt
at the institutional level and more or less irrelevant to the common citizen.
It does not even indicate the reader as a *you*, as would be logical given the
target readership, the distribution context, and the apparent purpose of the
text. Instead, we only find either impersonal, generalizing sentences (*ci si può
rivolgere* [one may ask]) or sentences whose subjects, topic, or theme are *gli
operatori* or *il personale* [staff]. The service user is never mentioned or even
addressed, only indirectly implied by the very existence of an information
desk staffed with people who are supposed to provide answers and solutions.
The neutral, impersonal face granted by the absence of personal addresses is
combined with a rather formal register and the use of non-elementary syntax
and lexicon: e.g. the noun clause *modalità di accesso a ricoveri* [mode of access to hospitalization] could be rewritten into a more transparent *come fare
se devi essere ricoverato/a* [what to do if you need to be hospitalized]. All
this may make the text difficult to read for non-native Italian speakers, who,
however, are the addressees of the five translated versions. It also makes the
text unappealing and builds a distance between the reader on the one hand
and both the AUSL and the hospital on the other.

The features highlighted in the previous paragraph may appear to point
to a text that claims to be I2U, but actually seems to target other institutional

levels and serve hidden institutional interests, such as showing AUSL top managers that the AUSL's public relations office is doing its job. Even if this were true, however, in this particular case it would not be terribly relevant for the translators, since AUSL top managers are very likely to be Italian native speakers and therefore, the only text that may fulfil the shadow purpose with the shadow target would be the Italian one, not its translations. A translator, then, would have no other option than to adhere to the official brief and make the text relevant and functional for the stated readership. In the case of the English translation, for instance, this would imply lowering the register as well as addressing the reader directly. When confronted with similar working situations, it might be a good idea to explain to the client that target language and culture conventions call for a friendlier, more informal image. Only if the client states that the source institution's dignified and authoritative image must not be altered in any way is the translator relieved of the responsibility of functionally adjusting the text.

On top of that, in example 20a hidden agendas can hardly be said to be the reason why the reader is kept at a distance from both the source and the object of promotion, and the text can hardly be said to be I2I. Why? Because, as already mentioned, from a public institution Italian readers expect more power distance and a more dignified face than most native speakers of English do. Italian readers, who tend to look suspiciously at what is uncertain, may also appreciate a reassuringly traditional institutional image that changes only slowly, without putting on a new face all of a sudden. In fact, in the past few years Italian public health units have been managed in a more entrepreneurial, money-driven way than in the past: the first A in the Italian acronym AUSL, introduced in the 1990s, stands for *azienda*, that is to say 'business', 'enterprise'. Their promotional style, however, is likely to forfeit the traditional image of a stately, somewhat bureaucratic, health authority and take on the characteristics of nimbler B2C communication only gradually, if at all.

This is why, even in the face of an information density that is lower than that of most B2B texts, the information-to-persuasion ratio of example 20a still appears comparatively high, because persuasive devices of the kind used in B2C promotion are accurately avoided. Similarly, the absence of personal deixis and the formal, bureaucratic register, which seem to run counter to any persuasive attempt, are consequences of the Italian target readership's cultural and linguistic expectations, or the addresser's suppositions about them. The translator who produced example 20b did recognize personal deixis as something that she could bring back into her English text, but did not effect more radical changes that would have decreased the information-to-persuasion ratio or at least simplified the information content, making the text more functional both for native readers of English, who come from small-power-distance cultures, and for the migrant population using English as a lingua franca, who might find example 20b linguistically difficult. In theory, such changes would have been possible here, since example 20a contains very few translational anchors, and none of them technical or monoreferential. However, since we do not know the details of the brief and the opportunities that the translator had to negotiate her choices with her client, it is impossible to conclude whether extensive rewriting or trans-creation were in fact an option in this particular translation commission.

As mentioned before, Italy being a national health system country, Italian private healthcare centres, too, often choose to present a reassuring image and comply with the neutral, impersonal discourse of health public authorities rather than with B2C personal and boosting techniques. The short excerpts in example 21 come from the homepage of a private Milan-based centre and the corresponding Russian, Arabic and English translations, listed in the same order in which they appear on the website. Once again, when compared with the original, the three translations do not show significant rewriting or trans-creation, especially in virtue of the presence of highly technical anchors in the second paragraph. Each one of them, however, is adapted in some respect to the expectations of the target readership. For instance, personal deixis is introduced in the English text, but not in the Russian one, Russians being used to even higher power distance than Italians, according to Hofstede and Hofstede (2005). The Russian one, on the other hand, features an instance of added lexical boost, 'полностью оборудован' [fully equipped], rather than just 'equipped' or *attrezzato* in the original.

Example 21a
From the homepage of Poliambulatorio Sanpietro, http://www.poliambulato-riosanpietro.it

La qualità della prestazione sanitaria si giova della presenza di apparecchiature medicali di grande contenuto tecnologico nonché dell'elegante comfort di questa Struttura.
Il Centro Medico, con una superficie superiore a 380 mq, è attrezzato per visite spe-cialistiche, diagnostica multidisciplinare e chirurgia ambulatoriale, check up, esami clinici in un giorno, fisiochinesiterapia, trattamenti laser, Thermage ed altro.

In conclusion, when translating Italian healthcare promotion into other languages, although the source texts are intentionally made impersonal and distant, almost I2I-like, functional rewriting is possible and actually advisable if the target language and culture suggest a different kind of approach to patients and prospective service users. Of course, it is always better to negotiate radical choices with the client.

This is not only valid when one translates from large power distance languages and cultures into small power distance ones; obviously, the reverse applies, too. When translating healthcare promotion material from English into

---

Example 21b

Russian translation of 21a, from http://www.poliambulatoriosanpietro.it/home_ru.htm

---

Высокое качество медицинской эффективности достигается благодаря наличию технологически нового медицинского оборудования и комфортных условий предлагаемой структуры.

Этот Медицинский Центр, площадью свыше 380 кв.м., полностью оборудован для проведения специальных медосмотров, установления комплексной диагностики и амбулаторной хирургии, для комплексного обследования состояния здоровья, для сдачи необходимых клинических анализов в течении 1 дня, для проведения физиокинезитерапии, лазертерапии, термажа и тд.

Example 21c

Arabic translation of 21a, with minor adjustments. From http://www.poliambulatoriosanpietro.it/home_lb.htm

---

نوعية الخدمات الصحية ناتجة عن وفرة ألآلات الطبية الحديثة والمُتقدِمة تكنولوجياً، هذا بالإضافة أيضاً إلى وسائل الراحة والترفية الذي يتمتع بها المستوصف.

ألإمتيازات

المركز الطبي تزيد مساحته عن 380 متر مربع،

مُجهَّز للكشف الطبي، تحاليل وتشخيص لجميع الحالات وللعمليات الجراحية، كشف طبي عام، الطب السَّريري اليومي، علاج لتدليك وإعادة حركة الجسم علاج باللايزر ،الترماج و غيره.

Example 21d

English translation of 21a, with minor adjustments. From http://www.poliambulatoriosanpietro.it/index_eng.html

---

The excellent quality of our services is due to the advanced technology of our medical equipment as well as to the comfort of our Medical Center.

Our Medical Center, which is more than 380 square meters, is equipped for specific medical examinations, image diagnostics, day surgery, check up examinations in one day, physiokinesitherapy, laser treatments, Thermage and more.

Italian, for instance, it would be appropriate to downplay the friendly attitude that the source institution or private centre may show in the original, make the target text as impersonal as possible, and re-focus its theme/rheme structure. For instance, the topic of many sentences may need to be shifted from a probable *us* to a neutral but authoritative general term, such as 'il Centro' [the Centre]. Even better, emphasis can be shifted from the source organization to its qualities, services, equipment, staff or the like, channelling the readers' attention into the rational arguments that should advocate the health centre's reliability and professionalism. For instance, a sentence like *We'll greet you by name when you come to our office, because we want you to feel at home* (an adaptation from real-life websites of American private healthcare and dentistry centres) may become in Italian 'I servizi e l'accoglienza sono sempre personalizzati in modo da far sentire l'utenza a proprio agio' [Services and reception are always customized in such a way that users feel at ease].

It appears, then, that healthcare promotion, like CVs and job application letters (§ 4.2.1 and § 4.2.2), is one of those promotional genres where, for the target text to meet its function, not only linguistic conventions, but the very information-to-persuasion ratio of the original text may need to be adjusted to the expectations of the target readership. In countries where uncertainty avoidance is high and power distance is large, and where healthcare institutions are perceived as authorities, this kind of promotion may resemble I2I, whereas in countries that have low uncertainty avoidance and small power distance, public healthcare bodies produce texts that are clearly I2U. In countries where private health centres do not tend to imitate public institutions' discourse, perhaps because there is no established or centralized public health system, the promotional materials of those private entities is actually more similar to B2C, with lexical boost, questions, exclamations, imperatives, reported speech vouching for the object of promotion, wordplay and idioms.

To provide just one example, a Google search for the phrase 'we cater to cowards' finds hundreds of matches referring to promotional websites of American dentists' offices and dental clinics. There is even a dentist's called 'Cater to Cowards' in Glendale, Arizona, and the conspicuous headline of one dental website reads 'Are you a big chicken?'. Needless to say, such catchphrases would require thorough and careful rewriting for a target that is not used to be addressed with such familiarity, and is probably not prepared to associate such a fun approach with sensitive topics like personal health or the pain associated with dental care. Besides Italian, target languages that according to Hofstede and Hofstede (2005) correspond to cultures with high uncertainty avoidance and large power distance (but not necessarily to countries having a public healthcare system) include French, Spanish, Portuguese, Greek, Korean, Japanese, Russian and most East European languages, Turkish, and Arabic. As a rule of thumb, when translating from English into such languages, it is better to read and analyse a certain number of original parallel texts coming from the target culture(s) before going for a translation that uncritically sticks to the rhetorical and information structure of the source text. The same applies to all I2U promotional texts whose source or object of promotion can be associated with some sort of public authority: embassies, governmental or ministerial agencies, public-owned enterprises or private *de facto* monopolies (e.g. the Italian railway company), local governments and their emanations, chambers of commerce, etc.

6.1.2.2 Tourist promotion

Tourist promotion material can come in a variety of formats and distribution contexts: brochures, websites, newsletters, free guides and other free material that can usually be found at tourist promotion agencies or downloaded from their websites. It can even be found in distribution contexts that do not presuppose intentional contact by the addressee, like promotional posters or advertising in the media, although for translators this is a relatively rarer case and can be approached following the guidelines of § 7.1.2 rather than the ones found here. Guides and other tourist material that are available at a price and are therefore supposed to objectively inform the reader about the strengths and weaknesses of a given destination obviously do not qualify as promotion. In Italy and in other countries where foreign tourism covers a considerable proportion of the country's GDP, the tourist industry, both institutional and B2C, can collectively be one of a translator's best commissioners.

The source of I2U tourist promotion can be a public agency whose mission is or includes the promotion of a nation or a given area (e.g. tourist boards), or a private consortium of hotels or other stakeholders that promote its members as a group and not as individual enterprises. The target is the individual tourist who is already in the area, or preferably, from the source's point of view, the prospective tourist who browses the web or goes to international tourist exhibitions to choose the destination for the next holiday trip. In other words, the target is a non-specialized reader who is likely to collect and compare several materials before deciding what to see or where to go. For this reason, functional tourist promotion texts tend to avoid over-technical content and attract and involve the reader with emotional devices and other B2C-like strategies, even in the face of a distribution context where contact is usually initiated by the addressee. Consequently, although in tourist promotion information can be rather dense and at times become specific or even monoreferential (especially in the case of longer guides that cover local cuisine, folklore, handicrafts or other peculiar traits), the information-to-persuasion ratio of this text type is, on average, comparatively lower than that of the promotional genres we have seen before.

We have already seen a practical example of tourist promotion translation (example 2 in chapter 2). In that case, the focus was the importance of negotiation and multiple versions when the source institution has hidden agendas that may have to do with its institutional position rather than with the purpose of the text. Such issues, therefore, will not be mentioned again here.

In tourist promotion, just like in healthcare promotion, cultural issues are important to determine the persuasive impact of the target text on the target readership. Tourists expect to find certain things in certain destinations and become oriented towards a country or area because they want to find there what they expect. Good tourist promotion copywriters know this and accommodate their source texts to the kind of tourists they want to attract. Target profiling is vital for tourist promotion; in this regard, this genre is similar to B2C. This is why, in countries and areas with a highly developed tourist industry, tourist boards and consortia produce materials catering for the interests of special categories of tourists (e.g. schools, congress convenors, gourmets, cyclists, trekkers) or promoting selections of destinations that correspond to specific tourist profiles (churches and monasteries, wildlife parks, castles and cities of art, holiday farms, hotels offering special packages to families with children and the like).

In destinations whose economy relies heavily on incoming tourism, local identities are restyled or in some cases designed from scratch to accommodate tourist expectations. If you work for a tourist promotion board or consortium and you are responsible for the copywriting, revision and/or adaptation of promotional material for a foreign target readership, choosing or revising the selection of the local features and identity traits to be promoted is the first step of your work. There is a vast literature on the translation or creation of local identities for the benefit of tourists: for a sociological discussion of how tourist experiences are actually crafted by mediators, such as tourist brochure copywriters and translators, see Ooi (2002); for a translation-oriented perspective, see Fuentes-Luque and Kelly (2000).

The example of the Italian town of Casola Valsenio (example 22) is a straightforward illustration of what I mean by selection of identity traits. In this case, the selection was decided by the local administrators, but similar marketing operations might be decided downstream by copywriters and/or translators. Moreover, Casola is an easy case in that its selected identity is fairly unambiguous, while larger or more complex tourist destinations, such as Rome, London, or broader areas, can be promoted under hundreds of different lights, all of which virtually relevant and approved by the respective local authorities.

Even if identity trait selection does not fall within your jurisdiction, because you think you are just a translator and you may well want to leave copywriters and/or board or consortium officials such a hot potato, things may not be so easy as they seem. In the standard tourist translation scenario, you have a ready-made source text which, in the best of possibilities, was already developed to accommodate the interests and expectations of a carefully targeted kind of tourists. The target of the source text, however, is more often than not assumed to be national tourists, while you need to produce a text that is functional for a foreign pool of (prospective) tourists who may well have expectations that differ from those of national tourists, not only in terms of what to see and where to go, but also in terms of what is an appealing visual and writing style. The moral is that in tourist promotion major rewriting

---

Example 22

Identity trait selection in tourist promotion. An easy case: Casola Valsenio

---

Casola Valsenio is a medieval town in the hills near Ravenna, surrounded by an idyllic landscape. During World War II it was caught between the Nazi-fascist retreating armies and the liberation forces, including Italian partisans, for 5 months; the nearby hills were the theatre of many battles that might be defined as epic (one of them, particularly fierce, lasted for as many as 16 days). However, unlike other Italian towns with a similar history, Casola did not construct a public face based either on its fancy medieval air or its painful war history. Instead, it recently acquired a totally different image that marked it out in the tourist scene and linked back to increasingly popular movements such as Slow Food or sustainable farming. Building on a herbal garden originally used for educational purposes, opened to the public in 1975 and included in the local museum circuit as late as 2003, the town started organizing several yearly herb and fruit festivals as well as guided tours and theme dinners on the same topic. It also took the official title *Paese delle erbe e dei frutti dimenticati* [Town of herbs and forgotten fruits], which appears prominently on the town's webpage, http://www.comune.casolavalsenio.ra.it. A trait of a road leading to the town was transformed into a panoramic route lined with lavender and accordingly renamed *Strada della Lavanda* to reinforce the link with aromatic plants and provide an appropriate backdrop for the town's festivals and events, mainly clustered in the lavender flowering season. Thus, the identity traits selected for the town's public image also impacted heavily not only on its production and trading activities, which were directed towards traditional herbs and fruits to make the most of incoming tourism and institutional promotion, but also on its very landscape, not to speak of its population's memory and self-perception as a community.

---

and possibly suggestions about the restyling of layout and pictures are often necessary. Trans-creation may go as far as to involve the contents, even the technical anchors of the text, although substantial changes in the information content should always be negotiated with the client. If the working context prevents negotiation, then a more conservative attitude may be preferable, but this should never lead to an uncritically literal translation.

Once again, the only reliable way of obtaining indications on how to re-write the text is to read and analyse as many texts as possible originally written in the target language and for a target readership that is comparable to that of the text to be translated. If translating tourist promotion becomes, or already is, one of your specializations, building a corpus or a set of corpora specifically tailored to your needs can be a good investment. Comparative analysis of original texts written in different languages is not only useful to detect specific linguistic patterns, but also to assess the average information-to-persuasion ratio of similar texts across different cultures and tourist markets.

An easy example of how partial rewriting may become necessary is the treatment of **realia tantum,** i.e. words that refer to things that exist only in the source culture. Realia include some, but by no means all, terms relating to local food, folklore, handicrafts, art, and architecture and often require additional explanations to be understood by a foreign readership. For instance, when translating a guide to the delicacies of an Italian destination, translators will generally not have too many problems in leaving terms such as *mozzarella* or *spaghetti* untranslated and without a gloss, but anything beyond that will require a choice between two alternative strategies. One has to either domesticate the term into the nearest equivalent in the target language and lose all the flavour of exoticism (and exotic flavour may well be the intended effect of the text), or leave the term in the source language and add a short explanation. The second choice is generally more functional, but to prevent the text from becoming somewhat pedantic, boost additions, punctuation revision and rhythm adjustment might be advisable, especially in those target languages where tourist promotion traditionally has a lower information-to-persuasion ratio.

Example 23 is a case in point. It comes from my professional experience and is a good example of several aspects of the translation process, in particular: the functional partial rewriting of texts with a high density of realia; client collaboration; and the successful management of space constraints. The client was a unit of the mixed-ownership regional tourist promotion board, the Azienda di Promozione Turistica (APT). I kept direct contact with two extremely collaborative members of the APT staff, who were also directly responsible for the publication of the brochure in all languages including Italian. Initially no space constraints were specified, because the guide had not been laid out yet; both the Italian and the English versions were to be laid out at the same time, and I had received the original as a series of Word files. The brief was to make the text enticing as well as clear for English-speaking readers and complete (i.e. I could only suggest or negotiate, but not independently effect any information omissions). High quality standards were required: I knew the client to be perfectly able to identify their own needs and assess whether translations complied with them. Time constraints were severe and did not leave me any leeway for self-revision: I only had about 15 days for what turned out to be a 150-page pocket-sized guide, luckily including pictures. For all these reasons, I sought the professional assistance of two British revisers whom I knew to be curious and critical travellers. In order to make the most of my investment in terms of my own professional image, I also immediately informed the client that I was providing them a quality insurance service at no additional price.

In the layout phase, the two APT members of staff who kept contact with me, and were both proficient in English and competent in tourist promotion copywriting, downsized those parts of the guide that exceeded the allotted frames, working directly on the page layout program file. The printout was then sent back to me for proofreading and the finishing touches. In example 23b you will find the version I originally sent out, while example 23c contains the final version after the client's downsizing and my proofreading.

Example 23a

From page 57 of the guide "Città d'Arte dell'Emilia Romagna", 2005 edition, Bologna: Unione di Prodotto Città d'Arte, Cultura e Affari. Also available as Web text at http://www.cittadarte.emilia-romagna.it/citta/bologna/buona_tavola.php

---

Narra la leggenda – una delle tante – che l'inventore del tortellino sarebbe stato un albergatore che, ammaliato dall'ombelico di Venere apparsagli in sogno, avrebbe cercato di riprodurlo inventando la pasta ripiena. Favola o realtà? Di sicuro i tortellini in brodo, famosi in tutto il mondo, sono, insieme alla Mortadella di Bologna IGP, il piatto più tipico della città. Ergo: obbligo assaggiarli nel luogo dove sono nati.

Per il resto, si sa, Bologna è popolare come "la grassa"! Attenzione però: "grasso" non si riferisce alla pesantezza del cibo, bensì alla gioia di vivere, alla capacità di godere i piaceri della vita.

E la lista dei piaceri enogastronomici è assai lunga. Dopo i primi piatti, a base di pasta all'uovo fatta in casa, come le popolari tagliatelle al ragù, arrivano i secondi di carne. Fra i prodotti freschi ecco il vitellone bianco dell'Appennino Centrale IGP.

Example 23b

English translation of 23a (original version provided by the translator). Parts that were eliminated in the final version are marked in bold

---

Legend **(or at least, one version of the legend)** has it that tortellini were invented by an innkeeper who, after dreaming about Venus, tried to re-create the beauty of her navel and ended up with this world-famous shape of pasta, stuffed with several kinds of minced meat, eggs, nutmeg and parmigiano. Maybe it's just a fancy story, but all the same, tortellini **(**served in broth, **according to the original recipe)** is one of the main specialities of Bologna, as is IGP Mortadella di Bologna (also known elsewhere as Bologna or baloney). Local hand-made tortellini are entirely different from the export product, so don't waste an opportunity to taste the real thing.

After all, Bologna is called La Grassa (The Fat **one**), not because its cuisine is especially heavy, but because the Bolognese love to live it up and enjoy the pleasures of life – and of the table. The list is long: first of all, hand-rolled pasta, like *tagliatelle al ragù*, universally (and very poorly) imitated under the name of Spaghetti Bolognese. Then, fresh meat from local certified breeds (such as **the** IGP *vitellone bianco dell'Appennino Centrale*, **a variety of young beef)** [...]

Example 23c
*Final version of the translation of 23a after the client's downsizing to accom-
modate the brochure format. From page 57 of the English guide "Cities of Art
of Emilia Romagna", 2005 edition, Bologna: Unione di Prodotto Città d'Arte,
Cultura e Affari. Also available, with some graphic differences, at http://www.
cittadarte.emilia-romagna.it/citta/bologna/buona_tavola.php?lang=en*

Legend has it that tortellini were invented by an innkeeper who, after dreaming
about Venus, tried to re-create the beauty of her navel and ended up with this
world-famous shape of pasta, stuffed with several kinds of minced meat, eggs,
nutmeg and parmigiano.
Maybe it's just a fancy story, but all the same, tortellini served in broth is one
of the main specialities of Bologna, as is IGP Mortadella di Bologna (also
known elsewhere as Bologna or baloney). Local hand-made tortellini are entirely different from the export product, so don't waste an opportunity to taste
the real thing.
After all, Bologna is called La Grassa (The Fat), not because its cuisine is
especially heavy, but because the Bolognese love to live it up and enjoy the
pleasures of life – and of the table. The list is long: first of all, hand-rolled
pasta, like *tagliatelle al ragù*, universally (and very poorly) imitated under
the name of Spaghetti Bolognese. Then, fresh meat from local certified breeds
like IGP *vitellone bianco dell'Appennino Centrale* [...]

Let us start with a reale tantum that is treated in a way that would be
absolutely indefensible in a normal working context. The use of an unglossed
'IGP' instead of the English acronym PGI (Protected Geographical Indication:
a quality European label) is certainly incorrect, as both the English and Italian
terms are monoreferential equivalents (i.e. technical anchors) sanctioned by
European Union laws. In this particular case, however, the Italian acronym
featured as a picture in a 'Key to symbols and acronyms' that appeared in the
first pages of the guide and could not be eliminated or changed. The client
therefore recommended that the acronym be used as such throughout the text,
and glossed as 'Protected Geographical Indication' only in the key to symbols
at the beginning of the book.

Let us now proceed to compare the two English versions. Version 23c
was made shorter, but the layout frame allowed as many as 1186 characters;
23b has 1299, the Italian text only 883. The clients made sure that only
secondary parts were culled, so that, in the end, 23c reads more easily than
23b. It therefore responds better to the mandate to make the text enticing,
even if it is slightly less complete. Completeness, however, was secondary to
persuasion for the client, and moreover, only low-information-content parts
were eliminated. The first omission, the interpolated clause *una delle tante*,
originally translated as 'or at least, one version of the legend', was present
in the source text and carried the implicit boost that there are several legends

about tortellini, which adds to their mythical nature. The loss of this instance of indirect boost, however, is made up for in the following, where explicit or implicit boost is systematically added to the English text (we will see how, and why, in a moment). The other two extensive culls are added explanations, whose elimination, however, does not hinder the full understanding of the corresponding realia, nor does it decrease boost. All other explanatory parts of the original translation were left unchanged, since they are important not only to ensure that readers uninitiated in the pleasures of Italian cuisine can understand the topic of discussion, but also to make it relevant for them as English speakers rooted in their own culinary cultures and markets.

The realia in the text are made relevant for the intended readership through additions. The easiest way to explain a *reale* is by adding a very concise description of what it is either before or after it, thus creating a couplet consisting of the *reale* itself, which remains in the original language, and its explanation. One such couplet can be found at the end of example 23c: 'fresh meat from local certified breeds like IGP *vitellone bianco dell'Appennino Centrale*', where 'local certified breeds' glosses the original *vitellone bianco dell'Appennino Centrale IGP*.

But there are more complex additions that imply rephrasing and, most prominently, emphasis shift. In the following, additions and substitutions will be marked in bold and considered one by one:

23a: la pasta ripiena [i tortellini]

Literal translation: this shape of stuffed pasta

23c: this **world-famous** shape of pasta, **stuffed with several kinds of minced meat, eggs, nutmeg and parmigiano**

The initial 'world-famous' is not, in fact, an addition but a relocation of the phrase, *famosi in tutto il mondo*, that in Italian appeared in the following sentence. The second lengthy addition is mainly explanatory: it lists the main ingredients of tortellini filling for the benefit of those who do not know tortellini and are wondering what they are, but also to give insider knowledge to those readers who do know the shape of pasta but never quite considered the ingredients. Revealing readers things that somebody who is inexperienced about the promoted destination is not likely to know, sharing with them the secrets or curiosities of the land, is a way to involve them, to give them the impression that they already partake of the destination's (selected) identity. Now that our readers know how tortellini are made and served, as well as their story, they already feel more into Bolognese cuisine than the average glocal consumer who buys industrial tortellini in supermarkets and seasons them with canned sauce. The following example pushes this even further, stating that one has to come to Bologna to say one has tasted the real thing:

> **23a:** i tortellini in brodo [...] sono [...] il piatto più tipico della città. Ergo: obbligo assaggiarli nel luogo dove sono nati.

> **Literal translation:** tortellini served in broth are the most typical dish of the city. Hence: tasting them where they were invented is a must.

> **23b and 23c:** tortellini served in broth is one of the main specialities of Bologna [...]. **Local hand-made tortellini are entirely different from the export product, so don't waste an opportunity to taste the real thing.**

The main plus of tortellini in the second sentence of 23a is their being the culinary symbol of Bologna, a must-eat for every Italian tourist who not only wishes to eat well, but also to capture a piece of the city's identity, as well as the very essence of tortellini. In 23c, the emphasis shifts as the element of local identity disappears and the reason why one would come to eat tortellini right in Bologna is that only there they are 'the real thing', and implicitly, something to boast about back home. First of all, they are hand-made (an indication that is superfluous to Italian readers, but not to people who are likely to be familiar only with industrial versions) and nothing that can be found outside Italy compares with them. Coming to Bologna without eating tortellini, then, would be a wasted occasion. The reference to the lesser 'export product' makes the tortellini experience something relevant (and desirable) specifically for tourists coming from outside Italy, while the allusion to 'the real thing' refers to authenticity, a key quality for any tourist experience.

The strategy of mentioning an 'export product', which makes readers feel that the text was written specially for them, is echoed by two other additions:

> **23a:** Mortadella di Bologna

> **23b and 23c:** Mortadella di Bologna **(also known elsewhere as Bologna or baloney)**

and

> **23a:** le popolari tagliatelle al ragù

> **23b and 23c:** *tagliatelle al ragù*, universally **(and very poorly) imitated under the name of Spaghetti Bolognese**

Both additions are interpolated clauses that, from a strictly linguistic point of view, may as well have been eliminated from 23c. They were not, however, because they establish a strong link of relevance with the target language and culinary cultures. The first example highlights that in English mortadella is often called by the popular name of Bologna or its phonetic distortion, 'baloney', thus implying that the mortadella of Bologna is, once again, the only real thing. The second adds relevance by establishing a link between *tagliatelle al ragù* and the popular recipe of Spaghetti Bolognese; at the same time, by explicitly belittling the international version of the dish and stating that it is an 'imitation', it implicitly boosts what is supposed to be the original and authentic recipe. In the same example, explicit boost is also added, by transforming *popolari* [popular] into an instance of lexical boost, 'universally ... imitated'. As we have already seen, adding boost and other B2C devices (exclamations, questions, imperatives, direct addresses, puns and the like) has the effect of decreasing the information-to-persuasion ratio of the text not by decreasing information density, which is difficult if one is briefed to be as complete as possible, as I had been in example 23, but by diluting it with persuasion-oriented strategies.

Does one really need to add boost when translating tourist promotion material from Italian into English? Not necessarily, if one translates for a global audience (as is often the case with tourist brochures) whose cultural profile and linguistic conventions cannot be determined. Yes, if one is briefed to produce a text that is enticing for English native speakers. As we have seen (§ 6.1.2.1), unlike Italians, English native speakers are likely to expect institutions to produce assertive, personal texts. Following Hofstede and Hofstede (2005), one may say that this happens because English native speakers typically come from highly masculine countries with small power distance. This theoretical conclusion is confirmed by practical studies on corpora of tourist brochures such as that by Sumberg (2004), who found that French tourist promotion texts tend to be more informative than persuasive while the British readership is used to shorter, less dense and catchier texts.

The good news for translators is that in tourist promotion the extent to which boost needs to be added or reduced, register to be lowered or raised, and personal deixis to be introduced or eliminated, is usually less dramatic than with healthcare promotion. Even in large-power-distance cultures, in fact, tourist boards usually have softer public images: they are not generally seen as public Molochs and are likely to keep less distance from their target public. For instance, in Italian tourist brochures, personal deixis standards are much more flexible than in healthcare promotion. Texts are often impersonal, but readers can be addressed with a plural second person *voi*, which, however, is not an indicator of formality, but rather betrays that service users are collectively seen as a nondescript mass instead of a set of individuals. It is not unusual to find occasional texts using the singular second person form *tu*, typical of B2C, if the target is particularly young or the source wishes to put on a particularly informal, friendly face. If you translate from English into Italian, the main rules are, first of all, to adjust the deictics to the general register and tone intended for the target text, and secondly, not to mix up the plural and the singular, and not to shift from the impersonal to the singular *tu* in the same brochure.

Before concluding the section on the translation of tourist promotion, perhaps another short practical example can make things clearer. The excerpt below comes from the same guide as example 23, from the 'Handicrafts' section of the chapter about Forlì and Cesena. This time, I will provide a literal translation of the Italian text that may help readers who do not understand Italian follow what happened in the translation process, but I will leave the analysis to you. In particular, how is the reader addressed in the Italian and English texts, respectively? How is explicit or implicit boost added in the English version? Can you spot instances of lexical boost (i.e., words whose meaning is inherently superlative, even if their grammatical form is not)? And in what other ways is the target text made more assertive?

Example 24

From page 92 of the of the guide "Città d'Arte dell'Emilia Romagna" and its English version, "Cities of Art of Emilia Romagna", 2005 edition, Bologna: Unione di Prodotto Città d'Arte, Cultura e Affari. Also available, with some graphic differences, at http://www.cittadarte.emilia-romagna.it/citta/forli_ cesena/artigianato_e_shopping.php and http://www.cittadarte.emilia-romagna. it/citta/forli_cesena/artigianato_e_shopping.php?lang=en

Italian: La scelta del souvenir da portare a casa non è sempre facile. Ma basta entrare in una delle varie botteghe di ceramica d'arte da Forlì a Cesena, da Modigliana a Portico di Romagna e Gambettola per non avere più troppi dubbi. È difficile, infatti, resistere a certi piatti con decorazioni rinascimentali o ad altre maioliche, spesso a produzione limitata.

Literal translation: Choosing a souvenir to take back home is not always easy. But it is enough to enter one of the many fine ceramics shops from Forlì to Cesena, from Modigliana to Portico di Romagna and Gambettola, to not have too many doubts. As a matter of fact, it is difficult to resist certain dishes with Renaissance decorations or other majolica products, [which are] often [produced] in limited numbers.

English: Choosing a souvenir to take back home is often a difficult task, but set foot in one of the fine ceramics shops in Forlì, Cesena, Modigliana, Portico di Romagna or Gambettola and you'll have no problem. The local ceramic or majolica dishes with Renaissance patterns are simply irresistible, and often production is limited, making them more valuable.

6.1.2.3 Awareness-raising

I2U also includes publicity produced by NGOs and governmental agencies whose aim is to change the addressees' behaviour in respect to an issue of public interest, in other words, awareness-raising campaigns. Examples might be ministerial or governmental campaigns to give up smoking, cancer prevention, road safety and the like; also, calls for action and awareness-raising publications and websites of not-for-profit organizations such as the WWF, Greenpeace, national heritage leagues, etc.

Awareness-raising material can come in a variety of formats and distribution contexts that may presuppose intentional contact by the addressee (brochures, leaflets, websites, newsletters) or mass distribution and unintentional contact, like in aggressive forms of B2C promotion (flyers, billboards, street stickers, Internet banners or pop-ups, and advertising in all media). As we have seen, the two kinds of distribution context require different approaches. If addressees are meant to intentionally seek the promotional material, meaning that they are already interested in or curious about the topic and wish to find information, then the information-to-promotion ratio is likely to be higher than that of texts that primarily need to attract and retain the reader's attention. Brief mass-distributed genres are best approached following the guidelines in § 7.1.2; in this section, we will only deal with comparatively longer texts that usually presuppose an intentional contact by the addressee, and therefore can afford a more developed argumentation of the reasons why one should contribute to fulfilling the source organization's mission. Persuasion patterns, as we will see, are usually more explicit in awareness-raising than in the other promotional genres we have seen so far. Highly informative parts can be clearly distinguished from highly persuasive parts, but the two are closely linked because raw, objective facts are used as the argumentative platform on which persuasion is based. The categories of right and wrong are a prominent issue in awareness-raising.

Generally, the distinction between highly informative and highly persuasive elements is best observed at a macro-level. The source organization, for instance, may produce reports and studies as well as calls for actions, and all those texts collectively contribute to its overall campaigning image. In several texts, however, both information and promotion can be found.

Example 25 is a good illustration of all this, both at the verbal and visual levels. Here, it is quite easy to separate informative, factual chunks that convey a sense of objective truth from more emotional parts. An analysis will be provided below, but before going on reading, try and separate the paragraphs and visual elements that are meant to be objective from those that use more emotionally involving language. Pay special attention to personal deixis, exclamations, informal expressions vs. impersonal sentences, formal or technical language, and figures.

Example 25
Greenpeace Italy's campaign for compact fluorescent lightbulbs (CFLs), http:// www.greenpeace.it/incandescenti/

Transcription of the verbal elements of the main text in example 25, excluding the logo, buttons and links to other documents (emphasis as in the original, coloured text rendered as bold):

1	**Al bando le lampadine a incandescenza!**
2	**Non mandare i tuoi soldi in fumo: salva il clima adesso!**
3	È giunta l'ora di mettere al bando le lampadine incandescenti che mandano in fumo i nostri risparmi e soffocano il pianeta. Le utilizziamo da oltre un secolo. E la tecnologia è sempre la stessa: sprecona.
4	Una lampadina incandescente tradizionale disperde sotto forma di calore oltre il 90 per cento dell'energia elettrica: solo il 10 per cento si trasforma in luce. Oggi sono sempre più diffuse le **lampade fluorescenti compatte** che, a parità di luce diffusa, permettono di abbattere i consumi elettrici dell'80 per cento.

5	Con le **lampade fluorescenti compatte** (LFC) risparmi un sacco di soldi in bolletta. **Calcola quanto puoi risparmiare!**
6	[*first caption*:] **Il risparmiometro di Greenpeace** [*second caption*:] INDICA A SINISTRA QUANTE LAMPADINE VUOI CAMBIARE E SCOPRI A DESTRA **QUANTO PUOI RI-SPARMIARE** PER TE E PER IL CLIMA [*followed by a calculator; the captions on the left indicate the voltage of every traditional bulb to be replaced, the captions on the right read*:] INVESTIMENTO INIZIALE _____ EURO RISPARMIO ANNUO IN BOLLETTA _____ EURO/ANNO RISPARMIO DOPO 6 ANNI _____ EURO RISPARMIO DOPO 10 ANNI _____ EURO EMISSIONI DI CO2 EVITATE _____ KG CO2/ANNO
7	Passare alle LFC permette di risparmiare soldi ed **emissioni di gas serra** responsabili del cambiamento climatico, la più grave emergenza ambientale del momento.
8	In tutta Europa Greenpeace sta chiedendo di **mettere al bando le incandescenti**, facendo pressioni su governi, produttori e rivenditori. La **grande distribuzione** ha un ruolo cruciale nel rimuovere al più presto dal mercato le lampadine sprecone e puntare sulla vendita di lampade a risparmio amiche del clima. Il mondo non ha bisogno di più energia, ma di utilizzare meglio quella che già c'è. Permettere la vendita di prodotti altamente inefficienti è un lusso che non possiamo più permetterci. **Al bando le incandescenti!**

Literal translation of the verbal elements in example 25, for illustrative use only (emphasis reproduced as in the original):

1	**Away with incandescent lightbulbs!**
2	**Don't let your money go up in smoke: save the climate now!**
3	It's time to do away with incandescent lightbulbs that send our savings up in smoke and choke the planet. We've been using them for over a century. and the technology is the same: wasteful.
4	A traditional incandescent bulb wastes over 90% of the power [it consumes] in the form of heat: only 10% is transformed into light. Today, there is an increasing use of **compact fluorescent lamps** that grant the same amount of light with an 80% power saving.
5	With **compact fluorescent lamps** (CFLs) you save a lot of money on energy bills. **Work out how much you can save!**

6	[*first caption:*] **Greenpeace's save-o-meter** [*second caption:*] MARK ON THE LEFT THE NUMBER OF BULBS YOU WANT TO REPLACE AND FIND OUT ON THE RIGHT **HOW MUCH YOU CAN SAVE** FOR YOURSELF AND THE CLIMATE [*followed by a calculator; captions on the left indicate the voltage of every traditional bulb to be replaced, the captions on the right read:*] INITIAL INVESTMENT _____ EURO YEARLY SAVINGS ON ENERGY BILLS _____ EURO/YEAR SAVINGS AFTER 6 YEARS _____ EURO SAVINGS AFTER 10 YEARS _____ EURO CO2 EMISSIONS SAVED _____ CO2 KG/YEAR
7	Switching over to CFLs is a way [*literally:* allows one] to save money and lower **greenhouse gas emissions** that cause climate change, the most serious environmental emergency at this time.
8	All across Europe Greenpeace is asking to **do away with incandescent lightbulbs,** by putting pressure on governments, producers and retailers. The **large-scale retail trade** plays a crucial role in removing guzzler bulbs from the market as soon as possible and relying on the sale of environmentally friendly, energy-saving bulbs. The world does not need more energy, but a better use of the energy it has. Allowing the sale of highly inefficient products is a luxury we can no longer afford. **Away with incandescent lightbulbs!**

Paragraphs 4 and 7 clearly seem to be more factual and objective than other paragraphs. They are impersonal and devoid of exclamations, imperatives or other devices that may elicit the reader's direct involvement. Moreover, the register appears comparatively higher than the informal language recurring elsewhere (e.g., *sprecona/e* in paragraphs 3 and 8, *un sacco di soldi* in paragraph 5). Paragraph 4 also contains two percentages that, being figures, count as objective data *par excellence*.

Other parts of the text may seem slightly more ambiguous, nonetheless they break quite easily into informative and emotional parts. Take for instance paragraph 6, which is made up of the 'save-o-meter' and its captions. We have seen that figures and lists of noun phrases are generally presented as inherently objective and neutral facts. This applies to the left- and right-hand columns of the calculator, where the concept of factuality is further highlighted by the square boxes that contrast with the rounded angles of the frame enclosing the calculator as a whole.

The main captions placed outside and inside the calculator, on the other hand, seem to include typically B2C features. The first caption, in particular, is a neologism, a new word coined following productive word formation rules: *risparmiometro* comes from *risparmio* [saving] plus the suffix *-metro*

[-meter], which tells us that it is something that measures savings. The fact that it is an entirely new term, however, requires the reader's active involvement in deciphering it. Moreover, in Italian the suffix -*metro* is usually attached to classical Greek roots to form words that indicate scientific measurement tools, as in *tachimetro* [speedometer] or *cronometro* [chronometer]. *Risparmio*, however, is not a lexical root and cannot boast any classical origin, so that *risparmiometro* appears ironical because of the word-formation anomaly and the register clash between the two morphemes. Quite obviously, irony is not typical of objective, neutral discourse, which is normally employed to persuade the reader that its contents are serious and indisputably credible rather than unconventional and fun.

The second caption, too, is markedly non-neutral, mainly due to the conspicuous use of the second person singular, which is not usual in other Italian I2U genres, as we have seen, while it is typical of Italian B2C promotion. The reader is addressed as a second person singular in paragraphs 2 and 5 as well. In paragraphs 3 and 8 an even greater degree of personal involvement is reached through the use of the inclusive *we*, which highlights that the addresser and the addressee are part of the same community and context. This device, too, is typical of B2C communication in several languages and generates a level of identification that is second only to that of first-person accounts (of the 'Because I'm worth it' kind). In paragraph 8, the inclusive *we* is further highlighted by a particular trope that is called chiasmus: the sentence where it is used starts and finishes with two forms of the same verb *permettere*. The use of tropes is once again typical of B2C, as is the final payoff, normally a noun clause or another instance of ellipsis. Here it reads *Al bando le incandescenti!* [Away with incandescent lightbulbs!], with further emphasis being provided by the bold typeface and by the exclamation mark.

At the same time, the first part of paragraph 8 is, once again, factual and neutral. All in all, there are as many as four shifts from high information-to-persuasion ratio parts of text to low-information-to-persuasion-ratio chunks, and vice-versa: the first between paragraphs 3 and 4, the second between paragraphs 4 and 5, the third between the second caption of paragraph 6 and the 'save-o-meter', and the fourth between paragraphs 7 and 8. Needless to say, from a translator's point of view each such shift implies a shift in the translation approach: more objective parts of the text may require an approach that preserves factual anchors, such as figures, and a neutral stance (although the latter may need some adaptation when the text is transferred to other languages and cultures, as we will see in a moment); while emotional bonds and direct addresses require full functional adaptation to make sure that the target is moved as effectively as in the original.

It is impossible to compare example 25 with an official translation or source text. Like other large multinational NGOs such as Amnesty International, Save the Children, or the World Wildlife Fund, Greenpeace has national chapters which manage their own campaigns and texts, adapting the organization's overall mission and communication strategy to national situations. It is a strategy that resembles that of glocalization, which we have already seen in example 12 of § 5.1.1.2, only here it is referred to the non-profit sector and exploited to its full potential. National chapters of Greenpeace do not translate their websites and documents from a common source text: rather, copies are written from scratch directly in the national languages, drawing from the central organization's global reports and briefs. Visuals, too, may be largely taken from a common pool produced by the central organization, but national chapters are generally free to choose the final look as well as the contents of their sites, brochures and ads, provided that they comply with the organization's general image. The same strategy, as we will see in § 7.1.2, and as emerges from example 3 in chapter 3, is followed by several large multinational companies.

Example 26 is the closest to example 25 that can be found on Greenpeace's international website. It is a text that, like the previous one, has the purpose of urging readers to switch to high-efficiency lightbulbs, but this time the action is presented as the first step in a seven-step 'energy [r]evolution'. Once again, before reading on, try and separate factual bits of text (the kind that was recurrent in B2B promotion) from parts characterized by the emotional or creative devices that we have by now learnt to associate with B2C communication. Can the two be separated as neatly as in example 25? Also, are the two kinds of approaches to the reader equally recurrent in the English text when compared to the Italian one?

(DO NOT READ HERE BEFORE LOOKING AT THE EXAMPLES!)

In example 26, factual information does not seem to be separated from emotional calls for involvement as clearly as in example 25. Here, facts do not seem to need impersonality and formal neutrality to be presented as credible argumentative bases. For instance, the factual nature of paragraph 5 is announced by the bold *Consider this*, which, however, is an imperative that addresses the reader directly and makes the following data relevant for him/her. In the same paragraph, the objective, impersonal potential of facts and figures is further mitigated by the inclusive *we*, the final exclamation, and the informal register (notice, for instance, *dirty* instead of *polluting*). Similarly, in paragraph 9, the sentence starting with *Most governments* reports factual information referred to third persons, but at the same time contains the contraction *they'll*, which is typical of informal writing. Such contractions are consistent throughout the text, together with the inclusive *we*, which is a feature we have already encountered in example 25 but here is ubiquitous: it is used whenever there is no direct reference to a *you* marking a call for action. As a whole, the English text seems to be more consistently oriented towards a low information-to-persuasion ratio than the Italian one, which on the other hand seems to draw a clear-cut line between factual, informative chunks and more emotional bits.

Example 26

Greenpeace's 7 steps towards the Energy [R]evolution, http://www.greenpeace. org/international/campaigns/climate-change/take_action/7steps/7steps-about

Transcription of the main text, excluding logos, buttons and links to other documents (emphasis as in the original, coloured text rendered as bold):

1	**Energy saving [r]evolution - first 7 steps**
2	**We need to kick start an energy [r]evolution! By burning fossil fuels for energy, we're altering our atmosphere – causing climate change. To reverse it, we'll need to stop burning so much coal and oil. Renewable energy like wind and solar power is part of the answer, but the fastest (and most cost effective) way to reduce our global warming pollution is simply use less energy.**
3	**What's so revolutionary about that?**

4	Sure, energy efficiency is only common sense. But the idea that with smarter technology we can have growing economies while using less and less energy is new and bold. It's the sort of thing that might even happen without us if we had the time to wait. But we don't. The effects of climate change are already starting to pile up, construction begins on new power plants literally every week and billions of energy wasting lightbulbs are still sold every year.
5	**Consider this:** A simple switch to energy saving bulbs in the EU alone, would save 20 million tonnes of CO_2, equal to shutting down 25 medium-size dirty power plants; and this is before we consider the efficiency of other household products, or even cars!
6	**It's not only about changing lightbulbs**
7	Specifically, it's not about your lightbulbs. Changing your lightbulbs is just an easy way to get started. Plus, it saves you money. Think of it as step one.
8	Revolutions start with individuals getting together for a common goal. That's why the next steps are about sharing this idea with your friends and community. Then you'll be ready to **challenge governments** and **influence businesses**.
9	It's all easier than you might think. Most governments already support energy efficiency to some degree - a few (like Canada, Australia and the Netherlands) have already said they'll phase out energy wasting lightbulbs eventually. With a little helpful push, we can get them to act now.
10	We're asking you to start with lightbulbs simply because they are so wasteful, and better alternatives are so easy to install. Soon, we'll take on other energy wasting products.
11	**Why today is the day**
12	Every ton of carbon dioxide pumped into the atmosphere, every coal burning power plant built and every energy wasting lightbulb installed makes it harder for us to stop climate change. Each one is one more thing we'll need to undo. Better to do it right the first time. Use an energy saving CFL so we'll need less electricity, avoid building another dirty power plant and protect our planet.
13	That's an energy revolution. Your energy revolution.

Of course two parallel texts are no basis at all to draw any kind of conclusion about regularities in Italian and English texts promoting NGOs' campaigns. If the characteristics outlined in examples 25 and 26 were confirmed in larger corpora, however, some conclusions could be drawn about the interlinguistic and intercultural treatment of factual vs. emotional contents in awareness-raising texts. In particular, Italian readers would seem to attach more reliability and authoritativeness to facts that are universally valid rather than especially relevant for them; specific relevance implicitly makes facts, and the arguments based on them, non-universal, therefore less than absolutely true. English-speaking readers, on the other hand, would tend to interpret such universal facts as less worthy of interest, because they are abstract, and do not refer to the immediate and local context. If such regularities emerged from extensive corpora of comparable texts, then, it might be concluded that the information-to-persuasion ratio of awareness-raising texts can be fine-tuned, or even require fine-tuning, when translating between Italian and English. This finding would, in turn, confirm Hofstede and Hofstede's (2005) classification of English-speaking countries as cultures where power distance is relatively small, and Italy as a country with high uncertainty avoidance accustomed to larger power distance.

At the same time, we have seen that overall differences between Italian and English levels of (in)formality and (non-)neutrality are not dramatic. Examples 25 and 26 show more similarities than differences: both signal the transition to factual bits, although with different devices: the explicit *Consider this*, and mainly with impersonal discourse in Italian. And both feature, although with different degrees of consistency, the inclusive *we*, which has not been found in the Italian promotional texts analyzed until now; exclamations; informal and creative language; and a final payoff that, in the English text, is marked out by paragraphing (whereas it was in bold in example 25), and employs repetition and syntactic parallelism to add emphasis and facilitate memorization. In the light of such similarities, then, is translating awareness-raising across languages and cultures relatively straightforward? Not really. In the following chapter, we will meet some of the features we have just listed and many more, and we will see that they often require thorough trans-creation to function well in the target language and culture, as is common for all texts with a low information-to-persuasion ratio. It is in the rendering of emotional, idiomatic and creative language, then, that lies the main difficulty of translating awareness-raising campaigns and other I2U genres that take on B2C-like characteristics: but we will tackle this problem in the following chapter.

7. Translating Promotional Material
Business-to-Consumer

This chapter presents and illustrates the main characteristics of business-to-consumer (or B2C) promotional texts, focusing in particular on the creative use of language and the challenges it poses for translators. It then examines in more detail two exemplary types of B2C promotional translation, i.e. brochures and websites, and advertising.

7.1 Business-to-consumer (B2C): creative and emotional language

Business-to-Consumer (or B2C) promotion is usually issued by private companies selling products or services, and addressed to individual prospective consumers who are not supposed to have in-depth knowledge about the object of promotion. B2C promotion, therefore, does not tend to be technical; when technical or highly specific language is used for a general readership, the reasons for this choice often go beyond that of informing the reader. The information-to-persuasion ratio of B2C promotion, then, is quite consistently low, even if it changes according to field (promotional texts for technological and medical products or services, for instance, may have slightly higher information-to-persuasion ratios) and target group (usually, the narrower and better defined the target, the more specific the information provided). This accounts for more immediate, boastful, creative and catchy language and tells translators that B2C translation is usually best approached with functional trans-creation than with the kind of close translation required by most B2B texts or other texts where anchors make rewriting difficult or less desirable by the client. When anchors are not an issue, either because they are not present in the source text, or because the brief is to ignore them and provide a creative translation, the emotional effect of the text on the addressee, the generation of interest or curiosity or desire towards the object of promotion, in other words the motivation to buy it, is virtually the only thing that matters.

The ability to recreate that motivation to buy in B2C translation can only be achieved through the critical observation of large amounts of B2C texts in the target language and culture. This arguably applies to all kinds of texts, promotional or otherwise, but it is particularly relevant for the translation of B2C and other promotional genres that require thorough rewriting. For example, to be able to translate B2C websites in a functional way, one should navigate and read as many B2C websites of the same kind as the source text, originally written in the target language for the target culture. And no advertising translator can afford not to look at ads in magazines, or to switch channel when commercials are broadcast on TV or the radio. If promotional advertising becomes a constant source of income, building and comparing corpora of B2C texts in one's source and target languages may well become a good investment. What follows in this chapter is meant as a series of general indications, not as a replacement for direct observation.

Before we move on to some practical examples, it is worth explaining what I mean by the terms 'creative language' and 'emotional language', two groups of stylistic features that are particularly important in advertising and B2C as a whole. Let us start with creative language. What I will call 'creative' language or style should actually be termed 'purposeful use of non-standard language'. This definition simply means that language is not used in normal (grammatical or logical) ways, but this does not constitute a mistake, because this non-standard usage follows alternative rules, like the rules of games, which are alternative to those of the real world. Several tropes or figures of speech are instances of creative language. Creative language captures the addressees' attention and enhances memorization by actively involving them in the (re)construction of meaning. The translation of creative devices requires trans-creation; it often happens that what appears as a metaphor in the source text cannot be possibly rendered with a metaphor – not even an entirely different one – in the target text without losing its effectiveness. This, however, is not a problem for an agile translator (§ 2.1) because instances of creative language are interchangeable. If creativity and addressee involvement is what makes the metaphor in the source text important, then that metaphor can be replaced with another creative device that engages the reader with equal intensity. On the other hand, the translator can choose to use non-creative language instead of the problematic metaphor, and introduce a new instance of creative language elsewhere. Either way, the rendering of creative language is the perfect example of the usefulness of alternative versions for both commissioners and translators (who can evade the responsibility of choosing one single solution that has fewer chances of being accepted, and use the multiple versions as tangible proof of the higher effort required by promotional translation, and negotiate a price accordingly).

One creative use of both verbal and visual language is metaphor. A metaphor is the transfer of a quality from a primary subject to a secondary subject. For instance: crude oil (primary subject) is often called 'black gold', where gold is the secondary subject: the transferred quality is preciousness. The same applies to 'time is money', 'she's a pearl', etc. Well-thought out metaphors are powerful indicators of the naturalness and efficacy of a promotional text, but extremely difficult to translate as they require re-contextualization and often thorough re-writing. Metaphors can sometimes be difficult to detect because frequent usage wears them out, until they die. That is, people do not perceive them as metaphors any longer, and use them routinely, usually as idioms, as happens with 'black gold', 'time is money' and 'she's a pearl'. Dead metaphors, however, can be brought back to life; this process makes them more involving for the reader who suddenly realizes the oddity and irony of their literal meaning, usually taken at face value. Dead metaphors can be revitalized by expansion, e.g. 'She's a rose of a girl, but what about her bunch of friends?'. Another way to bring a dead metaphor back to life is through a literal visual translation: for instance, if a non-precious product is called 'a jewel', and the accompanying visual shows a woman wearing it around her neck, the jewel metaphor is interpreted literally and the reader becomes aware of its usual non-literal meaning. In such a case, if the jewel metaphor does not work in the target language but changing the visual is an unfavourable option or not an option at all, a different metaphor or other creative device must be developed around the same visual, perhaps selecting the neck element rather than the jewel concept. The same principle applies to all other instances of verbal-visual interaction that do not work in the target language.

Another creative device is punning. One makes a pun by switching a word that would normally be used in that context with another one having the same sound, but different spelling (homophony) or the same written form, but a different meaning (homonymy). One example of the creative use of homophones is Baloo the bear's song in Disney's *The Jungle Book*, 'Look for the bear necessities'; and in the mid-1990s, a British ad for Stella Artois beer featured the headline, 'Poor homme', accompanied by a black-and-white picture of a man's naked torso and head that would have been perfect in an ad for a perfume *pour homme*. This case of interlinguistic homophony is also an example of intertextuality between beer ads and perfume ads (see below). An example of how homonyms can be used in advertising is the headline in a British ad for Jacob's crackers from the mid-1990s, 'You can wear anything when you're crackers', where the visual depicted cracker biscuits wearing toppings arranged to resemble clothes.

A third device is the creation of new words or neologisms, which is frequent in the creation of brand-names which carry semantic meaning. In English, neologisms can be created using prefixes or suffixes, some of which are separated with a dash, as in Juice-o-matic, Fruit-tella or Jell-o. Less visible, but equally important, neologisms are created using more productive affixes, such as in 'ultra-matte' (an adjective used in English advertising and product names to describe cosmetic foundations that are supposed to give the skin a non-shiny, non-oily look). Compounding produces brand-names such as PlayStation, ColorFix, or the adjective 'stay-fresh'. Sometimes it is difficult to tell if a word is the result of compounding or affixation: for instance, the '(-o)-rama' suffix is derived from the word 'panorama' and often carries the meaning not of the Greek root, *-orama* [view] but of *pan-* [all], as in the name of the restaurant chain Steak-o-rama, which probably means 'all types of steaks', rather than 'come and see our steaks'. Similar to compounds, but with phonological and graphic contraction, are the so-called portmanteau words that result from the process of blending: examples include Swatch (Swiss watch) and Intellution (Intelligent solution). Clipping or shortening is another productive way to produce informal-sounding neologisms, as in Crocs ('croc' being short for 'crocodile'; an American brand of plastic clogs). A form of neologism creation that is particularly sought after in brand-naming and advertising is the grammatical shift that turns proper names (brand names or company names) into common nouns, adjectives or verbs of everyday use. Historical examples are the verb '(to) hoover', which means 'to clean a carpet or floor with a vacuum cleaner', and 'kleenex', which refers to 'a small paper handkerchief'. Of course this grammatical shift ensures that the general public is constantly reminded that the brand in question is *the* brand in its field; this is why advertising may try to force the process in jingles and payoffs, as in 'make it a Blockbuster night'.

Using language creatively does not only mean playing with words (and visuals), but also with sounds, for instance, through assonance and consonance, i.e. the repetition of the same vowel or consonant sounds, of which rhyming is an advanced version. The payoff 'Have a break, have a Kit-Kat' is an example of consonance, further highlighted by the repetition of 'have a'. Alliteration, on the other hand, does not involve sounds but written letters, as in 'Zurich. Because change happenz', which is also an ironical play on (Swiss) German pronunciation. Onomatopoeias or transcribed sounds are also present in B2C, as in 'Pringles. Once you pop, you can't stop', where the onomatopoeia 'pop' rhymes with 'stop'.

Another level where one can play with language is syntax, for instance through parallelism. Parallelism is often reinforced by verbatim repetition, which achieves cohesion, enhances memorization and gives more relevance to the repeated element. Examples of both devices are the slogans 'Open minds. Open Amstels'; 'Pure clean. Pure beautiful. Pure me' (Ivory soap); 'To know your bank, know your man. Down to earth, down to business' (ABN Bank). Syntactic parallelism without repetition can be observed in 'It Tastes Good. It Costs Less' (Basic cigarettes).

Syntax can be further used in non-standard (although not particularly playful) ways by generating free-standing incomplete or elliptical clauses that, like metaphors, require the addressee's active reconstruction of meaning from the non-linguistic context. This is especially common in headlines and payoffs, such as in 'Shell. Made to move'; 'Aromatherapy by Fairy'; or 'Dry, oily skin?' (Johnson's Clean&Clear, which also contains a question, see the section on emotional language below).

Play with language, however, does not end with syntax; it can go as far as the textual level, where it takes the name of intertextuality. Intertextuality is the reference to another text genre, either through verbatim or modified quotation, or through the adoption of the stylistic conventions of that genre. For instance, advertising may borrow (pseudo) scientific or (pseudo) technical jargon to achieve an impression of reliability; or an ad for convenience food can be masked as a recipe. The Stella Artois ad described above exploits the irony generated by the clash between the imitated text type (perfume ads) and the nature of the object of promotion (beer, which is clearly contrasted with perfume). The use of proverbs can also be listed in this category, as proverbs are texts in their own right that have the advantage of being immediately recognizable as something familiar by virtually all native speakers of a given language. In any case, it is important that the intertextual reference can be easily decoded by the target readership, or the ad will appear pedantic or just strange. For instance, when Levi's launched an international TV commercial based on lines from Shakespeare's *A Midsummer Night's Dream*, after a few unsuccessful showings a subtitle carrying the Italian title of the play had to be added for the benefit of the Italian audience. *A Midsummer Night's Dream*, in fact, is not as popular in Italy as in English-speaking countries, and the commercial did not feature any visual cues that might have helped viewers decode the reference, since the actors were dressed and acted as contemporary young people in an urban ghetto.

But what should a translator do when faced with an intertextual reference? First of all, one should be able to identify it, which is not a simple task, as shown by the case of the Levi's commercial. The popularity of genres and single works may not travel well across cultures. Then, if reference is made to an entire genre rather than a single specific work, the translator should reproduce the conventions of the imitated text type that apply in the target language, which may differ from those of the source text. Think about the difference between Italian and American CVs and application letters pointed out in § 4.1; the genre label is the same, but the actual texts might look rather different. At that point, however, translation difficulties and opportunities are not specific of promotional or advertising language, but of the text type that is reproduced. If the imitated text type is not established in the target language or genre system, as might happen for instance with Haiku poetry or Limericks, or if the imitated work is not immediately recognizable by the target readership, as happened with Shakespeare in the Levi's commercial, then this should be pointed out to the commissioner, and negotiations for a different intertextual reference or an altogether different approach (and consequently, better remuneration and longer deadlines) may be initiated.

Example 27 is an excerpt from a Sony Vaio C-series website that is written to resemble the style of fashion magazines, as is further highlighted by the visual at the top of the page. The choice of the imitated genre is functional to the way in which the target is profiled: the advertised notebook is specifically targeted to young women who care for their looks. Example 28, on the other hand, verbally and visually mimics American comic books in order to ironically associate the boost provided by exclamations, exaggerated expressions, and graphic emphasis with a trivial situation such as oven cleaning. The reference to the (pseudo) medical field is less structural, but nonetheless it contributes to extend the medical metaphor which is present in the product's brand-name, Dr. Beckmann Rescue, and reiterated in the payoff, 'First aid for ovens', complemented by the visual symbol of the Greek cross.

Use examples 27 and 28 as translation exercises from English into your **active working language(s)**, rewriting the copies so that they resemble a fashion magazine article and a comic, respectively. Pay particular attention to the rendering (or substitution, or neutralization where necessary) of instances of creative language. Before translating, it might be useful to identify and perhaps underline such instances to make sure that they are not overlooked. You can also come back to examples 27 and 28 after reading the following on emotional language, which is also extensively used in the two examples, especially in example 27.

Example 27

Intertextuality: Sony Vaio C-Series website

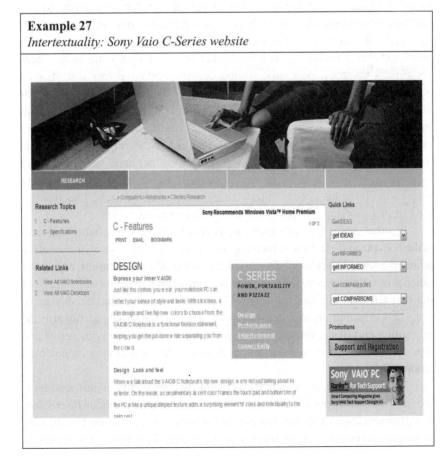

Transcription of the 'Design' section:

Express your inner VAIO®
Just like the clothes you wear, your notebook PC can reflect your sense of style and taste. With slick lines, a slim design and five hip new colors to choose from, the VAIO® C Notebook is a functional fashion statement, helping you get the job done while separating you from the crowd.

Design Look and feel
When we talk about the VAIO® C Notebook's hip new design, we're not just talking about its exterior. On the inside, a complimentary accent color frames the touch pad and bottom trim of the PC while a unique dimpled texture adds a surprising element of class and individuality to the palm rest.

Go from drab to delicious
You crave individuality. You exude style and take pride in your taste. So why buy a notebook that looks like all the rest? Designed for those who aren't afraid to add a touch of color to their computer, the VAIO® C Notebook offers five unique, hip styles to accessorize and energize your life with power, portability and pizzazz.

Espresso Black
Sleek and professional, the Espresso Black VAIO® C Notebook has striking copper accents, invigorating the touch pad and base.

Urban Gray
Sleek as a racecar, the Urban Gray VAIO® C Notebook has vibrant orange accents, to match your active lifestyle.

Glacier Blue
Calming yet playful, the blue/gray tones of the Glacier Blue VAIO® C Notebook reflect peaceful feelings of rediscovery and inner balance.

Blush Pink
Playfully chic, the Blush Pink VAIO® C Notebook is for free-spirited, fun-loving fashionistas and romantics who feel pretty in pink.

Spring Green
The Spring Green VAIO® C Notebook emits an organic Zen-like feeling of growth, renewal, health, and calmness.

Seashell Silver
Convey a light, wholesome impression with grace and elegance. The Seashell Silver VAIO® C Notebook will refresh your mind and impress your friends.

Example 28

Intertextuality: Dr. Beckmann Rescue ad, Good Housekeeping UK *December 1998, p. 374*

After identifying the stylistic features of action comic books in your target language, including punctuation, the use of bold script, and the treatment of the 'sigh' onomatopoeia, make a copy of this page, cover the ballooned text with correction fluid, and write your translation in the balloons trying to imitate the kind of lettering that is used in action comics in your target language. This will help you see if your target text is too long.

You can also experiment with the bodycopy between the comic and the packshot (i.e. the image of the product), progressively introducing or reducing the amount of boost, emotional language, and creative devices. What version(s) sound better in your target language? Why do you think they do?

Transcription of the bodycopy:

'Dr Beckmann Rescue is the powerful remedy for baked on grease and grime. And unlike other oven and grill cleaners, it's safe on the skin and releases no harmful vapours. Simply spray on, leave, then wipe off to a brilliant finish.'

Leaving aside creative language for the moment, emotional language is another important part of advertising discourse. The most obvious instances of emotional style are emotionally charged terms such as 'dream', 'fantastic', 'magic' and the like; superlatives and comparatives, lexical boost (i.e. inherently superlative terms that are not grammatically superlative, such as 'paramount', 'number one'); and terms with clear positive or negative connotations. A similar instance of emotional language is the use of the definite article *the*, which makes the object of promotion or its producer/provider unique, wiping out competitors from the scene. All such devices focus on the qualities of the advertised product or service. There are several other strategies, however, that focus on the reader rather than the product; they can be used to involve addressees emotionally, making the object of promotion relevant for them.

One such strategy, which we have already extensively observed in chapters 4-6, is the use of first- and second-person personal deictics (*I/we, you, my/our, your*), which creates the intimacy of face-to-face conversation. Particularly binding forms are the inclusive *we* that brings together the addresser and the addressee, or first-person reported accounts that promote identification between the addressee and the person allegedly vouching for the product, as in L'Oreal's payoff, 'Because I'm worth it'. Other deictics (indications of place, time, etc.) such as *this, that, so, such, today/yesterday,* and the like suggest that the addresser and addressee share the same space and time, the same attitudes and judgement about something, or even a secret. For instance, if 'those days' are mentioned without an explicit referent in an ad for sanitary towels or tampons, the assumption is that the reader can interpret the reference as 'menstruation'; if the reference is not recognized, then the reader surely does not belong to the target group of that particular ad.

Two devices that address the reader directly, thus eliciting personal involvement, are imperatives and questions, both real and rhetorical. Examples abound, here are just two of them: 'Drink Cuervo Gold today' (which also contains the time deictic 'today'), and 'Do you want caffeine… or decaf with that headache?' (Tylenol caffeine-free pain reliever).

Generally speaking, in B2C, in order to involve addressees and shorten the distance between them and the addresser, style and register are usually kept informal and tend to resemble oral speech. This, however, does not apply uniformly across languages and cultures: in German advertising, for instance, register can be more formal than in English or Italian ads, and even personal deixis is more often oriented towards the formal second person plural rather than the second person singular, except in ads or promotional campaigns specifically targeting young audiences. Where the general principles of informality and quasi-orality apply, however, these are achieved through a number of devices, some of which may be:

- high-frequency, generic, colloquial and short terms which are more immediate and add rhythm. In English, these are usually mono-syllabic Germanic (as opposed to Latinate) words such as 'new', 'good', 'get', 'give', 'take', 'feel', 'find'. In Italian, adverbs ending in *–mente* (which are the majority) are usually avoided in favour of shorter, more basic ones;
- simple verbal forms. In English and Italian B2C texts, the simple present is favoured in bodycopies because of its immediacy and be-cause it places the product and its qualities out of time, while shorter non-finite forms (infinitives, gerunds, or participles) are more usual in headlines and payoffs. This also links back to the use of ellipsis (see above, in the part about creative language);
- lack of grammatical cohesion, preference for implicit coordination through juxtaposition and punctuation rather than subordination. This, too, often borders with syntactic ellipsis, as in 'Boddingtons. The cream of Manchester'.

In the following sections, text types will be divided according to their dis-tribution context. Once again, websites and brochures (§ 7.1.1) will be grouped together because their distribution context presupposes that contact is initiated by the addressee, although, arguably, B2C brochures are also often handed out rather than picked up independently by the addressee. Websites and brochures are also comparatively longer than ads, which means that potentially they can contain more information, presented in a more argumentative way. Print advertising (§ 7.1.2), on the other hand, due to more severe space constraints and fiercer competition for the addressee's attention and memory, makes the most of the visual level as well as of emotional and creative language. As anticipated in § 1.5, advertisements meant for media other than the press will not be treated here. While this book is intended to be a general introduction to the main issues of promotional and advertising translation, discussing the translation of promotional and advertising material across different media would require an in-depth analysis of the constraints and opportunities for trans-creation offered by each medium. If you are interested in the translation of TV or radio commercials, the indications of this book can be complemented with those contained in Díaz Cintas and Remael (2007).

7.1.1 *B2C brochures and websites*

B2C websites and brochures are longer texts than ads; for this reason, they can afford a slightly more narrative or argumentative style, but ideally should never overtax the reader's attention with very dense or specific information, except when information density or specificity is what is expected (e.g. in websites or brochures for products whose main benefit is being high-tech or professional). We have seen that, even in the website of a technological product such as a PC where technicality is not the main claim (example 27), technical specifications can be presented as secondary to other characteristics that are thought to be more relevant for a non-geek target. The Vaio C-series website does include more technically-oriented sections that were not transcribed in example 27, but they, too, are interspersed with non-objective, non-technical persuasive language; moreover, they appear below the Design section and, unlike it, do not contain visuals.

One big risk in B2C website or brochure copywriting and translation is to be tempted by the amount of space potentially available and bore readers with long descriptions, thus losing their attention along the text. For this reason, the verbal texts of B2C brochures and websites are often kept short and persuasive and complemented with prominent visuals which attract attention but, at the same time, also carry both information (i.e. the visual description of the product) and persuasion (enticing the viewer through the use of lights, angles, etc.). Images and layout, then, are an integral part of the promotional text as a whole, and should never be ignored when translating a B2C text. Albeit to a lesser extent, this also applies to promotional texts in general (see for instance example 1 in chapter 2).

Examples 29a through 29f (reproduced here in the same order as the respective languages appear on the English main website) were accessed by navigating Intersport's site www.wherefootballstarts.com, which in August 2008 carried the UEFA Euro 2008 Adidas campaign. The English text (29a) is to be considered the source text of all other versions, but these were adapted by native speakers of the respective languages who might have looked at other non-English versions, too.

The six examples promote the official UEFA championship ball, therefore they contain specific terminology that is likely to be familiar to football fans but perhaps not to the general public. In the previous sections, we have learnt to treat such terminology as translation anchors that force the translator to go for a close translation rather than creative rewriting. To a certain extent, this applies here too, meaning that monoreferential terms are rendered rather accurately in all versions, but stylistic features – what we have called creative or emotional devices – seem to hold sway over accuracy, sometimes leading to strategic omissions or expansions for the sake of syntactic symmetry or other stylistic effects. This persuasion-oriented approach is the reverse of what we have encountered in B2B websites and brochures (with the notable exception of Zoratti's website), where information generally has priority over persuasive style, i.e. accuracy of rendition is usually more appreciated than creative rewriting.

Before reading on, compare the English text with any other version you understand, separating field-specific or semi-specific terms from creative and emotional language (for instance, underlining them in different colours). Note how the two categories were approached in translation. Remember that punctuation, grammar and syntax may contribute to boost and creative or emotional style as substantially as the lexical level.

Example 29a

Adidas Europass football web page, English version, http://www.adidas. com/campaigns/eurocup08/content/adipuresilver/index.asp?strCountry_ adidascom=com

Transcription of the verbal text:

THE SCIENCE OF CONTROL
EUROPASS
THE OFFICIAL MATCH BALL OF UEFA EURO 2008™

MORE TEXTURE, MORE CONTROL, MORE GOALS

The EUROPASS is the most accurate football ever. No other ball delivers more power, swerve and control, shot after dribble after pass, in the air and on the ground, regardless of the weather.
Faster attacks, crisper crosses, more accurate passing and more precise, powerful shots on goal are yours to be enjoyed! Explore and discover the science behind the world's first flawless football!

Example 29b

*Adidas Europass football web page, French version, http://www.adidas.
com/campaigns/eurocup08/content/adipuresilver/index.asp?strCountry_
adidascom=fr*

Transcription of the verbal text:

LE CONTRÔLE ULTIME
EUROPASS
LE BALLON OFFICIEL DE L'UEFA EURO 2008™

NOUVEAU REVÊTEMENT, PLUS DE CONTRÔLE, PLUS DE BUTS

L'EUROPASS est le ballon de football le plus précis des tous les temps. Aucun
autre ballon n'offre autant de puissance, d'effets et de contrôle, tir après drible
après passe, au sol ou en l'air, et par tous les temps. Une plus grande rapidité en
attaque, une plus grande précision des centres, des tirs au but ultra puissants...
voilà ce qui t'attend! Découvre la science qui a donné naissance au premier
ballon de foot parfait!

Example 29c

Adidas Europass football web page, German version, http://www. adidas.com/campaigns/eurocup08/content/adipuresilver/index. asp?strCountry_adidascom=de

Transcription of the verbal text:

DIE WISSENSCHAFT DER BALLKONTROLLE
EUROPASS
DER OFFZIELLE SPIELBALL DER UEFA EURO 2008™

NOCH MEHR STRUKTUR. NOCH MEHR KONTROLLE.

Der EUROPASS ist der präziseste Ball, den es je gab. Mit keinem anderen Ball hast du so viel Schusskraft, Drall und Ballkontrolle. Jeder Spielzug, jedes Dribbling, jeder Pass und jeder Kopfball wird mit diesem Ball effektiver. Und das bei jedem Wetter. Glänze durch verbesserte Schusskraft und größere Schnelligkeit, präzisere Pässe und härtere Torschüsse! Probier ihn aus und entdecke den technologischen Vorteil des ersten wirklich perfekten Fußballs.

Example 29d

*Adidas Europass football web page, Spanish version, http://
www.adidas.com/campaigns/eurocup08/content/adipuresilver/index.
asp?strCountry_adidascom=es*

Transcription of the verbal text:

LA CIENCIA DEL CONTROL
EUROPASS
EL BALÓN OFICIAL DE LA UEFA EURO 2008™

MÁS TEXTURA, MÁS CONTROL, MÁS GOLES

El EUROPASS es el balón de fútbol más perfecto que existe. Ningún otro balón
ofrece mayor potencia, regate y control. Disparo después del regate y tras el pase,
tanto en el aire como sobre el terreno, indipendientemente del clima. Podrás
disfrutar de ataques más rápidos, centros más enérgicos, pases más precisos y
disparos más directos y potentes para conseguir el gol. Explora y descubre la
ciencia que se oculta tras el primer balón de fútbol perfecto.

Example 29e

Adidas Europass football web page, Italian version, http://www.adidas. com/campaigns/eurocup08/content/adipuresilver/index.asp?strCountry_ adidascom=it

Transcription of the verbal text:

LA SCIENZA DEL CONTROLLO
EUROPASS
IL PALLONE UFFICIALE DELL'UEFA EURO 2008™

PIÙ RESISTENZA, PIÙ CONTROLLO, PIÙ GOAL

EUROPASS è il pallone più preciso mai realizzato. Nessun altro pallone offre maggiore potenza, controllo ed effetto, conclusioni a rete dopo un dribbling o un passaggio, in aria o sul terreno di gioco, indipendentemente dalle condizioni climatiche. Attacchi più rapidi, cross più calibrati, passaggi più precisi e accurati, tiri potenti: ora è tutto a tua disposizione! Scopri le tecnologie che stanno dietro al primo pallone al mondo privo di difetti!

Example 29f

*Adidas Europass football web page, Dutch version, http://www.adidas.
com/campaigns/eurocup08/content/adipuresilver/index.asp?strCountry_
adidascom=nl*

Transcription of the verbal text:

DE WETENSCHAP VAN CONTROLE
EUROPASS
DE OFFICIELE WEDSTRIJDBAL VAN UEFA EURO 2008™

MEER STRUCTUUR, MEER CONTROLE, MEER DOELPUNTEN

De EUROPASS is de nauwkeurigste voetbal ooit. Er bestaat geen enkele bal
die meer kracht, wendbaarheid en controle biedt, schot na dribbel na pass, in de
lucht en op de grond, ongeacht de weersomstandigheden. Snellere aanvallen,
perfecte voorzetten, zuiverder passes en nauwkeuriger, krachtiger schoten op
het doel. Ontdek de wetenschap achter's werelds eerste perfecte voetbal!

The fact that the way in which anchors are approached here is different
from what happens in B2B emerges right from some of the headlines. As you
might have noticed in example 27, in B2C websites and brochures (and, as we

will see, in ads) headlines, emphasized titles that break the copy, and payoffs or final sentences are the points where creative and emotional devices tend to cluster and to stand out more prominently, mainly thanks to more conspicuous layout. These parts, therefore, are the ones to be approached more functionally, and the ones for which clients are more likely to require a higher number of alternative versions.

The first headline, *The science of control* in 29a, is rendered closely in all versions except the French one, where it becomes 'Contrôle ultime' [Ultimate control]: the *science* element is omitted. This omission, however, does not seem to alter the meaning in any significant way: in this headline, the term *science* is meant to add objectivity to the claim, a generic notion that is perfectly conveyed by the lexical boost contained in 'ultime'.

More interesting is the treatment of the sub-headline *More texture, more control, more goals*, where the problematic term *texture* is variously rendered as 'textura' (Spanish), 'Struktur' and 'structuur' (German and Dutch), 'resistenza' (Italian: notice that resistance is a quality resulting from texture or structure, but not synonymous with them), and 'revêtement' (French: here, too, there is a metonymical shift, since the covering of the ball is mentioned instead of its qualities – texture or structure). Once again, what matters here is not the closeness of the translation of a potential anchor, but the inherently positive connotation of each term and the parallelism of the three noun clauses, reinforced by the repetition of *more*.

In the German translation, apparently, an additional concern was to make the sub-headline fit into one line; for this reason, the last of the three elements was simply cut out, and the parallelism of the remaining two parts was further highlighted by the use of full stops that mark longer rhythmical pauses than commas. In B2B, this would count as a major omission and, more likely than not, it would be contested by the commissioner: after all, *goals* is a very field-specific term and scoring more goals is certainly a key benefit for footballers. In this text, however, the result is a sub-headline that appears more effective than those which take up two lines, and even than the English, Spanish and Italian ones which do fit in one line each, but whose claims appear to have slightly less impact. In B2C, then, it would seem that less (quantity) often spells more (effect).

Compare the German solution with the French one, where all three elements are retained, but the clause *More texture* is translated as 'Nouveau revêtement' [new covering], which is certainly not a bad translation in itself, but breaks the triple repetition and parallelism. In such a case, then, one other solution might have been to omit the first part of the sub-headline, leaving a shorter but more effective 'plus de contrôle, plus de buts'; the 'revêtement' element, then, could have been recovered in the bodycopy below, space constraints permitting. It is impossible, however, to judge a translation without knowing the working situation in which it was produced: in this case, for instance, the *texture* element of the English version might have been indicated as one of the highlights of the promotion, and its omission in the sub-headline might have been discouraged by the commissioner.

One other characteristic of example 29 is the peculiar way in which grammar and syntax are used to add boost. In the bodycopy of 29a, for instance, elements are arranged in incremental structures that build up impact and positive connotations into a general impression of absolute performance. Boosting nouns come first by the three, as in *power, swerve and control*, and then by the four, as in *Faster attacks, crisper crosses, more accurate passing and more precise, powerful shots on goal*. In the latter series, phrases start having two elements bound by consonance (*faster attacks, crisper crosses*), and then become longer and longer, reaching a sort of boosting climax. The same incremental effect is achieved by juxtaposing specific syntactic constructions such as the symmetric repetition *shot after dribble after pass*, which suggests a very long succession of actions, or the parallelism of *in the air and on the ground*, where two non-gradable opposites are presented together to cover all play situations. In the same sentence we also find two structures that participate in building the boosting climax: *No other ball delivers more...*, which categorically excludes all competitors from the level of performance of this ball, and *regardless of*, which encompasses all kinds of (weather) conditions.

This kind of boosting climax is present in all versions, even when major restructuring is carried out. In the French text, for instance, the four-element series of boosting noun phrases is downsized by one element, probably to accommodate space constraints: 'Une plus grande rapidité en attaque, une plus grande précision des centres, des tirs au but ultra puissants'. The climax-building potential lost with the fourth element, however, is recovered by increasing the boost of the last element, which becomes a more absolute 'des tirs au but ultra puissants' [ultra powerful shots on goal] rather than just *more precise, powerful shots on goal*. Moreover, the list of performance enhancements is made virtually endless by the three dots; and instead of the crosses and passes of the English version, in 29b we find 'centres', perhaps less appealing for a defender but much more relevant for an attacker and in general for the young amateurs who play one-to-one football in their backyards (and probably are the main target of the promotion). Once again, in B2C completeness and accuracy of rendition are not as important as the overall persuasive effect of the target text, and the order in which informative and persuasive bits appear in the source text is often irrelevant: losing and then regaining boost is just as effective as preserving it in the same position as in the original text.

In all versions, the boost-piling is further complemented by more obvious instances of lexical boost such as, in English, *the ... first* and *flawless*, superlatives such as *the most accurate ... ever*, and a number of comparatives that implicitly compare the object of promotion with all other footballs produced to this day. In the headline, the definite article is used to highlight the unique-ness of the product, as it is *The [only] official match ball* of the European championship; this device is reproduced in all versions. Personal addresses that highlight why buying the advertised football would be particularly relevant for the reader are concentrated towards the end of the text, to capitalize on the boost built to that point, the message being more or less 'this is the best football ever – *and* you can have it'. Second person deictics are complemented by imperatives and two exclamations, although the latter change across the six versions: the Spanish page does without them, in Dutch only the second one is preserved, while the German version retains the first exclamation but ends with a full stop.

This variation is likely to be connected with whether the individual adapt-ers thought that as many as two exclamations might seem too much in the target culture. Exclamations (like graphic emphasis relying on large character size or heavy bolding) are a particularly explicit, little-refined kind of boost that is usually unsuitable for products, brands or fields that are promoted or perceived as elegant, up-market or authoritative, especially in cultures with large power distance. Thus, if in the target culture football is an elitist sport, or wherever the advertised ball is clearly positioned in the up-market segment (away from the purchasing power of children and teenagers, for instance), then it is better to avoid exclamations or keep them to a minimum. The same applies if on a given market the brand is assigned a consistently cool, self-conscious face that would be threatened by blunt addresses such as exclamatory imperative sentences.

In the particular case of the Adidas ball, however, and in similarly glocal-ized instances of promotion, such considerations are left to national marketing departments rather than decided at a centralized level. It is difficult, then, to establish if the Spanish decision to eliminate exclamations was more influenced by the Spanish market's perception of the Europass ball, Adidas, and football, than by what Adidas national marketing managers thought about the Spanish market's perceptions, or even by their personal stylistic preferences. In a real working situation, then, to tackle issues such as exclamations and other blunt promotional devices, a translator should infer or ask the commissioner as many details as possible about the target (including age, education and income level), the brand's and product's intended positioning on the target market, and the addresser's position vis-à-vis the addressee (items 2-4 of the model brief in table 1). If such information is not clear enough, then translation choices may be negotiated with the end client when possible; or, if multiple versions are foreseen in the brief, each version might contain a different treatment of such devices. Each alternative version should of course be carefully motivated specifying the kind of target and product/brand image it is meant for.

7.1.2 B2C advertisements

One might assume that the only B2C advertising campaigns that need translation are those launched by large multinationals that are present on several national markets. National-only or even highly local B2C companies, too, however, may require multilingual advertising if they operate in countries that are officially or unofficially multilingual. In such cases, copies and visuals may be developed in-house, with results of varying quality. Example 30, for instance, is a campaign circulated on several local free papers of the Italian region of Emilia-Romagna between January and March and September and October of 2005. The source company is Moreno, a used-car dealer based in Faenza, a town near Forlì. Although the source text of the three versions (a simple sentence that runs, more or less, 'at our dealer you will find cars in perfect conditions and at low prices') was in Italian, no Italian corresponding text was circulated, as Moreno's Italian ads are usually less straightforward and rely more on creative devices. The three texts in example 30, on the other hand, are aimed at migrants living in Italy, who are not familiar with Italian and might even use Russian, Chinese or Arabic as linguae francae. For this reason, creative style, whose comprehension can be difficult for non-native speakers, is avoided.

Example 30a
Moreno's 2005 Russian ad on the local free press of Emilia-Romagna

Example 30b

Moreno's 2005 Chinese ad on the local free press of Emilia-Romagna

MORENO MOTOR COMPANY

提供状况良好、

价格低廉的两手汽车，

机不可失。

Alfa 145 1,6 IE L A/C	Benzina	95	rosso	€ 1.900	Renault Clio 1.2 RN 5P	Benzina	96	blu	€ 2.600
Audi A4 1,8	benzina	96	blu	€ 4.000	Fiat Marea 1.9 td 100 sx sw	Diesel	96	argento	€ 4.500
Citroen ZX break 1,4	Benzina	95	grigio	€ 1.200	Renault Megane coach 1.6 RT A/C	Metano	97	blu	€ 3.200
Ford Mondeo SW 1.8 ghia A/C	Benzina	95	verde	€ 1.700	Renault Trafic 2,1 D 9 posti	Diesel	97	Bianco	€ 4.000
Honda Civic 1.5 I LSI 2 porte A/C tetto apribile	Benzina	95	nero	€ 3.200	Toyota avensis sw 2.0 td	Diesel	99	Bianco	€ 5.000
Mitsubishi Carlsma 1.9 Tdi 4 porte A/C	Diesel	97	nero	€ 4.200	Subaru impreza 1,6 compact wagon	Benzina	95	verde	€ 3.000
Peugeot 206 3Pt 1,9 XTD A/C	Diesel	99	grigio	€ 7.000	Toyota Corolla 5 porte 1.4 VVTi SOL A/C	Benzina	01	blu	€ 6.000

autlet ® OCCASIONI AUTLET **FAENZA** VIA CELLE I (Angolo via Emilia Ponente) 0546.620917

Example 30c

Moreno's 2005 Arabic ad on the local free press of Emilia-Romagna

MORENO MOTOR COMPANY

تجد لدينا فرص شراء السيارات

ذات الحالة الجيدة

و بالأسعار المدهشة بالفعل

Alfa 145 1,6 IE L A/C	Benzina	95	rosso	€ 1.900	Renault Clio 1.2 RN 5P	BENZINA	96	blu	€ 2.600
Audi A4 1,8	benzina	96	blu	€ 4.000	Fiat Marea 1.9 td 100 sx sw	DIESEL	96	argento	€ 4.500
Citroen ZX break 1,4	Benzina	95	grigio	€ 1.200	Renault Megane coach 1.6 RT A/C	METANO	97	blu	€ 3.200
Ford Mondeo SW 1.8 ghia A/C	BENZINA	95	verde	€ 1.700	Renault Trafic 2,1 D 9 posti	DIESEL	97	Bianco	€ 4.000
Honda Civic 1.5 I LSI 2 porte A/C tetto apribile	BENZINA	95	nero	€ 3.200	Toyota Avensis sw 2.0 td	DIESEL	99	Bianco	€ 5.000
Mitsubishi Carlsma 1.9 Tdi 4 porte A/C	DIESEL	97	nero	€ 4.200	Subaru impreza 1,6 compact wagon	BENZINA	95	verde	€ 3.000
Peugeot 206 3Pt 1,9 XTD A/C	DIESEL	99	grigio	€ 7.000	Toyota Corolla 5 porte 1.4 VVTi SOL A/C	BENZINA	01	blu	€ 6.000

autlet ® OCCASIONI AUTLET **FAENZA** VIA CELLE I (Angolo via Emilia Ponente) 0546.620917

Leaving the local for the multinational level, it often happens that the copywriting, translation and adaptation of large international advertising campaigns are managed by specialized agencies. Such agencies usually require translators first of all to be as creative as possible and adjust the target text to the target culture, and secondly to provide multiple versions, often with literal back-translations and detailed comments about any deviation from the original (e.g. omissions, puns introduced in the target language, revitalized metaphors or idioms, etc.). Ready-made grids can be sent as part of the brief to make sure that every version and element is clearly labelled. A simple working grid is provided in table 3 at the end of this chapter: you can use it for your translation exercises. Remember that fewer alternative versions might be required for bodycopies, while thorough trans-creation and more versions are usually expected for headlines and payoffs.

Sometimes, however, trans-creation does not necessarily entail the use of creative language. Instead of relying on creativity, some ads give out information and raw facts, with a preference for figures and (pseudo) scientific or medical terms, so that the superiority of the product or service comes out naturally. This is a technique that we have already encountered in B2B (§ 4.2) and in the factual parts of awareness-raising texts (§ 4.3.2.3). Neutral, objective advertising style works particularly well with products advertised as high-tech or scientific, especially when their image includes other traits associated with no-nonsense rationality and reliability: for instance, if they are made by a German brand that is internationally expected to go for functionality rather than fanciness (see chapter 5 for the exploitation of national identities as advertising benefits). In such ads, neutrality and impersonality build a distance between the addressee and the advertised object or brand, thus connoting the latter as an authority in its field. Even if thorough rewriting remains a valid option, in such cases it is rarely aimed at introducing creative devices, unless this is stated in the brief. More frequently it is aimed at reproducing an objective, neutral style that appears to state facts rather than catch attention or elicit identification. The neutral, impersonal stance can be safely altered only when retaining it would clearly sell poorly: for instance, if the target market has a different profile than the one for which the source text was developed, or when the brand or national identity the source campaign relies on has a negative connotation in the target culture, or when the kind of product presented under a neutral and factual light would clearly require a more emotional approach to meet target consumer expectations.

Consider for instance example 31. The headline contains a revitalized metaphor (an idiom) and the sub-headline features one instance of explicit lexical boost; lexical boost can also be found in the last sentence of the bodycopy. The bodycopy, however, mainly lists technical specifications in noun clauses separated by full stops, with only one subordinate clause containing one finite verb and no first- or second-person deixis. On the other hand, it has as many as four figures, some of which count as instances of implicit boost, and several technical terms arranged in non-oral-like constructions that would not be out of place in the appliance user's manual, such as *tubo flessibile integrato, sistema di filtraggio, filtro di classe 'S', accessori in dotazione*, plus two popular science words, *acari* and *microparticelle*.

The visuals also serve the same purpose: the main one depicts the appliance with its outstanding feature (the flexible hose) in evidence, while the three smaller pictures at the top of the page describe three possible uses of the product. Although a human figure is present in the three small photographs, the element in the foreground is the appliance, not the woman, and there is no eye contact between the reader and the woman in the photos, who is never portrayed in a close-up. In fact, in two of the pictures we cannot even see her head, and in the third one we find her looking away from the reader at the nozzle of the product, the main focus of the image. Thus, even in the visuals, emotional involvement and identification do not seem to be an issue; the object of promotion is the only thing that matters and its qualities are not argued for but shown as absolute facts, not as something that is especially relevant for the reader. This is in line with the image that Siemens has created for itself in Italy, capitalizing on its Germanness.

If Italian is one of your **passive languages**, translate example 31 into your active language(s) using the grid in table 3 to provide three versions with different degrees of informality and objectivity. Remember that the ad is intended for mid-market, non-glossy women's periodicals targeted at adult women with all kinds of education and income status. The answers to items 3, 4 and 5 of the model brief in table 1 can be inferred from the text itself. Which of your versions do you think would be more persuasive for the intended target group and brand image in your target culture(s), and why? Do all of your versions fit in well with the visuals? If not, how should the visuals be changed to match the verbal text? Do you think it would be worthwhile for the end client to invest money in new visuals, i.e. would your versions that require new images sell significantly more products than the other versions that do not entail visual modifications?

Intermediate approaches that combine figures and technical terminology with more emotional structures are also possible. Example 32 is a case in point: the bodycopy is written as a first-person singular narrated account, and we are led to think that the narrating subject is the woman who looks directly at us from the top of the page. This is aimed at generating the reader's identification and emotional participation in the account, which is made relevant for a supposedly real woman who uses the informal, sometimes spoken-like style that she would use with a friend (*So it was a joy to hear...*, *comes top*, *What's more*, and the like), except when she refers to product characteristics, as in *while re-circulating the water for minimum detergent wastage* or *the Acoustic*

Example 31

Siemens Converto Italian ad. From Donna Moderna, *September 8, 1999, page 14*

Transcription:

[*Headline*] Mette il naso dappertutto.

[*Sub-headline*] CONVERTO. L'unica scopa aspirante* con tubo flessibile integrato.

[*Bodycopy*] Tubo flessibile integrato estensibile fino a 1,20 metri (Mod. VR 42A20 e VR 41A20).
Ultrapotente: 1.300 Watt (Mod. VR 42A20).
Sistema di filtraggio a 6 stadi con il filtro di classe "S" che trattiene acari e microparticelle restituendo aria pura al 99,997% (Mod. VR 42A20).
Estremamente versatile grazie agli accessori in dotazione.

* Della gamma Siemens.

[*The payoff position is not transcribed as it relates to country-specific information*]

Literal English translation:

[*Headline*] Pokes its nose everywhere.

[*Sub-headline*] CONVERTO. The only floor cleaner* with an integrated flexible hose.

[*Bodycopy*] Integrated flexible hose extensible to 1.20 metres (Mod. VR 42A20 and VR 41A20).

Extra powerful: 1,300 Watt (Mod. VR 42A20).
6-stage filtering system with "S"-class filter that keeps in mites and micro-particles letting out 99.997% pure air (Mod. VR 42A20).
Extremely versatile thanks to the accessories supplied in the kit.

* Of the Siemens range.

[*The payoff position is not transcribed as it relates to country-specific information*]

Comfort technology decreases noise level by 25%. In this way, a compromise is struck between objective data, supported by three figures in the form of percentages, and the reader's involvement. The typography of the headline, sub-headline, and logo, where square fonts and capitals are mixed with curvy lines and typeface resembling handwriting, also confirm that both the product and the brand image are a blend of solid reliability and user friendliness.

Using the grid in table 3, translate example 32 into your passive working language(s), providing at least three different versions. Remember that the target and media plan are the same as in example 31 and here, too, the degree of closeness/distance to the reader and authority can be deduced by what we have just pointed out about the source text. In the first version of the headline, try and recreate the parallelism and repetition that you find in the source text, while in the remaining versions you can experiment with other creative devices or make the headline less creative but more emotional, by introducing, for example, first-person singular deixis. In all versions of the sub-headline, leave the model name – Candy Activa – unchanged, but provide target-language solutions for the 'Acoustic Comfort' technology (tip: it does not need to be two words in all versions, although it is better to keep it as short as possible, and the concept of quietness should not be lost). In the bodycopy, experiment with different kind of deixis or impersonal discourse and, depending on the degree of closeness to the reader induced by the deictics you use (remember to make them consistent throughout the text), increase or decrease the amount of boost, creative and emotional devices. Accordingly adjust the degree of creativity and emotional appeal of the payoff, too, remembering that it does not refer only to the advertised product, but to the brand as a whole. For this exercise, the first alternative version of all parts should be as close to the original as possible, but already functional in the target text and culture; successive versions should introduce incremental changes, until the last version is thoroughly trans-created. You can go as far as suggesting layout variations or modifications to the visuals; in this case, write a motivation for such suggestions.

Example 32
Candy Activa British ad. From Good Housekeeping UK, *October 1998, page 246*

Transcription (emphasis in the bodycopy as in the original, check the visual for different graphic encodings in the other parts):

[*Headline*] Top marks for the top performer.

[*Sub-headline*] New Candy Activa
Acoustic Comfort

[*Bodycopy*] **I expect nothing less than a spotless performance** from my washing machine. So it was a joy to hear that my new Candy Activa comes top in the cleaning stakes.
The double speed wash makes for a **Grade A wash performance.** Plus the Activa wash system guarantees perfect cleaning results, while re-circulating the water for minimum detergent wastage. All the while using 30% less water. Nothing short of brilliant.
What's more, the **Acoustic Comfort Technology** decreases noise level by 25%, making my Activa one of the quietest machines around.
With a washing machine I can rely on 100%, my life has taken a turn for the better. That's why **I've chosen. It's Candy.**

[*Payoff*] Candy. Choices for life.

In examples 31 and 32 we have had a sample of the importance of the visual level on the interpretation and rendering of B2C ads. It is now time to see how pictures and layout not only influence translation choices, but can actually be exploited as translation materials and tools.

In example 29 we have seen how what we had previously treated as technical or semi-technical anchors to be rendered as closely as possible, in B2C become more malleable material that can be omitted, substituted or altered in other functional ways. The same applies to images (as shown by example 3 in chapter 3) and even to factual or descriptive qualities attributed to them. In other words: even when a visual cannot be changed, in some cases I can just give it the meaning I need. This is better shown through an example than explained. In the three versions of example 33, you will find the same picture with different captions. Look closely at them.

Example 33a
British Maybelline Smooth Foundation print ad, circulated on glossy magazines such as Marie Claire *in early 2002*

Transcription (emphasis in the bodycopy as in the original, check the visual for the graphic encoding of other parts):

[*Caption*] Melina Kanakaredes
Melina is wearing Smooth Result in Apricot Beige.

[*Headline*] Smooth away your first tiny lines. A younger look instantly.

Smooth Result

[*Bodycopy*] It does more than smooth away the appearance of those first tiny lines.

Enriched with a triple complex of **Vitamins A, C** and **E**, it also boosts your complexion thanks to its light refracting particles and moisturising agents.

Sun protection: **SPF 18**. Lightweight formula.

The result: **Reduced appearance of lines. For a youthful radiant looking you**.

[*Payoff*] Maybe she's born with it. Maybe it's Maybelline.
Maybelline New York

Example 33b
Italian Maybelline Smooth Foundation print ad, circulated on glossy magazines such as Marie Claire *in early 2002*

Transcription (emphasis in the bodycopy as in the original, check the visual for the graphic encoding of other parts):

[*Caption*] "Una pelle più liscia, più radiosa... sei tu più giovane."
Melina Kanakaredes

Melina indossa Smooth Result Nude n° 21

[*Headline*] New Maybelline Smooth Result

Fondotinta levigante effetto ringiovanente

[*Bodycopy*] Fa molto più che **minimizzare le piccole rughe**.

Agenti idratanti e un mix di **vitamine A,E,C** risvegliano la luminosità del tuo viso.

L'indice di **protezione solare IP 18** protegge il futuro della tua pelle. **Formula ultraleggera**.

Il risultato? Neanche più l'ombra di una ruga... **sei tu più giovane**.

[*Payoff*] Il make-up N° 1 negli U.S.A.
Maybelline New York Gemey
It's you. It's new. It's Maybelline New York.

Literal translation:

[*Caption*] "A smoother, more radiant skin... It's a younger you."
Melina Kanakaredes

Melina is wearing Smooth Result Nude n° 21

[*Headline*] New Maybelline Smooth Result

The smoothing foundation that makes you look younger [*literally*: Younger-making effect smoothing foundation]

[*Bodycopy*] It does much more than **minimize tiny lines**.

Moisturising agents and a mix of **vitamins A,E,C** highlight your complexion [*literally*: awaken the luminosity of your face].

The **sun protection index SPF 18** protects the future of your skin. **Ultra-lightweight formula**.

The result? Not a shadow of a line left... **it's a younger you**.

[*Payoff*] The N° 1 make-up in the U.S.A.
Maybelline New York Gemey
It's you. It's new. It's Maybelline New York.

Example 33c
Russian Maybelline Smooth Foundation print ad, circulated on glossy magazines such as Marie Claire *in early 2002*

Transcription (emphasis in the bodycopy as in the original, check the visual for the graphic encoding of other parts):

[*Caption*] Мелина Канакаредес
www.maybelline.com

Мелина использует разглаживающий тональный крем Смус Резалт оттенок Опаловый и помаду Колор'н Фикс оттенок 17 Капучино.

[*Headline*] Первые морщинки?
Разгладьте. Омолодитесь.

Новинка
Smooth Result
Разглаживающий тональный крем Смус Резалт

[*Bodycopy*] Он может больше чем просто разгладить Ваши первые морщинки...

Увлажняющие вещества + комплекс витаминов A, E, C – и цвет лица пробуждается.

Фильтр UVB 18. Защитит кожу и обеспечит ей безупречное будущее. Воздушная формула.

Результат: ни тени от морщинки. Ваш цвет лица излучает молодость.

[*Payoff*] Все в восторге от тебя. А ты от Мэйбеллин.
Мэйбеллин Нью-Йорк

Literal translation:

[*Caption*] Melina Kanakaredes
www.maybelline.com

Melina uses the smoothing foundation Smooth Result shade Opal and the lipstick Color'n'Fix shade 17 Cappuccino.

[*Headline*] First tiny lines?
Smooth away. Get younger. [*second person plural imperatives*]

New
Smooth Result [*in Latin letters*]
Smoothing foundation Smooth Result

[*Bodycopy*] It can do more than just smooth away Your [*plural*] first tiny lines...

Moisturizing substances + A, E, C vitamin complex – and the complexion blossoms [*literally*: the colour of the face awakens].

UVB 18 filter. Protects the skin and grants it an impeccable future. Air-light formula.

The result: not a shadow of a line. Your [*plural*] complexion radiates youth.

[*Payoff*] All crazy for you [*singular*]. And you [*singular*] for Maybelline.
Maybelline New York

As you may have noticed, the actress endorsing the foundation is said to be wearing three different shades of the product. Clearly, the colour mentioned in each ad is the one which is expected to sell best in the respective target market, and is advertised as the celebrity's choice. This kind of operation has the advantage of accommodating local marketing needs and does not require any substantial modification of the visual, except perhaps slightly darkening or lightening it depending on the foundation shade that is mentioned. Of course the responsibility for choosing which models, colours or versions of a product should be advertised on the target market does not lie with translators; and the fact that the variable here is a foundation colour is not a central point. What this example shows is that the relationship between images and verbal elements can be manipulated to generate more effective target texts. (For more details about pictures as signs that can be used by translators, see Torresi 2008, from which example 33 is taken.)

Let us take another, more subtle but perhaps more fitting instance of how the visual-verbal interaction can be altered. Whereas at the verbal level the English and Russian Maybelline texts promote the reader's identification and emotional involvement only by addressing her with second-person deictics, the Italian version includes a statement that is presented as Kanakaredes' reported speech, although it does not explicitly include first-person deixis: it is in quotation marks, placed directly under the photograph, and the actress's name follows it in the way that is customary to indicate the author of a quotation or aphorism. This personalization of the message is in line with the use of the second person singular both in the alleged quotation and throughout 33b, and also with the way in which the picture is encoded: it is a very close shot of Kanakaredes, who looks out of the page making direct eye contact with the reader, thus promoting her identification and involvement. In 33b, then, we can conclude that the verbal text expands the sense of intimacy that is inherent in the visual; probably the new element of the reported quotation would have seemed more awkward with a less participatory picture.

Inherently intimacy-inducing as the picture may be, the interpretation provided in 33b is not the only possible one. The same visual, in fact, is an equally fitting match for the Russian ad, where the reader is addressed with a formal plural *Вы*, which does not foster identification or closeness between the addresser and the reader (and, incidentally, contrasts with the singular *ты* repeated twice in the payoff). The Russian formality is not accidental: at the time when the campaign was issued, the pricing and brand positioning of Maybelline were comparatively higher in Russia than in Great Britain and Italy. This accounts for a more refined brand image that finds tangible expressions not only in more formal personal deixis, but also in the visibly more sober layout of 33c. The verbal elements of the Russian Maybelline ad are never in bold and, unlike in the Italian text, here the *New* element, *Новинка*, is in lower case, smaller non-slanted print, and in shaded white rather than dark red, which makes it less blatantly conspicuous. Quite clearly, then, the Russian translators or trans-creators attributed a different meaning to the picture simply by changing the layout and formality level of the verbal text. Of course a new visual that could reinforce the refined image that accommodates Maybelline Russia's specific marketing needs would lead the product to sell better on the target market. On the other hand, advertising pictures, especially those involving celebrities, have high production and copyright costs, and the end client is likely to accept a suggestion to change a ready-made visual only if using it would be disastrous for the brand image in the target culture (see chapter 5) or if the additional sales induced by a more carefully targeted ad can cover the expenses. Maybelline Russia's example shows how minor problems of visual re-targeting can be overcome and also teaches us that layout changes, such as re-arranging emphasis patterns, can be employed rather freely in advertising translation, especially when they do not entail additional expenses for the end client.

The three texts in example 33 also differ in a number of other aspects. This campaign is another instance of glocalization – the development of national or local versions from an international brief, set of visuals, and generally an English original draft that may very loosely count as a source text but is generally not circulated as such. This leaves the adapters who work at or with the relevant marketing departments of the multinational commissioner relatively free to omit or change even technical anchors, for instance the *light refracting particles* that appear in the British version but not in the other ones. The Russian and Italian versions, in turn, feature a virtue of the sun protection factor that is especially relevant to cultures with high uncertainty avoidance, namely that it protects the skin from future lines (*protegge il futuro della tua pelle*, *обеспечит ей безупречное будущее*). And stating that the product will 'smooth away all traces of lines' (*Neanche più l'ombra di una ruga*, *ни тени от морщинки*) is not just opting for more boost – it is a radically different claim from *Reduced appearance of lines*, and a potentially dangerous one, since all customers may see for themselves that traces of their lines do remain even after using the foundation. Once again, this shows that what in other texts would be seen as informational or factual anchors can be modified more freely in B2C ads. An even more radical choice can be observed in example 3 (chapter 3), where the very name and nature of the main ingredient of the advertised product was changed to accommodate the expectations of the respective target markets and cultures.

A less technical but equally important element that we do not find uniformly distributed across all versions is the product's Americanness, which is hinted at by the choice of the actress endorsing the product and explicitly stated in the brand name (Maybelline New York), but significantly expanded in the Italian text. In 33b, several additional text parts reinforce the brand's national identity, starting from the initial line of the payoff, *Il make-up N° 1 negli U.S.A.*. Additionally, English language – which in this context counts as a metonymical trait of the product's American identity – is employed in two points of the Italian text. In the headline, we find a *New* in bold slanted capitals; it is printed in the same dark red as *N° 1* below, so that the colour code links two reminders of Americanness. English also appears in the payoff *It's you. It's new. It's Maybelline New York* that, interestingly, is not used in the British version. Being American, therefore, is clearly presented as an inherently positive trait of the brand identity, conveying a certain cool and state-of-the-art quality. The product's Americanness, however, is only boasted in the Italian ad, while it is kept to a minimum of visibility in the British and Russian ones. This suggests that the implication that a make-up product is superior to competitors because it is American might have failed to convince British and Russian readers, due to different stereotypes associated with the American national identity in the respective target cultures.

Even if not all campaigns are glocalized rather than translated, cases such as examples 33 and 3 show that when translating B2C ads, translators and adapters are substantially more free than in any other promotional text type, and that even in dealing with technical or highly informative texts or parts of texts, accuracy of rendition is secondary to the intended purpose. Translating an ad might mean re-writing it for a completely different target if the commissioner indicates that the product in question is positioned differently in the target market with respect to the market for which the source text was developed. As we have seen, layout and images become tools that translators and editors can, and sometimes must, use to achieve coherence and cohesion across all modes of expression, both verbal and visual. Of course, in a scenario that is so rich in potential opportunities, but also in potential pitfalls, negotiation and a correct use of alternative versions for different targets or brand/product images become vital (§ 2.2).

Additionally, as shown by the case of the Americanness trait, product characteristics that are seen as positive among a given target and in a given culture may be less appealing for other targets and cultures. For this reason, in advertising translation, cultural aspects are even more important than in the translation of other promotional genres, because the target culture influences addressees' expectations not only in terms of the linguistic style to be employed, but with regard to the very values and stereotypes to be exploited to generate a motivation to buy. Once again, one might think that deciding on which values a campaign should be based is not a translator's responsibility. In advertising translation and promotional translation in general, however, a translator is not just a translator (§ 2.1), but partakes of the copywriter's status. Being able to suggest changes that are motivated by one's knowledge of the target culture as well as the target (verbal and visual) language is usually appreciated, and sometimes required, by agencies and end clients with some experience in international advertising and localization. Some key cultural aspects of advertising and promotional translation will be discussed in the following chapter.

Table 3. *Working grid for B2C advertising translation*

	Translation	Back-translation (literal)	Comments
1.			
2.			
3.			

8. Translating Persuasion across Cultures

In this chapter, the term 'culture' means the set of values, traditions, beliefs and attitudes that are shared by the majority of people living in a country or, alternatively, in a local community that is distinguished from the rest of the national society by major traits such as language, religion, or political and legal system. All translators know that conveying a message across languages also usually means carrying it across cultures, meaning that different cultures may have different ways of encoding information, emotion expression/elicitation and the like. Sometimes the concept of cultural expectations overlaps with that of language-specific genre conventions. We have seen, for instance, that British tourists seem to expect to be persuaded and enthused by tourist brochures, while the French primarily seek information in the same promotional text type (see § 6.1.2.2 and Sumberg 2004). Similarly, American employers and interviewers usually expect to find much more boost in CVs and cover letters than Italian applicants are prepared to put in their personal promotion literature (§ 4.2.1 and § 4.2.2). And Italian patients would find it difficult to trust private healthcare or dental centres promoting themselves through funny, creative, B2C-like communication of the kind that is, conversely, popular in American private healthcare promotion (§ 6.1.2.1). We have already discussed how Hofstede and Hofstede's (2005) notion of cultural dimensions can help explain such cross-language differences among genre conventions in terms of cultural expectations.

Another, more generalized cultural convention that is not strictly genre-specific but can be applied to the whole of low information-to-persuasion ratio promotional text types (such as B2C, prominently ads) is the national or local degree of acceptance of highly creative and emotional texts. In § 7.1 we have discussed the prominent role that creative and emotional language has in B2C copywriting and translation. Creative devices involve readers in the (re)creation of the advertising message and thus ensure better attention and message retention; emotional devices promote identification and participation, thus making the message relevant for the target. For this reason, it is important that promotional and advertising translators learn how to render creative and emotional style in the target language in a way that is equally creative and emotional as in the source text. That, for instance, may well be the brief when one translates advertisements.

It should also be clear, however, that the overall amount of creativity and/or emotional appeal that is usual or expected in B2C and other low information-to-persuasion promotional text types varies across cultures. For instance, creative language is very common in British and American advertising as a whole, even in ads for products of everyday use. In Italy, on the other hand, advertisers complain that, with the exception of some notable up-market product categories such as fashion and spirits, their client companies generally tend to go for less brilliant but more reassuring solutions based on traditional values that are seldom presented under an ironical light, such as the family, the pursue of a high social status, and the like (Brancati 2002).

This also accounts for Italian ads offering a picture of social relations that tends to remain behind the times. When it comes to gender relations, for instance, at the time when I am writing it is still very uncommon for men to be depicted in Italian advertising doing housework or caring for babies (e.g. in ads for diapers or homogenized food). This contrasts with the recent developments of Italian society: for instance, separated husbands' associations have long lobbied for, and obtained, the legal institution of *affido congiunto*, meaning that after separation both ex-spouses have equal responsibility towards their offspring; children, even small ones, live alternately with each parent. Responsible fatherhood, however, does not seem to have been digested by advertising yet, perhaps in the fear that this cultural trait has yet been fully assimilated and families would not be attracted by a brand of diapers or homogenized food promoted as 'daddy's choice'.

This trend towards formally duller and conceptually more traditional advertising can be traced back to Italy scoring higher than English-speaking countries on Hofstede and Hofstede's (2005) uncertainty avoidance scale. From the viewpoint of translation practice, this tells us that, when the source text sounds or looks too creative for the target culture, at least one of the multiple versions we are allowed to provide might be encoded in a less creative way, explaining the reasons for this choice. The reverse applies when the source text is judged too bland for the target culture: in this case, creative devices (perhaps inspired by the visual) may be introduced in one or more of the alternative versions. If alternative versions are not allowed, then translation choices may be negotiated with the client or, if this too is impossible, one might suggest in a separate comment a way in which the target text could be better adapted to the expectations of the target readers.

The same applies to emotional language: German advertising, for instance, perhaps with the exception of ads targeted only at young audiences, often uses formal register and the formal plural second person, while we have seen that in English and Italian the standard is informal register, emotional language, and the second person singular. When translating a German ad into Italian or English, or when localizing an English dummy ad created by a German client for a glocal campaign, the target version might therefore need to be personalized and made more informal; the reverse applies when translating into German. Of course, such invasive changes, which also have an impact on the brand and product image, might need to be explained to the client and carefully argued for in a comment or accompanying e-mail.

But how does one assess the degree of creativity and emotional appeal that the target culture is prepared to accept? Once again, the only valid indication in a world where national advertising trends change by the month is to keep a constantly keen eye on the advertising and promotional material circulated in one's working languages, collecting corpora of texts, looking at them critically and taking into account the verbal as well as the visual level, with particularly attention to the devices described in § 7.1.

A more obvious way in which the cultural dimension can impact the efficacy of a promotional text is the use of culture-specific references, which make the text specifically relevant for one culture. Of course, such references require heavy adaptation in order to avoid "culture bumps" (Leppihalme 1997) that would make it clear that the target text refers to a reality that is not relevant for the target culture. Culture bumps are perfectly acceptable in genres where **overt translation** (the opposite of covert translation) and foreignization are valid choices, but should normally be avoided in any consumer-oriented genre unless they are purposefully and conspicuously introduced to achieve an ironical effect, in which case they count as intertextual references to other cultures.

Examples of culture-specific references are realia tantum, whose rendering in tourist brochures we have already discussed in § 6.1.2.2, but which are carefully avoided in B2C whenever the particular national identity indicated by them is not an element of the product's identity or claim. In such cases, if the generic element of culture-specificity carried by the reale is important, then it can be replaced with a reale that is recognizably specific to the target culture and fits in the target context; otherwise, it can be neutralized and replaced by a non-culture-specific term. To give a simple food-connected example, in the 1980s a popular jingle for an Italian digestif, Digestivo Antonetto, went *spaghetti, pollo, peperoni, tre polpette, sei bignè* [spaghetti, chicken, peppers, three meatballs, six cream puffs], a parody of a popular song by the Italian singer Fred Bongusto, where *spaghetti* was not used to specifically convey Italianness but only as a typical first course in a typical, albeit heavy, meal. To the best of my knowledge, that jingle has never been translated into other languages, but if it had been, *spaghetti* would of course have been replaced with the standard meal opening in the target community. Similarly, the division of the meal into a first and second course plus a side dish and dessert is typically Italian and would have been adjusted to the culinary habits of the target country. In fact, the only two elements to be left unchanged would have been, first, the generic meaning of 'complete and rather heavy meal', and second, the adjustment to (and possibly, the parody of) the accompanying tune – which, in its own turn, would ideally have been borrowed from local popular music.

Another instance of culture-specific references is the reference to national habits or traditions that may be present, but not equally widespread in other cultures. For example, in several former USSR republics, riding a bicycle is not perceived as a means of transport for people of all ages but as a children's game. Clearly, in such countries advertising a product through non-ironical visuals depicting adults on bicycles or metaphors based on cycling would not be a good marketing choice, unless the translator saved the visual and rewrote the copy around the involuntary ironical turn that it would acquire in the target culture.

Similarly, what in one community is a national sport, or a team sport usually played by children, in another community may be practised only by small groups or elites. In this sense, football (soccer) is to Italy as baseball is to the USA (compare the discussion of football as a popular vs. elitist sport in § 7.1.1). Now concentrate on your own mother culture and answer the following question in the most obvious way that you can think of: what is the sport that is popular with children and implies a lot of physical movement, including staining one's clothes with earth and possibly grass, grazing one's elbows and knees, and sweating a lot? If your answer was different from rugby (being Italian, for instance, I would have answered football), then Persil Performance Tablets would need to provide the kids in example 34 with different shirts if they were to advertise in your country.

Example 34
Persil Performance Tablets ad, from Good Housekeeping UK, *August 1998, page 131*

Q: **Sports kit is easy to clean, isn't it?**

A: *Really? And how many have you washed recently?*

New Persil Performance Tablets.

Culture-specific references also include visual or verbal taboos or words and concepts that are neutral or positively connoted in the source culture but negative in the target one, and as such are better avoided in translation. We have seen instances of this in § 3.1 with regard to brand name adaptation, e.g. the pronunciation of the Sega videogames brand in Italian commercials or the British misadventures of White Elephant batteries. Taboos and negative connotations are in no way limited to the verbal level only: colour and visual symbolism is a well-known source of intercultural misunderstandings. For instance, distinguished as the choice might appear to an Asian company, a website or company logo where the colour purple is associated with white chrysanthemums would only spell a death omen to Italian eyes.

A third way in which culture interacts with promotion has to do with the representation of national identities. We have already mentioned how some specific products are normally associated with national identities, because they are known to have been invented or are thought to be of better quality in a given country. This association can be exploited in brand-names (see the beginning § 3.1): for instance, giving an Italian-sounding name to French-made pasta, or an (American) English-sounding name to Italian-made chewing-gum or denims. Additionally, certain national identities are attributed, internationally or in given cultures, specific positive traits that are automatically transferred onto products or brands that capitalize on their real or fictitious origin. Thus, as we have seen in example 31, a German brand can choose to advertise its products in a neutral, objective way rather than insisting on creativity and emotional language, thus voluntarily confirming the international stereotype of the unemotional, over-serious, perhaps even boring, German. As a consequence, the ad implicitly confirms another trait of Germanness that is beneficial for the product and brand image: that of maximum professionalism, reliability and rationality, all positive qualities when associated with technical products and appliances. Conversely, in example 33b the Italian version of a Maybelline ad – unlike the British and Russian versions of the same campaign – stresses Americanness as a carrier of traits such as being metropolitan, hype, in fashion. (For more examples of how a national identity, specifically Italianness, can become a marketing capital, see Chiaro 2004.)

And finally, culture plays a fundamental role in advertising and all those promotional texts whose claim is based on widespread and uncritically accepted values and fears. Such crystallized values and fears can be called 'cultural stereotypes', i.e. assumptions that are not subject to conscious rational judgement but are handed down as naturally occurring and universal facts from parents to children, and passed on in peer groups. This does not only refer to negative or positive stereotypes that can be associated with a given nationality (as the ones mentioned above) or group of people, but to all pre-logical assumptions that we usually take for granted and expect to see confirmed in the media as well as in our daily experience. For instance, in most societies, if one has not taken religious vows, having a family is generally seen as a better or even more virtuous condition than living as a childless single person until the end of one's life. In some cultures more than others, ageing as a child-less single person is seen as a personal failure. This is why the happy family, made up of a varying number or members depending on the target culture, features regularly in advertising across the globe; the message is not only that the product is for families, but at a deeper, more unconscious level, that the product can help consumers fulfil the personal dream and social requirement of having a perfect family.

It is difficult to detect the culture-specificity of cultural stereotypes because they are often seen as universals by most members of a given culture, and may resist cross-cultural contact and rational arguments. Thus, many Italians will insist that doing without bidets and cleaning a regularly used bathtub less than once in a week connotes a whole people as dirty, which, they will maintain, is an inherently negative quality even if infectious disease incidence rates are not significantly higher among some of the world's bidetless, encrusted-bathtub national communities (while these might spend less time in household chores). Quite clearly, then, a home's cleanliness is to Italians a virtue that is transferred upon the people living in that home and a standard by which a person, and even a whole people, can be judged. Accordingly, in Italian ads for detergents, cleaning one's home is often presented as a moral duty, especially for women (!), and dirt or stains are variously visualized as devils or monsters, making it clear that they are evil. Such representations would completely miss the point in other cultures that are more relaxed about home cleaning and do not see it as a moral duty, nor as a standard by which a person or community can be judged. Italian translators or marketing managers, however, might fail to acknowledge the need to adjust the advertising message to such a culture, because they might perceive the moral virtue of cleanliness as a universal rather than as a cultural variable. (For more about the inter-cultural comparison of ads for cleaning products, see Torresi 2004.)

Advertising and B2C promotion would have a completely different face today if they did not rely on cultural stereotypes to sell products. Being pre-logical assumptions that can be taken for granted and simply hinted at to build a background that is familiar to the target, cultural stereotypes are a vital asset for short promotional genres such as advertisements. Moreover, culture goes as far as influencing consumer trends and desires. For instance, if culture is highly masculine, real jewellery sales will be predictably high, regardless of national income rates (De Mooij 1998/2005).

Thus, when translating advertising or promotional texts, the cultural stereotypes of the target culture, just like the standards and conventions of the target language and semiotic system, should be breached only with a clear purpose, after careful assessment, and never without informing the commis-sioner or negotiating with the end client. When the cultural target is missed, the advertising or promotional campaign is doomed. As a consequence of the marketing failure, the end client will not be very happy about losing the advertising investment, and will probably start looking for the person responsible for the disaster, or else for a scapegoat – and remember that for an advertising and promotional translator, invoking the 'I'm just a translator' defence strategy is rarely a good idea, because one is not expected to be 'just a translator' (except perhaps by some B2B clients).

And of course, there is no ready-made intercultural map of cultural stereotypes: the only way to become aware about them is, once again, to compare corpora of advertisements or other promotional texts collected in the cultures of one's working languages, and look very closely at the values and fears they rely on at the visual as well as the verbal levels. Boring as this might seem at first sight, it is a precious occasion to dig into one's own cultural and consumer values; a sort of treasure hunt that leads to ever new and unexpected findings.

Appendix

This appendix collects the additional versions of examples 10, 18, 19 and 20 for which there was no room in the main body of the book, but which are nonetheless interesting, especially for speakers of the languages accounted for by such examples.

Example 10: *other language versions, respectively downloaded from:*
http://www.olifrance.com/
http://www.oligmbh.de/
http://www.oliromania.ro/
http://www.olispain.es/

French

VN

CM

Extras

Photos d'application

Description

VN est un vibrateur à immersion à haute fréquence. VNP dispose d¿un puissant moteur électrique plus grand par rapport au VN car il monte un rotor et un stator plus grands. En outre sa masse vibrante est plus grande et son aiguille plus longue. VNP ne requiert pas de protection thermique car le moteur (plus grand de celui du VN) n¿atteint jamais 100°C.

Fonction

Pour garantir une pose parfaite du béton sur chaque chantier on utilise des vibrateurs à immersion. OLI® les produits depuis le début des années 60.

Performances et Caratéristiques Techniques - Avantages

- Protection du moteur par thermistances
- Diamètre de l¿aiguille : 36 mm, 50 mm, 60 mm, 65 mm
- Amplitude : de 1,2 mm à 3 mm
- Diamètre d¿efficacité : de 60 cm à 180 cm
- Aiguille en acier ou en Vulkolan
- Revêtement de l¿aiguille renforcée
- Basse consommation d¿électricité
- Hautement performant

- 2 ans de garantie

Options et Accessoires

- VN Line optionally with thermal protection
- Standard 42V/200Hz, option 230V/200Hz

German

VN

CM

Extras

Anwendungsfotos

Beschreibung

VN und VNP sind Hochfrequenz-Elektro-Innenvibratoren zur Betonverdichtung. Die VNP Professional Line entwickelt höhere Zentrifugalkräfte und verfügt über eine 4-fach (plus Nadellager) gelagerte Welle und ist somit für härteste Einsätze konzipiert. Beide Reihen sind mit 5m Schutzschlauch, 10m Kabel mit CE - Stecker und ABS Handschalter ausgestattet.

Funktion

Durch die enorm gesteigerte Verdichtungsleistung der VNP Professional Line resultiert ein optimaler Luftporenentzug, der die Anforderungen moderner Betontechnologie erfüllt.
Mit wahlweise 42V/200Hz oder 230V/200Hz mit sechs verschiedenen Flaschendurchmessern steht eine umfangreiche Palette zur Ortbetonverdichtung oder zum Einbau in Betonverdichtungsanlagen (Deckenfertigungsanlagen) zur Verfügung.

Leistungsdaten & Technische Merkmale - Vorteile

- 2 Jahre Garantie
- Motorvollschutz durch Thermosensoren, VN Standard Line
- Flaschendurchmesser: 36 - 50 ¿ 57 - 60 - 65 ¿ 70 mm
- Amplituden von 1,2 mm bis 3 mm
- Wirkungsdurchmesser von 60 cm bis 180 cm
- Stahl- oder Vulkolan-Spitze
- Flaschenmantel spezialgehärtet
- Geringe Stromaufnahme
- Starke Leistung

Optionen & Zubehör

- VN Line wahlweise mit Thermoschutz
- Standard 42V/200Hz, wahlweise 230V/200Hz

Romanian

VN

CM

Extras

Application Photographs

Description

VN este un vibrator de frecvență înaltă pentru beton. VN are motor electic de mare putere, un rotor mare și stator. În plus, are o masă vibratoare mai mare și vibropilă mai lungă. Nu necesită protecție termică, deoarece motorul electric mare nu ajunge niciodată la 100ºC (212ºF).

Function

Pentru a garanta sedimentarea perfectă a betonului proaspăt livrat, gata amestecat, pe fiecare șantier de construcție sunt necesare vibratoarele pentru beton (Pokers). OLI® fabrică vibratoare pentru beton (Pokers) de la începutul anilor 1960.

Performance & Technical Features - Benefits

- Protecție completă a motorului prin termistori
- Diametrele vibropilei : 36mm (11/2¿), 50mm (2¿), 60mm (2.3¿), 65mm (2.6¿)
- Amplitudine : 1,2mm (0.05¿) până la 3mm (0.1¿)
- Diametrul de eficiență : 60cm (2 ft) până la 180cm (6 ft)
- Fabricat din oțel sau Vulkolan
- Înveliș al vibropilei călit
- Putere absorbită mică
- Performanță ridicată

- Doi ani garanție

Technical Catalogue

Spanish

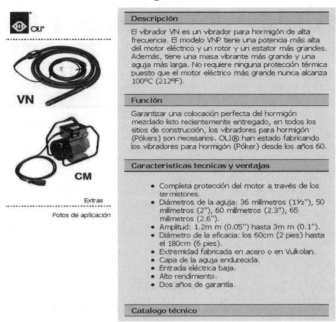

Example 18: *other language versions, downloaded from:*
http://smetypo3.stage-server.de/

Czech

About the project

Podporuje mobilitu pracovníkov v remeselných zručnostiach a MSP.

Vízia projektu ako súčasť Európskeho roka pracovnej mobility má podporiť kvalifikovaných pracovníkov, aby sa dobre rozhodli pri prijatí zamestnania v rôznych krajinách, či už dočasne alebo na stálo, alebo za účelom (zvýšenie kvalifikácie) alebo ako východisko z núdze (napríklad nezamestnanosť). Projekt môže pomôcť všetkým vekovým kategóriám zručných pracovníkom, aby získali pracovné skúsenosti v zahraničí, ktoré im značne zvýšia šance na spoločnom pracovnom trhu. Projekt taktiež pomôže Európskym MSP získavať vhodných zamestnancov pre ich potreby, ktoré opäť prispejú k naplneniu Lisabonských cieľov – konkurencie schopnosť a tvorba pracovných miest.

Projekt má za cieľ poskytnúť:

• vybrané informácie o požadovaných a o dodávaných zručných prácach
• porovnateľné údaje zručným pracovníkom, aby im pomohli rozhodnúť sa na základe solidných informáciach, ak chcú pracovať v zahraničí
• vzdelávací materiál, ktorý pomôže mobilným zamestnancov pre ich adekvátnu prípravu pre prácu v zahraničí
• platformu pre Európske získavanie zručných pracovníkov, na základe už existujúcich a funkčných databáz, ktoré manažuje EFKA.

Platforma bude poskytovať dodatočné služby: podnikatelia, ktorí sa zaregistrujú a prehlása možnosť poskytnutia pracovného miesta pre pracovníka zo zahraničia, získajú prehľad o Európskych pracovníkoch, ktorí sa zaujímajú o prácu a skúsenosti vo svojej profesii.

Danish

FAGLÆRT – MOBIL – EUROPÆER (FME) støtter mobiliteten hos faglærte håndværkere og FMEer

Som en del af d European Year of Workers' Mobility et europæiske år for arbejdstagernes mobilitet er det projektets hensigt at støtte kvalificeret arbejdskraft i at træffe velinformerede beslutninger om at søge ansættelse i et andet land, det være sig enten for en periode eller permanent, og enten med fuldt overlæg (som en del af ens karriereforløb) eller af nød (f.eks. på grund af arbejdsløshed). Projektet tilskynder unge og ældre faglærte arbejdere til at søge arbejdserfaring i udlandet for at øge deres chancer på arbejdsmarkedet i betragtelig grad. Projektet vil også hjælpe europæiske FMEer med rekruttere egnede medarbejdere til at opfylde deres behov, som igen vil bidrage til at nå målsætningerne fra Lissabon – konkurrenceevne og jobskabelse.

Projektet stiler derfor imod at kunne tilbyde:

- Målrettet information om udbud og efterspørgsel indenfor faglærte arbejdskraft
- Sammenlignelige data til faglærte, som skal hjælpe dem til at kunne træffe en beslutning baseret på pålidelige oplysninger, når de er interesseret i at komme til udlandet og arbejde
- Uddannelsesmateriale, der kan hjælpe mobile medarbejdere med at forberede sig i tilstrækkeligt omfang på at arbejde i udlandet
- En platform for europæisk rekruttering af faglært arbejdskraft baseret på en allerede eksisterende og fungerende database, der forvaltes af EFKA

Denne platform tilbyder en ekstra service: Virksomheder, der bliver registreret og er interesseret i at rekruttere arbejdskraft fra andre lande, vil have mulighed for at opnå synlighed overfor europæiske arbejdere, som er interesseret i at få arbejdserfaring indenfor deres felt.

Finnish

Projekti on osa hanketta, jonka avulla autetaan ammattitaitoisia työntekijöitä hakeutumaan töihin toiseen eurooppalaiseen maahan joko pysyvästi tai tilapäisesti.

Projekti rohkaisee sekä nuoria että vanhempia ammatti-ihmisiä hankkimaan työkokemusta ulkomailta, ja siten parantamaan mahdollisuuksiaan työmarkkinoilla. Samalla projektin tavoitteen on auttaa PK–sektorin työnantajia rekrytoimaan tarpeisiinsa sopivaa työvoimaa ja tukea Lissabonin sopimuksen tavoitteita – kilpailukyvyn ja työpaikkojen lisääntymistä.

Projektin tavoitteena on tuottaa

- täsmätietoa ammattitaitoisen työvoiman tarjonnasta ja tarpeesta
- vertailukelpoista tietoa ammattitaitoisille työntekijöille, jotta nämä voivat tehdä päätöksiä ulkomaille siirtymisestä luotettavalta pohjalta.
- aineistoa tukemaan liikkuvan työvoiman valmistautumista ulkomailla työskentelyyn
- EFKAn hallinnoima, jo toimivaan tietokantaan perustettava alusta ammattitaitoisen työvoiman rekrytoimista varten Euroopassa.

Alusta tarjoaa lisäpalvelun: rekisteröityvät ja muista maista haluttavan työvoimatarpeensa kertovat yritykset saavat näkyvyyttä, joka kattaa koko Euroopan alueella kansainvälistä kokemusta haluavat, ammattitaitoiset työntekijät.

Jotta kansainvälistä työvoiman liikkuvuutta ja vaihtoa voidaan edistää tehokkaasti, projekti keskittyy tiettyihin toimenpiteisiin ja työkalujen tuottamiseen. Niiden avulla pyritään helpottamaan työvoiman liikkumista maasta toiseen.

German

About the project

Mobilität von Arbeitnehmern in Handwerks- sowie kleinen und mittleren Betrieben (KMU) unterstützen

Im Rahmen des Europäischen Jahres der Mobilität der Arbeitnehmer will das S-M-E Projekt qualifizierte Arbeitnehmer dabei unterstützen, gut informierte Entscheidungen bei der Aufnahme eines neuen Arbeitsplatzes in einem anderen Land zu treffen. S-M-E bezieht sich sowohl auf sog. vorübergehende und permanente Schritte – Karriereschritte bzw. Ausweg aus der Arbeitslosigkeit.

Arbeitskräfte aller Altersklassen sollen ermutigt werden, Berufserfahrung im Ausland zu sammeln, um schlussendlich mit dieser Erfahrung auch auf dem heimischen Arbeitsmarkt wieder eine Chance zu haben. Ebenfalls im Rahmen des S-M-E Projekts wird europäischen KMU's bei der Rekrutierung geeigneten Personals geholfen – ein wichtiges Ziel der europäischen Strategie für mehr Wachstum und Beschäftigung

Ziele des S-M-E Projekts:

- Analyse von Angebot und Nachfrage qualifizierter Arbeitskräfte;
- Bereitstellung von geeignetem Datenmaterial, damit qualifizierte Arbeitskräfte eine Entscheidung für das Ausland mit zuverlässiger Information begründen können;
- Erstellung von Schulungsmaterial;
- Ausbau einer bereits existierenden Datenbank der EFKA Suhl, damit diese im Sinne der europaweiten Rekrutierung von qualifizierten Arbeitskräften nutzbar wird.

Hungarian

About the project

Dolgozók mobilitásának támogatása az Európai Unióban

A project küldetése az, hogy szakképzett dolgozók elég információval rendelkezhessenek ahhoz, hogy más országban vállalhassanak munkát, akár önszántukból, saját karrierjük fejlesztése érdekében, akár esetleg a munkanélküliség elkerülése érdekében. A program bátorítani akarja a fiatal és idősebb munkavállalókat arra, hogy külföldön végzett munka során növeljék tapasztalataikat, fejlesszék ismereteiket, ezáltal növelve munkaerő-piaci esélyüket. Mindez lehetővé teszi az uniós vállalkozásoknak, hogy megfelelő munkaerőt toborozhassanak a lisszaboni céloknak megfelelően, a versenyképesség növelése és a munkahelyteremtés érdekében.

Ezért a project céljai a következők:

- Pontos információk nyújtása munkaerő szükségletre és feleslegre vonatkozóan
- Információ nyújtása szakképzett emberek számára azért, hogy elegendő információval rendelkezzenek akkor, amikor külföldön kívánnának munkát vállalni,
- Képzési anyagok kidolgozása annak érdekében, hogy a dolgozók megfelelő en tudjanak felkészülni külföldi munkák vállalására.
- Az EFKA által fenntartott, már létező adatbázis számára platformot biztosítani.

A platform még a következő szolgáltatást is felajánlja: azok a vállalatok, vállalkozások, amelyek regisztráltatják magukat, lehetőséget kapnak arra, hogy az adatbázisban szerepelve külföldi munkaerőt toborozhassanak.

Italian

About the project

MOBILITA' DEL LAVORATORE QUALIFICATO EUROPEO
Supporto alla mobilità dei lavoratori qualificati e alle Piccole e Medie Imprese

Nell'Anno Europeo della Mobilità dei Lavoratori, il progetto "SKILLED-MOBILE-EUROPEAN"
ha l'obiettivo di offrire supporto a lavoratori qualificati nel prendere la decisione di
lavorare in un'altro Paese, in modo temporaneo o permanente, come scelta o per
necessità. Il progetto intende pertanto incoraggiare lavoratori qualificati, giovani e
adulti, ad intraprendere un'esperienza di lavoro all'estero per accrescere le loro
opportunità occupazionali nel mercato del lavoro. Favorisce inoltre le Piccole e Medie
Imprese a reclutare personale adeguato alle loro esigenze, contribuendo in tal modo a
raggiungere gli obiettivi di Lisbona, competitività e creazione di posti di lavoro.

Principali obiettivi del progetto sono l'offerta di:

• informazioni mirate sulla domanda e offerta di lavoro qualificato a livello europeo;
• conoscenze specifiche per aiutare i lavoratori qualificati a prendere la decisione di
  lavorare all'estero;
• materiale per il supporto alla formazione per sostenere i lavoratori nel prepararsi
  adeguatamente per un lavoro all'estero;
• una piattaforma per il reclutamento di lavoratori qualificati a livello europeo,
  basata su un database, già esistente e funzionante, gestito da EFKA (coordinatore
  tedesco per tutte le medie, piccole e micro imprese, organizzazioni e associazioni
  interessate a contatti, cooperazione e scambi a livello europeo).

La piattaforma offrirà alle imprese che si registreranno e dichiareranno disponibilità a
reclutare forza-lavoro da altri Paesi, l'opportunità di acquisire visibilità verso lavoratori
europei interessati a fare un'esperienza di lavoro nel loro settore.

Example 19: *other versions of page 5 of the brochure "Do you want to work in another EU Member State? Find out about your rights!", issued by the European Commission Directorate-General for Employment, Social Affairs and Equal Opportunities. Downloaded from http://bookshop.europa. eu/uri?target=EUB:NOTICE:KE7506930:EN. Languages appear here in alphabetical order.*

Czech

Úvod

Volný pohyb osob je jednou ze základních svobod zaručených právem Společenství. Občané EU se mohou přesouvat do jiného členského státu, aby tam pracovali nebo studovali, poskytovali nebo si nechávali poskytovat služby, založili společnost, usadili se tam na penzi nebo, pokud jsou nevýdělečnými osobami, tam pouze pobývali.

Tato příručka popisuje **pouze** právní postavení **osob, které se přesou- vají v rámci Evropské unie z důvodu zaměstnání.** Jejím cílem je poskytnout vám informace o vašich právech migrujícího pracovníka v podobě snadno srozumitelných otázek a odpovědí.

Chcete získat zaměstnání v jiném členském státě? Pracujete v jiném členském státě, a nevíte, jaká jsou vaše práva ve srovnání s pracovníky z dotčené země? Jak to funguje, když pracujete v jedné zemi, ale pobýváte v jiné? Tato příručka vám poskytne odpovědi na tyto a mnohé další otázky.

Tato příručka byla vydána v rámci Evropského roku mobility pracovníků 2006, je pořádán s cílem zvýšit povědomí a porozumění ohledně výhod práce v zahraničí.

Danish
Indledning

Den frie bevægelighed for personer er en af de grundlæggende frihedsrettigheder, som EU-lovgivningen sikrer. Borgere i EU kan flytte til en anden medlemsstat for at arbejde eller studere, levere eller modtage tjenesteydelser, starte en virksomhed, bosætte sig som pensionister eller for simpelthen at bosætte sig, selv om de ikke er økonomisk aktive.

I denne vejledning redegøres der **kun** for retsstillingen for **personer, som flytter inden for EU på grund af deres arbejde.** I form af letforståelige spørgsmål og svar indeholder den oplysninger om dine rettigheder som vandrende arbejdstager.

Ønsker du at arbejde i en anden medlemsstat? Arbejder du allerede i en anden medlemsstat og vil gerne vide, hvilke rettigheder du har sammenlignet med de indfødte arbejdstagere? Hvad sker der, hvis du arbejder i ét land, men bor i et andet? I denne vejledning finder du svar på disse og mange andre spørgsmål.

Denne vejledning udgives i forbindelse med det europæiske år for arbejdstagernes mobilitet 2006, som er blevet organiseret for at øge kendskabet til og forståelsen af fordelene ved at arbejde i udlandet.

Dutch
Inleiding

Het vrije verkeer van personen is een van de fundamentele vrijheden die in het EU-recht zijn verankerd. De burgers van de EU kunnen naar een andere lidstaat gaan om daar te werken of te studeren, diensten te verlenen of te ontvangen, een bedrijf op te richten of, voor gepensioneerden of economisch niet-actieve personen, gewoon om daar te gaan wonen.

In deze gids wordt **alleen** de rechtspositie beschreven van **personen die binnen**

de Europese Unie migreren om arbeidsredenen. Het is de bedoeling u in de vorm van gemakkelijk te begrijpen vragen en antwoorden informatie over uw rechten als migrerende werknemer te verstrekken.

Wilt u een baan in een andere lidstaat aannemen? Werkt u in een andere lidstaat en vraagt u zich af wat uw rechten zijn in vergelijking met werknemers van dat land zelf? Wat gebeurt er als u in een ander land woont dan het land waar u werkt? De antwoorden op die en nog veel andere vragen vindt u in deze gids.

Deze gids is gepubliceerd in het kader van het Europees Jaar van de mobiliteit van werknemers 2006, dat is georganiseerd om de voordelen van werken in het buitenland onder de aandacht te brengen en te verduidelijken.

Estonian
Sissejuhatus

Isikute vaba liikumine on üks ühenduse õigusega tagatud põhivabadustest. Euroopa Liidu kodanikud võivad ümber asuda teise liikmesriiki, et seal töötada või õppida, teenuseid osutada või saada, äriühing asutada, sinna pensioni ajaks elama asuda või kui tegemist on majanduslikult mitteaktiivsete inimestega, siis ka lihtsalt elada.

Selles juhendis kirjeldatakse **üksnes** nende isikute õiguslikku olukorda, kes **liiguvad Euroopa Liidu piires töötamise eesmärgil.** Juhendis jagatakse Teile lihtsalt mõistetavas küsimuste ja vastuste vormis teavet selle kohta, millised on Teie õigused võõrtöötajana.

Kas soovite asuda tööle mõnes teises liikmesriigis? Kas töötate teises liikmesriigis ja Teid huvitab, millised on Teie õigused samast riigist pärit töötajatega võrreldes? Mis juhtub, kui Te töötate ühes riigis, aga elate teises? Siit leiate vastused nii nendele kui ka mitmetele muudele küsimustele.

Juhend avaldati töötajate liikuvuse Euroopa aasta 2006 raames, mis korraldati eesmärgiga suurendada teadlikkust ja parandada arusaamist välismaal töötamisega kaasnevatest soodustustest.

Finnish
Johdanto

Henkilöiden vapaa liikkuvuus on yksi yhteisön lainsäädännön takaamista kansalaisten perusvapauksista. EU:n kansalainen voi muuttaa toiseen EU-maahan työskentelemään tai opiskelemaan, tarjoamaan tai ottamaan vastaan palveluja, perustamaan yrityksen, asettua sinne eläkevuosikseen tai – jos hän on työelämän ulkopuolella – vaikka vain asumaan.

Tässä oppaassa kuvataan **vain sellaisten ihmisten** oikeudellinen tilanne, **jotka muuttavat Euroopan unionin sisällä työhön liittyvistä syistä.** Tarkoituksena on antaa tietoja siirtotyöläisen oikeuksista selkeinä kysymyksinä ja vastauksina.

Kiinnostaako työnteko toisessa EU-maassa? Mitkä ovat toisesta EUmaasta tulleen työntekijän oikeudet verrattuna isäntämaan kotimaisten työntekijöiden oikeuksiin? Entä jos työskentelee eri maassa kuin asuu? Tässä oppaassa vastataan näihin ja moniin muihin kysymyksiin.

Opas on julkaistu osana Euroopan työntekijöiden liikkuvuuden teemavuoteen 2006 liittyvää toimintaa. Teemavuoden tavoitteena on lisätä ihmisten tietoja ulkomailla työskentelyn eduista.

French
Introduction

La libre circulation des personnes est une des libertés fondamentales inscrites dans le droit communautaire. Les citoyens de l'Union européenne (UE) ont la possibilité de se rendre dans un autre État membre pour y travailler, y étudier, y fournir ou y obtenir des services, y créer une entreprise, s'y établir lors de leur retraite ou, dans le cas de personnes économiquement inactives, simplement y résider.

Ce guide décrit **uniquement** le statut juridique des **personnes qui migrent au sein de l'Union européenne pour des raisons professionnelles.** Il a pour objectif de vous informer sur vos droits en tant que travailleur migrant, sous la forme de questions et réponses facilement compréhensibles.

Vous voulez occuper un emploi dans un autre État membre? Vous travaillez dans un autre État membre et vous vous demandez quels sont vos droits par rapport aux travailleurs de ce pays? Que se passe-t-il si vous travaillez dans un pays mais résidez dans un autre? Ce guide répond à ces questions et à bien d'autres encore.

Il est publié dans le cadre de l'Année européenne de la mobilité des travailleurs — 2006 —, organisée pour sensibiliser les citoyens aux avantages du travail à l'étranger et pour en améliorer leur compréhension.

German
Einführung

Der freie Personenverkehr zählt zu den vom Gemeinschaftsrecht garantierten Grundfreiheiten. EU-Bürger können sich in einen anderen Mitgliedstaat begeben, um dort zu arbeiten oder zu studieren, Dienstleistungen zu erbringen oder zu empfangen, ein Unternehmen zu gründen, um dort ihr Rentenalter zu verbringen oder, wenn sie nicht erwerbstätig sind, ganz einfach zu leben.

Dieser Leitfaden beschreibt ausschließlich die rechtliche Stellung von **Bürgern, die sich der Arbeit wegen in einen anderen Mitgliedstaat der Europäischen Union begeben.** Er informiert Sie in leicht verständlicher Form anhand von Fragen und Antworten über Ihre Rechte als Wanderarbeitnehmer.

Möchten Sie gern eine Arbeit in einem anderen Mitgliedstaat aufnehmen? Oder arbeiten Sie bereits in einem anderen Mitgliedstaat und wüssten gern, welche Rechte Sie im Vergleich zu Arbeitnehmern dieses Landes haben? Wie verhält es sich, wenn Sie in einem Land arbeiten, doch in einem anderen Land Ihren Wohnsitz haben? Hier erhalten Sie Antwort auf diese und zahlreiche weitere Fragen.

Dieser Leitfaden wurde im Rahmen des Europäischen Jahres der Mobilität der Arbeitnehmer 2006 veröffentlicht, das ausgerufen wurde, um den Bürgern die Vorzüge einer Beschäftigung im Ausland näherzubringen.

Greek
Εισαγωγή

Η ελεύθερη κυκλοφορία των προσώπων είναι μία από τις θεμελιώδεις ελευθερίες που εγγυάται το κοινοτικό δίκαιο. Οι πολίτες της ΕΕ μπορούν να μετακινηθούν σε άλλο κράτος μέλος με σκοπό να εργαστούν ή να σπουδάσουν σ' αυτό, να παράσχουν ή να λάβουν υπηρεσίες, να συστήσουν εταιρεία, να εγκατασταθούν κατά τη συνταξιοδότησή τους ή, στην περίπτωση οικονομικώς ανενεργών προσώπων, απλώς να κατοικήσουν εκεί.

Αυτός ο οδηγός περιγράφει **μόνο** τη νομική κατάσταση των **προσώπων που διακινούνται εντός της Ευρωπαϊκής Ένωσης λόγω απασχόλησης.** Στόχος του είναι να σας πληροφορήσει σχετικά με τα δικαιώματά σας ως διακινούμενου εργαζομένου με ένα εύκολα κατανοητό έντυπο υπό μορφή ερωτήσεων και απαντήσεων.

Θέλετε να αναλάβετε απασχόληση σε άλλο κράτος μέλος; Εργάζεστε σε άλλο κράτος μέλος και αναρωτιέστε τι δικαιώματα έχετε σε σύγκριση με τους εργαζομένους της συγκεκριμένης χώρας; Τι συμβαίνει εάν εργάζεστε σε μια χώρα αλλά κατοικείτε σε άλλη; Αυτός ο οδηγός θα σας απαντήσει σ' αυτές και σε πολλές άλλες ερωτήσεις.

Ο παρών οδηγός δημοσιεύτηκε στα πλαίσια του ευρωπαϊκού έτους κινητικότητας των εργαζομένων 2006, το οποίο οργανώθηκε για να βελτιώσει την επίγνωση και την κατανόηση των πλεονεκτημάτων της εργασίας στο εξωτερικό.

Hungarian
Bevezetés

A személyek szabad mozgása a közösségi jog által biztosított alapvető szabadságok egyike. Az EU polgárai munkavállalás vagy tanulás, szolgáltatásnyújtás vagy szolgáltatás igénybevétele, cégalapítás és nyugdíjasként való letelepedés, illetve – gazdaságilag inaktív személyek esetében – egyszerűen tartózkodás céljából is átköltözhetnek egy másik tagállamba.

Ez az útmutató **csak** azon személyek jogi helyzetét írja le, **akik az Európai Unión belül foglalkoztatási okokból vándorolnak.** Célja, hogy migráns munkavállalói jogairól könnyen érthető, kérdés-felelet formában tájékoztassa Önt.

Egy másik EU-tagállamban szeretne munkát vállalni? Egy másik tagállamban dolgozik, és szeretné tudni, milyen jogai vannak az adott ország munkavállalóihoz viszonyítva? Mi történik, ha más országban lakik, mint ahol dolgozik? Ez az útmutató ezekre és sok egyéb kérdésre ad választ Önnek.

Ezt a kiadványt a munkavállalók mobilitásának 2006-os európai éve keretében tették közzé, amelyet azért szerveztek, hogy a polgárok még inkább tudatában legyenek és jobban megértsék a külföldön való munkavállalás előnyeit.

Italian
Introduzione

La libera circolazione delle persone è una delle libertà fondamentali garantite dal diritto comunitario. I cittadini dell'Unione europea possono trasferirsi in un altro Stato membro per lavoro o per studio, per offrire servizi o usufruirne, per creare un'impresa, per trascorrervi la pensione o, nel caso di persone economicamente inattive, semplicemente per soggiornarvi.

Questa guida descrive **unicamente** la posizione giuridica delle **persone che si spostano all'interno dell'Unione europea per motivi di lavoro.** Intende fornire informazioni, sotto forma di domande e risposte di facile comprensione, sui diritti dei lavoratori migranti.

Volete iniziare a lavorare in un altro Stato membro? Lavorate già in un altro Stato membro e volete sapere quali sono i vostri diritti rispetto ai lavoratori di quel paese? Cosa succede se lavorate in un paese ma risiedete in un altro? La guida risponde a queste e a molte altre domande.

Essa è stata pubblicata in occasione dell'Anno europeo della mobilità dei lavoratori 2006, organizzato per fare meglio comprendere ai cittadini i vantaggi derivanti dal lavorare all'estero.

Latvian

Ievads

Personu brīva pārvietošanās ir viena no pamatbrīvībām, ko nodrošina Kopienas tiesības. ES pilsoņi var doties uz citu dalībvalsti, lai tur strādātu vai studētu, sniegtu vai saņemtu pakalpojumus, nodibinātu uzņēmumu, apmestos pensijas vecumā vai – ekonomiski neaktīvu personu gadījumā – vienkārši tur uzturētos.

Šī pamācība raksturo tikai tiesisko stāvokli, kas ir **personām, kuras pārvietojas Eiropas Savienības robežās darba dēļ.** Pamācības mērķis ir viegli saprotamu jautājumu un atbilžu veidā sniegt informāciju par tiesībām, kas jums ir kā migrējošam darba ņēmējam.

Vai vēlaties pieņemt darba piedāvājumu citā dalībvalstī? Vai strādājat citā dalībvalstī un vēlaties zināt, kādas ir jūsu tiesības salīdzinājumā ar tās valsts darba ņēmējiem? Kas notiek, ja strādājat vienā valstī, bet dzīvojat citā? Šī pamācība jums sniegs atbildes uz šiem un daudziem citiem jautājumiem.

Šī pamācība izdota Eiropas Darba ņēmēju mobilitātes 2006. gada ietvaros, kas tika organizēts, lai informētu un radītu sapratni par darba ārvalstīs pozitīvajiem aspektiem.

Lithuanian

Įvadas

Laisvas asmenų judėjimas yra viena iš pagrindinių laisvių, kurią užtikrina Bendrijos teisė. ES piliečiai gali išvykti į kitą valstybę narę dirbti arba studijuoti, teikti paslaugų ar jomis naudotis, įsteigti ten bendrovę, įsikurti išėję į pensiją arba, jei yra ekonomiškai neaktyvūs, tiesiog gyventi.

Šiame vadove apibrėžiamas teisinis statusas **tik tų asmenų, kurie migruoja Europos Sąjungoje profesiniais tikslais**. Informacija apie jūsų, kaip migruojančio darbuotojo, teises pateikiama lengvai suprantama klausimų ir atsakymų forma.

Norite įsidarbinti kitoje valstybėje narėje? Jau dirbate kitoje valstybėje narėje ir norite žinoti, kokios Jūsų teisės, palyginti su tos šalies darbuotojų teisėmis? Kas bus, jeigu dirbsite vienoje šalyje, o gyvensite kitoje? Šis vadovas padės rasti atsakymus į šiuos ir į daugelį kitų klausimų.

Šis vadovas skelbiamas Europos darbuotojų judumo metais (2006), siekiant informuoti ES piliečius ir padėti jiems geriau suvokti darbo kitoješalyje teikiamus privalumus.

Maltese

Introduzzjoni

Il-moviment ħieles tal-persuni huwa wieħed mil-libertajiet fundamentali garantit mil-liġi tal-Komunità. Iċ-ċittadini ta' l-UE jistgħu jmorru fi Stat Membru ieħor biex jaħdmu jew jistudjaw hemmhekk, biex iwaqqfu xi kumpanija, biex jistabbilixxu ruħhom u jirtiraw hemmhekk jew, f'każ ta' persuni li ma jkunux attivi ekonomikament, sempliċiment biex jgħixu hemmhekk.

Din il-gwida tiddeskrivi biss il-pożizzjoni legali tal-**persuni li jiċċaqilqu fi ħdan l-Unjoni Ewropea għal raġunijiet ta' impjieg**. L-għan tagħha huwa li, f'għamla ta' mistoqsijiet u tweġibiet li huma faċli biex wieħed jifhimhom, tipprovdilek l-informazzjoni dwar id-drittijiet tiegħek bħala ħaddiem li se tmur taħdem f'pajjiż ieħor.

Tixtieq tibda taħdem fi Stat Membru ieħor? Qed taħdem fi Stat Membru ieħor u qed tistaqsi x'inhuma d-drittijiet tiegħek meta mqabbla ma' dawk ta' ħaddiema minn dak il-pajjiż? X'jiġri jekk inti taħdem f'pajjiż imma tkun residenti f'pajjiż ieħor? Din il-gwida se tipprovdilek it-tweġibiet għal dawn il-mistoqsijiet u għal ħafna oħrajn.

Din il-gwida ġiet ippubblikata fil-qafas tas-Sena Ewropea tal-Moviment tal-Ħaddiema 2006, li ġiet organizzata biex tqajjem kuxjenza u biex wieħed jifhem iktar il-benefiċċji tal-ħidma barra mill-pajjiż.

Polish

WSTĘP

Swobodny przepływ osób to jedna z podstawowych swobód gwarantowanych przez prawo wspólnotowe. Obywatele UE mogą udać się do innego państwa członkowskiego, aby tam pracować lub studiować, świadczyć lub otrzymywać usługi, założyć firmę, osiedlić się po przejściu na emeryturę lub – w przypadku osób nieaktywnych zawodowo – po prostu w celu pobytu na terytorium wybranego państwa.

Niniejszy przewodnik opisuje **jedynie** sytuację prawną **osób przemieszczających się w obrębie Unii Europejskiej w związku z zatrudnieniem.** Celem niniejszego opracowania jest przedstawienie informacji o prawach pracownika migrującego w łatwo przystępnej formie pytań i odpowiedzi.

Czy chcesz podjąć pracę w innym państwie członkowskim UE? Czy pracujesz w innym państwie członkowskim UE i zastanawiasz się, jakie masz prawa w porównaniu z pracownikami pochodzącymi z tego kraju? Jaka jest Twoja sytuacja, jeśli pracujesz w jednym kraju, ale mieszkasz w innym? Niniejszy przewodnik zawiera odpowiedzi na te i wiele innych pytań.

Niniejszy przewodnik został opublikowany w ramach Europejskiego Roku Mobilności Pracowników 2006, ogłoszonego w celu szerzenia świadomości i wiedzy o korzyściach wynikających z pracy zagranicą.

Portuguese

Introdução

A livre circulação de pessoas é uma das liberdades fundamentais consagradas no direito comunitário. Os cidadãos da UE podem deslocar-se para outro Estado-Membro para aí trabalhar ou prosseguir estudos, prestar ou receber serviços, criar uma empresa, fixar-se após a reforma ou, no caso de pessoas economicamente inactivas, simplesmente residir.

O presente guia descreve **unicamente** a situação jurídica de **pessoas que migram no território da União Europeia por motivos profissionais.** O seu objectivo é prestar-lhe informações sobre os seus direitos enquanto trabalhador migrante, sob a forma de perguntas e respostas facilmente compreensíveis.

Gostaria de trabalhar noutro Estado-Membro da UE? Trabalha num outro Estado-Membro e quer saber quais são os seus direitos comparativamente aos trabalhadores originários desse país? E se trabalha num país e reside noutro? O presente guia dar-lhe-á repostas a estas e a muitas outras perguntas.

O guia foi publicado no âmbito do *Ano Europeu da Mobilidade Profissional* (2006), organizado no intuito de dar a conhecer aos cidadãos as vantagens de trabalhar no estrangeiro.

Slovak

Úvod

Voľný pohyb osôb je jednou zo základných slobôd zaručených právnymi predpismi Spoločenstva. Občania EÚ môžu ísť do iného členského štátu, ak v ňom chcú pracovať alebo študovať, poskytovať alebo využívať služby, založiť si spoločnosť, ak sa v ňom chcú usadiť v dôchodku alebo v prípade ekonomicky neaktívnych osôb jednoducho bývať.

Táto príručka opisuje **iba** zákonné postavenie **osôb, ktoré sa pohybujú v rámci Európskej únie z dôvodov zamestnania.** Jej cieľom je poskytnúť vám informácie o vašich právach migrujúceho pracovníka vo forme ľahko zrozumiteľných otázok a odpovedí.

Chcete začať vykonávať prácu v inom členskom štáte? Pracujete v inom členskom štáte a chcete vedieť, aké sú vaše práva v porovnaní s pracovníkmi z danej krajiny? Čo sa stane, ak pracujete v jednej krajine, ale bývate v inej krajine? Táto príručka vám poskytne odpovede na tieto a mnoho ďalších otázok.

Táto príručka bola uverejnená v rámci Európskeho roka voľného pohybu pracovnej sily 2006, ktorý bol zorganizovaný s cieľom zvýšiť informovanosť o prínosoch práce v zahraničí a prispieť k ich lepšiemu porozumeniu.

Slovenian

Uvod

Prosto gibanje oseb je ena temeljnih svoboščin, zapisanih v zakonodaji Skupnosti. Državljani EU se lahko preselijo v drugo državo članico, kjer lahko delajo ali študirajo, nudijo ali uporabljajo storitve, ustanovijo podjetje, preživljajo pokoj ali, v primeru ekonomsko neaktivnih oseb, tam preprosto prebivajo.

Ta priročnik opisuje **samo** pravni položaj **oseb, ki se selijo znotraj Evropske unije zaradi zaposlitve.** Namenjen je temu, da vam v enostavni obliki vprašanj in odgovorov poda informacije o pravicah, ki jih imate kot delavec migrant.

Se želite zaposliti v drugi državi članici? Ali delate v drugi državi članici in se sprašujete, kakšne so vaše pravice v primerjavi s pravicami delavcev, ki imajo stalno prebivališče v isti državi? Kako ravnati v primeru, ko delate v eni državi, medtem ko imate stalno prebivališče v drugi državi? Ta priročnik vam bo odgovoril na ta in na mnoga druga vprašanja.

Priročnik je bil objavljen v okviru Evropskega leta mobilnosti delavcev – leta 2006 – katerega cilj je poglobiti zavest in izboljšati poznavanje prednosti dela v tujini.

Spanish

Introducción

La libre circulación de personas es una de las libertades fundamentales inscritas en el Derecho comunitario. Los ciudadanos de la Unión Europea tienen la posibilidad de desplazarse a otro Estado miembro para trabajar, estudiar, proporcionar u obtener servicios, crear una empresa, establecerse tras su jubilación o, en el caso de las personas económicamente inactivas, sencillamente residir en él.

La presente guía describe **únicamente** la situación jurídica de las **personas que migran dentro de la Unión Europea por motivos de empleo.** Su objeto es informarle sobre sus derechos como trabajador migrante, en forma de preguntas y respuestas fácilmente comprensibles.

¿Desea trabajar en otro Estado miembro? ¿Trabaja en otro Estado miembro y se pregunta cuáles son sus derechos con respecto a los trabajadores de ese país? ¿Qué ocurre si trabaja en un país pero reside en otro? La presente guía responde a estas y otras muchas preguntas.

Esta guía se ha publicado en el marco del Año Europeo de la Movilidad de los Trabajadores (2006), organizado para dar a conocer a los ciudadanos las ventajas de trabajar en el extranjero.

Swedish

Inledning

Den fria rörligheten för personer är en av de grundläggande friheter som gemenskapslagstiftningen ger oss. Medborgare i EU kan flytta till en annan medlemsstat för att arbeta eller studera, tillhandahålla eller utnyttja tjänster, starta eget, bosätta sig där som pensionär eller helt enkelt för att vistas där även om man inte förvärvsarbetar.

Denna handbok gäller **enbart** den rättsliga ställningen för **personer som flyttar inom Europeiska unionen i samband med arbete.** Den innehåller information till dig om dina rättigheter som migrerande arbetstagare, i form av frågor och svar för att underlätta läsningen.

Vill du ta anställning i en annan medlemsstat? Arbetar du redan i en annan medlemsstat och vill veta vilka rättigheter du har jämfört med inhemska anställda? Vad gäller om du arbetar i ett land och bor i ett annat? I den här handboken hittar du svaren på dessa frågor och många andra.

Handboken ges ut i samband med Europeiska året för arbetstagares rörlighet 2006, som har utlysts för att skapa större medvetenhet och kunskap om fördelarna med att arbeta utomlands.

Example 20: *Other language versions, downloaded from:* *http://www.ausl.fo.it/tabid/444/Default.aspx*

French

A qui demander des informations

800.033.033
C'est le numéro vert gratuit à contacter pour reçevoir des informations sur l'hôpital.

Dans le hall du Pavillon « Morgagni » on peut s'adresser au guichet des informations. Les operateurs réponderont à toutes les questions relatives aux services offerts. Ils peuvent fournir des informations sur les modalités d'accés aux hospitalisations et analyses, visites et en lbre profession, temps d'attente, fonctionnement de toutes les structures opérationnelles et autres informations pour garantir la solution des problèmes relatifs aux services socio-sanitaires comme l'éxemption, remboursements, autres structures sanitaires à qui s'adresser. Le personnel favorise l'accueil, et il est disponible à l'égard des citoyens pour les écouter et comprendre leurs exigences, offre l'aide necessaire pour limiter les incommodités qui peuvent apparaître quand on bénéficie de ces services et résoudre éventuels problèmes pratiques liés aux préstations éffectuées par l'entreprise.

Chinese

如何咨询医院的服务情况

如果需要了解医院的情况, 请打 **800.033.033** 医院的绿线免费咨询电话.

-在 医院的**"Morgagni"**大厅, 设有医院服务咨询窗口, 窗口工作人员会给你提供一切有关医院的服务情况和回答有关的问题. *例如有关如何办理住院手术, 如何做检查,如何看门诊,及专科门诊, 和看一些自由职业医生门诊, 约会的时间等等医院所提供的各部门服务,另外作为公共社会福利医疗一部份,,保证尽力解决一切和公共社会福利医疗保健有关问题, 如何报销医疗费用,其他与医院有关卫生单位(如和公立医院有挂钩的私立医院的信息), 窗口的接待工作人员随时都会听取公民所提出的各种问题和要求,给予公民必要的帮助, 尽量减少公民可能在就医过程中出现的不便和困难.*

Albanian

Ku dhe si të kërkoni informacione

* **800 033 033** është numri i telefonit pa pagesë që mund të thërrisni për t'u informuar mbi spitalin.
* _ Në *hyrjen e Pavijonit Morgagni (Padiglione Morgagni)* mund të drejtoheni tek sporteli i informacioneve. Punonjësit do t'u përgjigjen të gjitha pyetjeve në lidhje me shërbimet e ofruara. Ata mund të japin informacione mbi mënyrat e shtrimit në spital, bërjen e analizave, vizitat mjekësore, shërbimet private, kohët e pritjes, funksionimin e të gjitha strukturave shëndetësore të Shoqërisë USL. Gjithashtu, punonjësit mund të japin informacione të tjera për të garantuar rrugëzgjidhjen e problemeve që lidhen me shër-bimet sociale e shëndetësore si p.sh.: mospagimin a rimborsimin i shërbimit apo orientimin në strukturat e tjera shëndetësore. Per-soneli mundëson pritjen e qytetarëve, është i gatshëm për dëgjimin dhe kuptimin e kërkesave të tyre, jep ndihmën e duhur për të pa-kësuar vështirësitë që mund të shfaqen gjatë dhënies së shërbimeve shëndetësore dhe ndihmon në zgjidhjen e problemet të mundshme që lidhen me shërbimet e dhëna nga Shoqëria USL.

Arabic

إلى أين يجب التوجه للحصول على المعلومات A chi chiedere informazioni

800.033.033 رقم الهاتف المجاني الاتصال به للحصول على معلومات المتعلقة في المستشفى في مدخل قسم المورغاني في الإمكان التوجه إلى قسم المعلومات والاستعلامات . الموظفين يجيبون على جميع الاسئلة المتعلقة في الخدمات المقدمة . في امكانهم تقديم المعلومات المتعلقة في كيفية البقاء في المستشفى عن الامتحانات والفحوصات الطبية، فحوصات طبية لدى العيادات العامة والخاصة وعن وقت الانتظار ، عن عمل جميع الاقسام الفعلية الموجودة في الشركة ومعلومات أخرى لضمان حل وتسهيل العقبات المتعلقة في الخدمات الصحية مثل الاعفاء من الدفع، الحصول على المبلغ الذي تم دفعة، أقسام صحية أخرى للتوجة اليها . الموظفين يكفلون الاستقبال وهم مستعدين لسماع حاجات المواطنين وفهم احتياجاتهم، يقدمون لهم المساعدة الضرورية لتقليل سوء الفهم والصعوبات التي يمكن ان تحدث خلال الاسافادة من الخدمات المقدمة زهم سيقومون في حل المشاكل العملية المرتبطة في الخدمات المقدمة من قبل الشركة .

A Glossary of Terms

Active (working) language: a language that one is able to translate into.

Adaptation: a form of translation that accommodates the conventions of the target language and culture, the canons of literary genres thereof, and the expectations of the target readership/audience. Commonly used as a hypernym of **localization** and **trans-creation**, it also subsumes the concepts of **covert translation** and **domestication**. It is commonly viewed as the preferred approach to **consumer-oriented translation**.

Agility: one of the qualities often required of advertising and promotional translators. It is the ability to recognize the pattern in which functions and purposes shift in the source text and follow or modify such pattern according to the use and function of the target text, without losing sight of coherence and cohesion.

Alternative versions: see **multiple versions**.

Anchor: a term used in this book only. An anchor is a usually technical or highly informative chunk of text (down to the word level) that normally requires close rendition in order to preserve its purpose. Anchors tend to make extensive rewriting difficult for the immediately surrounding text as well (hence the name), except in advertising and other low **information-to-persuasion ratio** texts, where they might be omitted, or changed, if this is thought to make the target text work better. **Monoreferential terms** and numerical data are examples of translation anchors.

B2B: see **business-to-business**.

B2C: see **business-to-consumer**.

Bodycopy (or **body copy**): in a print advertisement, it is the longer part of verbal text that follows the **headline** and precedes the **payoff**; it is printed in smaller or otherwise less visible characters.

Boost: as used in this book, this term generically indicates the use of words with a markedly positive connotation (but not necessarily a superlative meaning) in connection with the object of promotion. A hypernym, not a synonym, of **lexical boost**.

Brief: the information provided to the translator by the client and/or the agency or other intermediaries about their expectations regarding the target text. It may include the target audience (which is important for translation choices concerning personal deixis, lexis and register), the **media plan** (which is important for register and also for text length), and other specific requirements such as the recommendation to use specific keywords, concepts or puns that are linked to the brand or product image. In promotional translation more than in other translation types, the brief should always be respected or **negotiated** with the final client before handing in the target text. Intentional departures from the brief should always be motivated and offered as an alternative to one or more versions that adhere to it.

Business-to-business (or **B2B**): the promotion of goods or services done by businesses and aimed other businesses.

Business-to-consumer (or **B2C**): the promotion of goods or services done by businesses and aimed at individuals.

Consumer-oriented texts: a working category of texts that are focused on readers as consumers or users of something. They aim to affect consumers' behaviour in various ways and include a variety of genres, such as user manuals, tourist brochures, recipe books, and promotional texts. They require a purpose-oriented translation approach. (Hervey and Higgins 1992/2002; Hervey *et al* 1995/2006).

Consumer-oriented translation: the translation of **consumer-oriented texts**, whose aim is to serve in the target language and culture the same purpose fulfilled by the original texts in the source language and culture.

Copywriting: the act, or profession, of developing the *copy*, i.e., the verbal part of advertising texts. A copywriter usually works in close contact with an art director, who is responsible for the visual part of the same texts.

Covert translation: a concept developed by House (1977/1981) and closely linked to the concepts of **domestication** and the translator's invisibility (Venuti 1995). It means that the target text is not, or is not intended to be, recognizable as a translation, but is meant to appear as natural as possible in the target language and culture. The opposite of **overt translation**, a concept related to **foreignization**.

Creativity: one of the qualities often required of advertising and promotional translators. It is the ability to devise clever texts that play with language and visual cues, often within an extremely limited time frame. It also subsumes the ability to **trans-create** texts.

Domestication: a concept developed by Lawrence Venuti (1995, 1998a, 1998b) with main reference to literary texts and in opposition to **foreignization**. A domesticated text is translated in such a way that it is inserted as seamlessly as possible in the genre it is ascribed to in the target culture and language. In the process, the translator remains largely invisible and the author of the source text is given sole authorship.

Flexibility: one of the qualities often required of advertising and promotional translators. It means that translators should not be too fussy in terms of the extent to which their work is acknowledged. The target text may be transformed, further **trans-created** or even left aside by the end client. Visibility is seldom an option in advertising and promotional translation. This should not lead to frustration or spoil the translator's relationship with the client. Note that clients may give the term a variety of other meanings (e.g., readiness to accept low prices, adjust to impossible deadlines, etc.) that do *not* help promotional translators in their professional careers.

Foreignization: a concept developed by Lawrence Venuti (1995, 1998a, 1998b) with main reference to literary texts and in opposition to **domestication**. In the process of foreignization, the source text is translated in a way that does not accommodate the established canons of the target literature and language, but contributes to bringing about diversification in them. The translator thus acquires an active, visible role and authorship status.

Functionalism (in translation): see *Skopostheorie*.

Glocalization: a term used by Adab (2000:224) for the practice, adopted by several multinational companies, of developing local campaigns simultaneously from a **brief** that is as little culture-specific as possible.

Headline: the slogan at the opening of a print advertisement, usually appearing in larger or otherwise more visible characters.

I2I: see **institution-to-institution**.

I2U: see **institution-to-user**.

Information-to-persuasion ratio: a term used in this book only. It indicates the ratio between the information content and the explicitly persuasive intent of a text. In high information-to-persuasion ratio texts, such as CVs or business-to-business product information, persuasion is subordinate to (and sometimes dependent on) the specific or technical information conveyed by the text. Such texts usually require closer rendition than low information-to-persuasion ratio texts, and they are more likely to contain several translation **anchors**. Conversely, in the translation of low information-to-persuasion ratio texts, such as most business-to-consumer advertising, **persuasiveness** and extensive rewriting are usually more appreciated. See table 2 for a tentative collocation of promotional genres on the information-to-persuasion ratio continuum.

Institution-to-institution (or **I2I**): a term coined for this book (after **business-to-business**) to indicate texts that institutions produce to promote themselves with upper-level and/or funding institutions.

Institution-to-user (or **I2U**): a term coined for this book (after **business-to-consumer**) to indicate institutional promotion aimed at the general public.

Laws and restrictions: specific legal restraints about advertising and publicly distributed material that may apply in the target markets. Knowing them is often required of advertising and promotional translators who work in-house at agencies and companies, although freelance translators do not usually share this responsibility.

Lexical boost: a term first used by Teh (1986) and made more widely known by Bhatia (1993:51-52), which describes words that, although devoid of a superlative form, have an inherently superlative meaning. 'Superlative' is one such word: nothing can be *more superlative than something else, or *the most superlative. Other examples include 'optimize', 'maximize', 'minimize', 'absolute', 'winner', 'first', 'matchless'. The notion can be extended to phrases such as 'to have no/without equals', 'N° 1', and the like. The term is not synonymous with the term **boost** as used in this book.

Localization: the same as **adaptation**, but the term is market- rather than culture-oriented and only used for specific text types: for instance, websites, software, videogames, and advertising. The use of the term is motivated by the fact that a part of such texts is originally developed by multinationals that aim at global diffusion. When the texts reach local markets, however, they need to be adjusted to the conventions and expectations of each target market, not only from the verbal and cultural points of view, but also with reference to interfaces, navigation tools, **visuals**, and any other formal element.

Media plan: the detailed list of all media on which the advertising/promotional text or campaign will be distributed.

Monoreferential terms: terms that have only one referent in a given language. They are usually quite technical and in high **information-to-persuasion ratio** genres they often constitute translational **anchors** that do not lend themselves to rewriting.

Multiple versions: additional versions of a text or one part of it that may be required by the client, especially with texts with lower **information-to-persuasion ratio** such as advertisements. The client can choose between alternatives that have different nuances and therefore adjust to partly different target groups or convey partly different product images. See example 2 for a practical illustration of how the provision of multiple versions may be **negotiated** between the translator and his/her client.

Negotiation: any initiative that helps shape, integrate or modify the translation commission with a view to ensuring that the translator carries out his/her work as well as possible, or the client receives the best possible service (from the respective points of view). Eliciting a **brief**, asking for deadline extensions or for terminological assistance are examples of translator-initiated negotiation. Asking for a discount, alternative versions or revisions are examples of client-initiated negotiation. See example 2 for a practical illustration and § 2.2 for a detailed account.

Non-verbal elements: anything that constitutes a text apart from words. In the text types discussed in this book, examples of relevant non-verbal elements include **visuals**, layout, colours, typeface, and website navigability.

Overt translation: a term introduced by House (1977/1981) to refer to the opposite of **covert translation**. An overt translation is clearly recognizable as a translated rather than an original text in the target language and culture. It is closely linked to the concept of **foreignization** (Venuti 1995).

Passive (working) language: a language that one is able to translate from.

Payoff: the slogan at the end of a print advertisement, usually appearing in larger or otherwise more visible characters. While it was once given the function of facilitating product memorization, e.g., through rhymes, puns or the repetition of the same motto across different campaigns, in more recent times it is often replaced by a logo, website address, or other contact information (not necessarily in highly visible print).

Persuasiveness: one of the qualities often required of advertising and promotional translators. It is the mastery of an emotional or evocative style that helps lure the addressee into the desired course of action.

Realia tantum, **realia** (singular **reale tantum**, **reale**): things or concepts that exist only in one culture and the corresponding terms that, accordingly, exist only in one language. Realia are common in tourist promotion, where the usual translation strategy is to leave them unchanged but gloss them in the target language. In shorter genres, such as advertising, or wherever exoticism is not functional to the promotional purpose of the text, realia can be domesticated or avoided through **trans-creation**.

Skopostheorie: the theory that applies the notion of *Skopos*, a Greek word for 'purpose', to translation. Proposed in the late 1970s and early 1980s by Katharina Reiss and Hans J. Vermeer, it played a major role in the development of modern functionalism in translation studies. According to *Skopostheorie* a translation can be deemed successful only if it succeeds in having a certain intended effect on a given intended audience. (see Reiss and Vermeer 1984/1991; Nord 1997; Schäffner 1998, 2009).

Trans-creation: a type of **adaptation** that involves **copywriting** and, possibly, prompting the creation of new **visuals** for the promotional material, rather than relying on the same verbal and visual structures of the source text. In this approach, the translator is seen as a creative professional with highly developed language skills and an in-depth understanding of social, cultural, legal and promotional conventions currently in place in the target community.

Translation: a term whose semantic extension varies according to one's perspective. In daily usage, it is generally associated with the transformation of verbal elements (words) across languages, usually in the written mode. In my own perspective and in this book, it means the transfer of any kind of text and textual purpose across languages, cultures, signification systems, and markets.

Visual: each visual element of a (promotional) text. Also, the typeset version of a print advertising or promotional text, complete with pictures and any other visual material that accompanies the written text.

References

Works cited

Adab, Beverly (2000) 'Towards a More Systematic Approach to the Translation of Advertising Texts', in Allison Beeby, Doris Ensinger and Marisa Presas (eds) *Investigating Translation*, Amsterdam and Philadelphia: Benjamins, 223-234.

Bhatia, Vijay K. (1993) *Analyzing Genre: Language Use in Professional Settings*, London: Longman.

Brancati, Daniela (2002) *La pubblicità è femmina ma il pubblicitario è maschio: Per una comunicazione oltre i luoghi comuni*, Milan: Sperling & Kupfer.

Chiaro, Delia (2004) 'Translational and Marketing Communication: A Comparison of Print and Web Advertising of Italian Agro-Food Products', *The Translator* 10(2): 313-328.

Chuansheng, He (1997) *English for Trademarks*, Changsha: Hunan University Press.

Chuansheng, He and Xiao Yunnan (2003) 'Brand Name Translation in China: An Overview of Practice and Theory', *Babel* 49(2): 131-148.

De Mooij, Marieke (1998/2005) *Global Marketing and Advertising. Understanding Cultural Paradoxes*, London, Thousand Oaks and New Delhi: Sage, 2nd edition.

Díaz Cintas, Jorge and Aline Remael (2007) *Audiovisual Translation: Subtitling*, Manchester: St. Jerome.

Fuentes-Luque, Adrián and Dorothy Kelly (2000) 'The Translator as Mediator in Advertising Spanish Products in English-Speaking Markets', in Eija Ventola (ed) *Discourse and Community. Doing Functional Linguistics*, Tübingen: Gunter Narr, 235-242.

Hervey, Sándor and Ian Higgins (1992/2002) *Thinking French Translation. A Course in Translation Method: French to English*, London and New York: Routledge, 2nd edition.

Hervey, Sándor, Ian Higgins and Michael Loughridge (1995/2006) *Thinking German Translation. A Course in Translation Method: German to English*, London and New York: Routledge, 2nd edition.

Hofstede, Geert and Gert Jan Hofstede (2005) *Cultures and Organizations: Software of the Mind*. New York: McGraw-Hill.

House, Juliane (1977/1981) *A Model for Translation Quality Assessment*, Tübingen: Narr, 2nd edition.

Leppihalme, Ritva (1997) *Culture Bumps: An Empirical Approach to the Translation of Allusions*, Clevedon: Multilingual Matters.

Mossop, Brian (2001/2007) *Revising and Editing for Translators*, Manchester: St. Jerome, 2nd edition.

Nord, Christiane (1997) *Translating as a Purposeful Activity. Functionalist Approaches Explained*, Manchester: St. Jerome.

Ooi, Can Seng (2002) *Cultural Tourism and Tourism Cultures: The Business of Mediating Experiences in Copenhagen and Singapore*, Copenhagen: Copenhagen Business School Press.

Reiss, Katharina and Hans J. Vermeer (1984/1991) *Grundlegung einer allgemeinen Translationstheorie*, Tübingen: Niemeyer, 2nd edition.

Sandrini, Peter (2005-2007) 'Website Localization and Translation', in Heidrun Gerzymisch-Arbogast and Sandra Nauert (eds) *Challenges of Multidimensional Translation. Proceedings of the Marie Curie Euroconferences* MuTra: *Challenges of Multidimensional Translation – Saarbrücken 2-6 May 2005*, MuTra, http://www.euroconferences.info/proceedings/2005_Proceedings/2005_Sandrini_Peter.pdf.

Schäffner, Christina (1998) '*Skopos* Theory', in Mona Baker (ed) *Routledge Encyclopedia of Translation Studies*, London and New York: Routledge, 235-238.

Schäffner, Christina (2009) 'Functionalist Approaches', in Mona Baker and Gabriela Saldanha (eds) *Routledge Encyclopedia of Translation Studies*, London and New York: Routledge, 115-121.

Schopp, Jürgen F. (2002) 'Typography and Layout as a Translation Problem', in FIT (eds) *Translation: New Ideas for a New Century. Proceedings of the XVI FIT World Congress*, Vancouver: FIT, 271–275 (translated by John Hopkins), http://www.uta.fi/~trjusc/vancouver.htm.

Sumberg, Carolyn (2004) 'Brand Leadership at Stake: Selling France to British Tourists', *The Translator* 10(2): 329-353.

Teh, G.S. (1986) *An Applied Discourse Analysis of Sales Promotion Letters*, unpublished MA thesis, University of Singapore. Quoted in Bhatia (1993: 51-52).

Torresi, Ira (2004) 'Women, Water and Cleaning Agents: What Advertisements Reveal about the Cultural Stereotype of Cleanliness', *The Translator* 10(2): 269-289.

------ (2008) 'Advertising: A Case for Intersemiotic Translation', *Meta* 53(1): 62-75.

Venuti, Lawrence (1995) *The Translator's Invisibility: A History of Translation*, London and New York: Routledge.

------ (1998a) *The Scandals of Translation: Towards an Ethics of Difference*, London and New York: Routledge.

------ (1998b) 'Strategies of Translation', in Mona Baker (ed) *Routledge Encyclopedia of Translation Studies*, London and New York: Routledge, 240-244.

Further reading

Adab, Beverly (2001) 'The Translation of Advertising: A Framework for Evaluation', *Babel* 47(2): 133-157. *[with several examples from English into French]*

Adab, Beverly and Cristina Valdés (eds) (2004) *Key Debates in the Translation of Advertising Material*, special issue of *The Translator*, 10(2).

Bueno García, Antonio (2000) *Publicidad y traducción*, Soria: Vertere, Monográficos de la Revista Hermeneus.

Guidère, Mathieu (2000a) *Publicité et traduction*, Paris: L'Harmattan. *[with several examples from French into Arabic]*

Guidère, Matthieu (2000b) 'Aspects de la traduction publicitaire', *Babel* 46(1): 20-40. *[on the importance of semiotics in advertising translation, and with examples from French into Arabic]*

Torresi, Ira (2007) 'Translating the Visual. The Importance of Visual Elements in the Translation of Advertising across Cultures', in Kyongjoo Ryou and Dorothy Kenny (eds) *Across Boundaries: International Perspectives on Translation Studies*, Newcastle upon Tyne: Cambridge Scholars Publishing, 38-55.

On visual semiotics:

Kress, Gunther and Theo Van Leeuwen (1996) *Reading Images. The Grammar of Visual Design*, London and New York: Routledge.

On social semiotics:

Van Leeuwen, Theo (2005) *Introducing Social Semiotics*, London and New York: Routledge.

On geosemiotics:

Scollon, Ron and Suzie Wong Scollon (2003) *Discourses in Place. Language in the Material World*, London and New York: Routledge.

Websites

The Europass Curriculum Vitae (CV): http://europass.cedefop.europa.eu/europass/home/vernav/Europasss+Documents/Europass+CV/navigate.action

The Owl At Purdue. Free Writing Help and Teaching Resources: http://owl.english.purdue.edu/owl/resource/527/03/

Italian Langit: http://list.cineca.it/cgi-bin/wa?P1&L=langit

Index